What Others are Saying About Learning DOS for the Complete Novice

"Clear, concise, and cleanly written, this is one of the best beginner's books I've ever seen. It does everything those 'dummy' books do and more—and it does it better!"

  –Alfred Glossbrenner, author of over a dozen best-selling computer books including: DOS 6 [Random House, 1993], Power DOS! [Random House, 1993], File and Disk Management—From Chaos to Control [Osborne/McGraw-Hill, 1993], Glossbrenner's Master Guide to CompuServe [Brady Books/Prentice Hall, 1987]

"If you're a DOS user, this is the book to buy. One of the easiest books I've ever seen to learn to use DOS. Because of the wealth of information in Learning DOS For The Complete Novice, I feel I can recommend it to old timers as well."

  –Shareware Magazine, January/February 1993 issue, as reviewed by **Paul Mayer**, the past president of the Association of Shareware Professionals

"The ultimate beginner's guide on understanding and using DOS...Probably the first book a computer beginner should consider."

  –Jim Hood, author of PC-Learn, an award winning DOS tutorial

"I recommend Learning DOS For The Complete Novice to all DOS users, from the complete novice to the incomplete expert."

  –R.J.R. Rockwood, Ph.D., Sr. Product Information Analyst, Unisys Corporation, Atlanta Development Center, Norcross, Georgia

"The title says a lot but doesn't say it all...it is also a valuable reference for the experienced user."

  –William Chandler, M.D., Librarian for the Pasco Area Computer Users Group, Dade City, Florida

What Others are Saying...cont.

"Learning DOS for the Complete Novice is the best and easiest understood explanation of DOS that I have seen to date."
   –Judy B. Sparks, Computer Instructor, James L. Walker Vo-Tech, Naples, Florida

"What! Another DOS book? WAIT! As an experiment, I distributed some copies to some computer novices and asked them to use the book for two weeks. Afterward, I asked each person what they thought of the book and asked for its return. Not one person wanted to return it."
   –Bits & Bytes—Newsletter of the Pinellas IBM PC Users Group, November 1992 issue, as reviewed by **Jay Morris**

"The index alone makes this book superior to all others!"
   –Gary A. Cockrell, Pilot/Programmer, Tampa, Florida

"Steven has written a book so well organized and easy to understand that anyone should be able to master basic DOS easily. He has somehow been able to transport himself back in time; to think and especially speak to me as if he were in my shoes walking the new, sometimes frightening DOS path. He does it well and this is a great book! Thanks."
   –James H. McCreary D.D.S., Dayton, Ohio

"This book makes it so easy my 10 year old daughter can do it!"
   –Donald Pangburn, New Port Richey, Florida

"I'm in my first month of owning a computer and I have no idea how I could survive without this book!"
   –Jim Powell, Jim Powell Design, Muskegon, Michigan

"We have a collection of DOS manuals—a large collection, but in your book I have finally found the manual for me. You clearly explain and illustrate all that stuff that other manuals assume I know—or ought to know. I can't get over how much I have already learned just by browsing through the pages."
   –Lorraine Purnell, Coronado, California

Learning DOS
for the
Complete
Novice

2nd Edition

The Beginner's Guide
to DOS 3.2 through DOS 6

by Steven Woas

CELESTIAL
PRESS

Celestial Press, New Port Richey, Florida

Published by
Celestial Press
4424 Dohrcrest Dr.
New Port Richey, FL 34652
(813) 845-8522

Printed in the United States of America.

Library of Congress catalog card number: 93-72097

Publisher's Cataloging in Publication
  (Prepared by Quality Books Inc.)

Woas, Steven D.
  Learning DOS for the complete novice: the beginner's guide to
DOS 3.2 through DOS 6/ Steven Woas. -- 2nd ed.
  p. cm.
  Includes index
  ISBN 0-9623898-9-7

  1. Operating systems (Computers) 2. MS-DOS (computer file) 3.
PC-DOS (Computer file) I. Title.

QA76.76.063W67 1993   005.4'469
                                              QBI93-916

For information on ordering this book and special prices for bulk orders for educational institutions, retailers, wholesalers, and libraries, write to the above address or in the US call toll free 1-800-330-3311. Phone (813) 845-8522. Fax (813) 842-5636. Celestial Press is also a vendor of IBM and compatible shareware software. For a catalog of IBM compatible software, specify 5¼" or 3½" disk and write to the above address.

Trademarks: All product names and brand names mentioned herein are trademarks or registered trademarks of their respective holders.

Limits of Liability and Disclaimer of Warranty: The author and publisher have made their best efforts in preparing this book. However, the author and publisher make no warranties of any kind, expressed or implied, with respect to the documentation contained in this book. The book is sold "as is." Neither the publisher nor the author shall be liable in any event for incidental or consequential or special damages, arising out of the use of this information or material.

Contents

Part I Introduction

Part II Groundwork

Part III   DOS Basics

Part IV   Hard Drive Fundamentals

Part V   DOS 6 Section

Part VI   Reference

Acknowledgments

No project like this ever gets completed without a lot of help. I would like to thank the following people for their valuable suggestions and editorial efforts: Fred Brisard, Bob Glass, Betty Glass, Barbara L. Clarke, Ralph LoBianco, Ralph George who is a computer instructor at Traviss Technical Center in Lakeland, Florida, and Norman A. Peterson. Mr. Peterson teaches computering to technologically impaired novices in Clearwater, Florida. Thanks, too, to Karen Nolan, copy editor for THE REPORTER in Vacaville, California, for her editorial suggestions. The cartoons were drawn by artist Kirsten Rockwood of Atlanta, Georgia. I also want to thank all my customers over the years whose endless questions were the inspiration for this book. Douglas Wetterhall and Braxton Brooks gave very valuable leisure counseling...we went fishing. Most of all, thanks to my lovely wife Susy, who contributed ideas, enthusiasm, encouragement, and edited, to boot.

About The Author

Steven Woas has been involved with computers since the early 1980's. He authored a marine navigation program which has been sold commercially since 1982. Since 1987 he has been a distributor of shareware software. His company, Celestial Press/Software, has been an approved vendor of the Association of Shareware Professionals (ASP) since 1989. Every week he answers hundreds of questions about DOS from new users. Some of the most frequent questions appear in the section starting on page 15.

Part 1

INTRODUCTION

MOUSE DRIVER.SYS PARALLEL PARKING.

Introduction

There are plenty of comprehensive DOS reference books on the market. One of them may have come with your computer. The comprehensive DOS books are typically 600 - 1000 pages in length. These books usually do not tell you which DOS commands are important and which ones you will rarely use. For the novice, wading through a comprehensive DOS book can prove to be a loathsome task. Some of these books use cryptic notations that tend to confuse even seasoned users.

The beginner does not want to deal with all DOS commands, nor does he need to. This book is written for the new user as an introduction to DOS. It is not intended as a comprehensive work but contains the information on DOS to get a new user up and running with the least amount of work. Once you have mastered this book, the comprehensive DOS books will not be so intimidating. This book covers IBM and compatible computers only. Other kinds of computers, such as Apple or Atari, have entirely different operating systems.

What is DOS?

DOS stands for "Disk Operating System." It is a collection of programs that your computer uses so you can run other programs. Your computer would be a large paperweight without DOS. When you buy a computer with a hard drive, DOS usually has been installed on the hard drive by the dealer. You may also have DOS on one or more floppy disks. DOS is also called MS-DOS. The MS stands for Microsoft, the corporation that makes the operating system for IBM PC's and PC clones. The DOS for an IBM PC is called PC-DOS. Most IBM PC clones use MS-DOS. The commands we will be dealing with will work the same for versions of MS-DOS 3.2 through MS-DOS 6 (except where noted). Included is a special section on the important New DOS 6 Commands starting on page 190.

What does DOS do?

DOS performs many tasks.

- All software programs require an operating system (DOS).

- A blank floppy disk must be formatted before it can be used. You format a blank disk using a DOS command.

- You need DOS to show what programs are on a disk.

- You use DOS to access files on all the drives.

- When you want to copy a file or a disk, you use DOS.

DOS does many more things; but, as you can see, you will have to deal with DOS if you want to use your computer!

Assumptions

For the purpose of this book it is assumed that:

1. You have an IBM PC or compatible with a hard drive called C.

2. DOS has already been installed for you on your C drive.

3. DOS has been installed in a directory that is in your computer's PATH. Usually, DOS is installed in a directory called C:\DOS.

4. You have a floppy disk drive called the A drive. You may have more than one floppy disk drive, but you have at least one called the A drive.

The above constitutes the usual way an IBM compatible computer with a hard drive is set up. In order for you to use your computer, DOS must be installed. This is often more than a novice can do at first.

★ **NOTE**: To check to see if the C:\DOS directory has been installed in your computer's PATH, at any DOS prompt you can type:

path <ENTER>

That is, at the C> (or A> or B>) type the word PATH and then press the key marked <ENTER>. If the computer does not respond with a line of text showing C:\DOS somewhere on that line, you can turn to page 145 for a quick fix. Also, see pages 146 - 153.

Part 2

GROUNDWORK

How to Read this Book

It is highly recommended that you first browse through the **Table Of Contents** in the front of this book. When you need specific information, use the **Index** (in the back) to direct you to the right pages. A reference book like this one is rarely read straight through. In fact, it is just not done. If you do it, you will be violating a sacred custom. With this book and other computer books, use the index to find the section that covers the particular task at hand.

This book is meant to be used alongside your computer. **When reading this book, if you see something shown in angle brackets < >, it means press that key. For instance, if you see <ENTER>, it means push the key marked ENTER.** It should be understood that keyboards differ. On some keyboards the <ENTER> key is marked <RETURN>, and still others have a key that looks like ◄——┘ to indicate the ENTER key. Commands that the user types in will be indented near the center of the page, and these will be bold lower case letters. Incidentally, *DOS doesn't care whether you use upper or lower case to issue a command*. The computer responses to the commands will appear on the left side of the page. When file name extensions are presented in the text, they will be preceded by a period.

By far, the most frequent mistake a beginner will make is misspelling a file name or a DOS command. A file is a collection of information stored as a unit which has a unique file name. **DOS simply will not recognize a DOS command or a file name if you do not spell it exactly right.** When you want to run a program, you must be sure of the spelling. To see how a file name is spelled, you issue a directory command—**DIR <ENTER>**. When you issue a DIR command, there will be no periods that appear before the extensions. See page 40. However, DOS requires a period to separate the file name from the extension when you issue a DOS command. Therefore, in this book extensions will be preceded by a period as a *gentle reminder*.

Special Keyboard Keys

Angle brackets < > will be used to indicate a particular key on your keyboard. This convention will be used throughout this book.

< ENTER >   On some keyboards the <ENTER> key is marked <RETURN> and still others have a key that looks like ◄──┘ . You press the <ENTER> key after each DOS command.

< CAPS LOCK >   This key is somewhat like a shift lock key on a typewriter. <CAPS LOCK> shifts only letters to make capitals. Pressing <SHIFT> while <CAPS LOCK> is on creates lower case letters. Press <CAPS LOCK> again to turn it off.

< TAB >   You have a <TAB> key next to your Q key for tabulating. This is very similar to a tab key on a typewriter.

< ESC >   This is your escape key. Many programs use <ESC> to exit a program or to cancel an action.

< DEL >   This is the delete key. It will delete the character the cursor is on. *The cursor is the blinking character that shows you where you are on your screen.*

< ◄── >   There is a long left arrow key that is right above the <ENTER> key. This is the backspace key. It erases the character to the left of the cursor.

\<CTRL\>	The control key is used in conjunction with other keys. You hold down the \<CTRL\> key and push another key. Many computer books represent the \<CTRL\> key with the following character: ^. *It is precisely this kind of cryptic notation that tends to confuse the novice.*
\<F1\> ... \<F12\>	These are function keys. These keys are used in many programs as shortcuts—a single key to represent some function. The function key \<F1\> *is often used to get help in programs.* The one labeled \<F3\> is used to recall the previous DOS command.
\<NUM LOCK\>	This is used to lock the number keypad to use numbers. When the \<NUM LOCK\> key is engaged accidentally, it can cause panic! The keyboard should display a light to indicate that it is on. To turn the \<NUM LOCK\> key off, just press it again.
\<SHIFT\>	There are usually two \<SHIFT\> keys on most keyboards. Sometimes these are marked with up arrows instead of the word "shift."
\<PG UP\>	The page up key is often used to view the previous page of information.
\<PG DN\>	This is the page down key.
\<INS\>	This is called the insert key. In most word processor programs you can change from "typeover mode" to "insert mode" by pressing the \<INS\> key. To change from the "insert mode" back to the "typeover mode," press the \<INS\> key again. \<INS\> is a toggle key like \<NUM LOCK\>.

Special Key Combinations

Below are special key combinations. **This means that you have to hold down more than one key at a time.** To work one of these key combinations, you press down the first key; and, while that key is being held down, you press another key (or keys). Browse through this section even before you start DOS. Later you will want to come back to this section for further reference.

<CTRL> <BREAK>

This cancels whatever DOS was doing. To activate, you hold down the key marked <CTRL> and then press the key marked <BREAK> while still holding down the <CTRL> key. Suppose you issued the command:

format a: <ENTER>

To cancel this command just press <CTRL> <BREAK>.

<CTRL> C

Also cancels whatever DOS was doing. Some programs won't let you out with <CTRL> <BREAK> but will let you exit if you first hold down the key marked <CTRL> and, while holding down <CTRL>, press C. Occasionally, a program won't allow you to quit in a graceful manner, and you will have to restart your computer.

<CTRL> S

This combination functions the same as the <PAUSE> key. First press the key marked <CTRL> and, while holding down <CTRL>, press S. It is often used with the TYPE command to look at a text file. It will stop the scrolling. Press any other key to continue. See pages 46 - 47 for more about the TYPE command.

<SHIFT> <PRT SC>

The second key of this two key combination is sometimes labeled <PRINT SCREEN> or <PrtSc>. This combination prints any text that is showing on the screen. With many of the newer computers you don't have to hold down a <SHIFT> key. You can just press the <PrtSc> key. Also, see pages 52 - 55 for how to print out graphic screens.

<CTRL> <ALT> <DEL>

This three key combination causes the computer to do what is called a *warm boot*. To boot the computer is to start it up. If your computer locks up, this can be your best way to get back to work. Remember, for this three key combination to work, you have to press all three keys down at the same time. This is sometimes refered to as the "three fingered salute."

Introductory Computer Terms

For more computer terms see the section starting on page 288.

ACTIVE DIRECTORY: The current directory. This is the directory that DOS searches when it looks for files.

BOOT: To start the computer. Please don't kick your computer!

BYTE: A byte is a unit of measure for a computer's memory and also for disk data storage. A byte can store one letter or other character. The disks we buy are expressed in how many bytes of storage that they will hold.

COM1: The first serial port which is also called a communications port.

COMMAND LINE: The DOS system prompt. You know you are at the DOS command line when you see something like: A>, B>, C>, etc.

CURRENT DIRECTORY: The directory in which you are currently working. This is also called the active directory. DOS keeps track of the last current directory that you were in for each drive. If you change drives, DOS will take you to the last directory you were working in for that drive. If you had not used that drive since turning on the computer, DOS will take you to the root directory.

DEFAULT DRIVE: The current drive that is being used.

DEFAULTS: Programs often come with designated values which are called the default values. If you don't enter your own values, you can often just press <ENTER>; and the program will accept the *default values*.

DEFRAGMENTATION: A procedure where a special program rewrites files on a disk, so each file (and the parts of each file) are stored in contiguous sectors.

DESTINATION DISK: When you copy a file, the disk that you are copying the file to is called the destination disk. A destination disk is also called the target disk.

DIRECTORY: A directory can mean several things in computer jargon. Directory can mean a *list of files* displayed when you issue the DOS DIR command. Also, the files on a disk are organized in directories and subdirectories. So, a directory can also mean *an area on the disk where a certain group of files are stored*.

DOCUMENTATION: The instructions for running software are called the "documentation."

EXTENSION: The up to three letter suffix that helps identify file types. The extension comes after the file name. When you do a directory—DIR <ENTER>, you will see the list of file names with their extensions.

FILE: A collection of information that is stored on a disk as a single unit and has a file name.

FLOPPY DRIVE: A diskette drive. DOS users are likely to have either a 5¼" drive and/or a 3½" drive. Even though the 3½" disks are hard, they are not called hard disks because they are not fixed. They are removable. A 3½" disk is called a floppy disk.

FORMAT: Before a disk can be used, it must be formatted. When you format a disk, you prepare it for use.

HARD DRIVE: A large capacity disk (storage system) that is not removed from the computer. These usually range in size from twenty megabytes to one gigabyte. A hard disk is also called a fixed disk. See FLOPPY DRIVE above.

12

HARDWARE: Computer hardware is computer equipment and its physical components like: power supply, motherboard, disk drive, printer, etc. Computer programs are called software.

KILOBYTE (K): A unit of measure for computer memory. One kilobyte is 1,024 bytes. *K* is often used as an abbreviation for kilobyte.

LPT1: The first parallel port where you attach a printer. LPT stands for Line PrinTer.

MEGABYTE (MB): A unit of measure equal to 1,048,576 bytes. Note that a megabyte is equal to a little over one million bytes. An abbreviation for megabyte is *MB*.

PATH: The term PATH can have several meanings. PATH can mean *the directories that DOS searches to run programs when the programs are not in the active directory*. Path can also mean *the full directory name where a particular file is stored*. For example, C:\GAMES\PINBALL might be the directory where you keep your favorite pinball game. If that were the case, C:\GAMES\PINBALL would be the PATH to your pinball game.

ROOT DIRECTORY: The first or top level directory on a disk. This is the directory that was made when the disk was formatted.

SELF-EXTRACTING FILE: A self-extracting file is a compressed file. The file contains a file or group of files that has been compressed to save space. When a self-extracting file is run, other files pop out (emerge) from it. It is best to copy self-extracting files to the hard drive where they will have plenty of room to expand.

SHAREWARE: Shareware is a method of marketing software for the program's author. Shareware programs are copyrighted. The manuals for these programs are usually found on the disk in the form of a text file. You can print the manuals using your printer. You can obtain these programs for *trial use* from shareware distributors for a small copying fee (usually just a few dollars per disk). *Shareware programs require a separate payment to the author if found useful.* Shareware is a wonderful deal for the consumer because you get to "*Try before you buy.*" There are some great programs that are distributed as shareware. Excellent shareware programs are mentioned throughout this book.

SOFTWARE: The programs that are used in a computer. Software is to a computer what a record is to a record player. The computer would be a big paperweight without software. Just think how useless a record player would be without records. Also, see hardware above.

SOURCE DISK: When you want to copy a disk, the one you want to copy is called the source disk. The disk you want to copy the file or files to is called the target disk or destination disk.

SWITCH: A code in a command to indicate a particular way that the command is to be used. For example: DIR /W <ENTER>. The /W in this command tells DOS to show the directory in wide fashion.

SYSTEM PROMPT: This is also called the *command line*. See command line above. These are the characters that DOS displays on the screen to indicate that it is ready to accept commands. An example would be: C>.

TARGET DISK: When you are copying files to a disk, the disk that you are copying the files to is called the target disk. The target disk is also called the destination disk. Also, see source disk above.

WILDCARD: A DOS wildcard character is a special symbol that is used to represent any character. This is like the wildcards used in the game of poker. The asterisk looks like (*) and is used to represent any character or number of characters. The question mark (?) is used to represent any single character.

14

Questions and Answers

Below are some of the most frequent questions that new computer users ask. You may find your questions in here, too.

1. *I bought a box of new disks and tried to use them in my computer. It just wouldn't accept them. It gave me a cryptic error message like:*

   GENERAL FAILURE READING DRIVE A

   What am I doing wrong?

   Before a new disk can be used, it must be formatted. See pages 59 - 69.

2. *I just bought a new 486 computer. I went out and bought some 3½" disks. They will fit in the drive; but, when I try to format them, my computer just refuses to take them. What am I doing wrong?*

   You probably bought low-density disks (720K), and you have a high-density drive (1.44MB). Low-density 3½" disks have one small square hole in the top right corner. High-density 3½" disks have two square holes in the top. You can format low-density diskettes if you know the proper DOS commands. See pages 60 - 62.

3. *When I use the DIR command, the files seem to scroll too fast for me to read the ones in the beginning. Can the rest of the computing community read that fast, or is there some solution?*

   Try DIR /P <ENTER> which will **P**ause the directory when the screen is full. Also try DIR /W <ENTER> which shows the directory in **W**ide format. See the section starting on page 35.

4. *When I use the type command, often the words go by so fast I can't read them. Should I try to take back this computer and get a slower one? What can I do?*

If you press < PAUSE >, the text will stop scrolling; and you can read it. Press any *other* key to continue the scrolling. The TYPE command is really an obsolete command but will do in a pinch. See pages 46 - 47 for more about the TYPE command and also about using it with the MORE filter. You would do much better using an editor or shareware's great utility program called LIST. See the description of shareware programs on pages 256 - 263. Many DOS commands can be replaced by better shareware alternatives.

5. *I bought a disk from a mail order outfit, and "the code to get in" was not on the disk's label. How do I "break the code" to get into the program?*

You can do a directory on the disk—**DIR** < ENTER >—to see what files are on the disk. You can run files with **.EXE, .COM,** and **.BAT** extensions by simply typing the file name and pressing < ENTER >. I hate to interfere with your hacking, but you really shouldn't call this "breaking the code." Knowing a few file name extensions is the "key" to running programs. See pages 39 - 45, and remember to **read the manual** on the disk. See the section starting on page 46 for how to recognize and view the manuals.

6. *Sometimes when I do a directory on a disk, I see lots of files. I can run some of these files but not others. How do I run all the files I see on the disk?*

You can't run all files. Some files are used only by the main software program. The key is knowing about **file name extensions**. When you are looking for a program to run directly, look for files with .EXE, .COM, and .BAT extensions. See pages 39 - 45.

16

7. *When I try to run one of my programs, I can only get so far until the screen reads:*

PATH?

I have tried every password I can think of, including "straight and narrow"; but I still can't get past it. What am I doing wrong?

When a program asks for PATH, it often wants to know where you plan to store or retrieve data. See pages 144 - 148 for more on DOS PATHS.

8. *I often get the following error message when I try to operate my computer:*

BAD COMMAND OR FILE NAME

What does that mean?

The error message **"Bad command or file name" often means you misspelled a file or command.** DOS is very fussy about spelling. You can check the spelling of a file name by doing a directory—DIR <ENTER>. If you don't see the file, it may mean you need to change to the directory that has the file you want to run. See the section on directories starting on page 96.

9. *I bought a tape that has a lot of programs on it. I can get into some of them, but I can't run the one called CHECKERS.BAS. How do I run this checkers program?*

First of all, you probably mean disk and not tape. It is a mystery to me why people often call disks "tapes." Files with a **.BAS** extension require some form of BASIC program to run them. These BASIC files are run in a different way than most programs. See pages 181 - 184.

10. *I just installed DOS 6, and I can't seem to get my old BASIC programs to run using QBASIC. What am I doing wrong?*

QBASIC comes with DOS 5 and DOS 6. The problem is that QBASIC is not compatible with older versions of BASIC programs. If you still have an older version of GWBASIC, BASIC, or BASICA, you will find that the programs will run under DOS 5 or DOS 6 using the older versions of BASIC. If you have GWBASIC, you can save your GWBASIC files as ASCII text files; and many programs will then run without modification in QBASIC. See page 181.

11. *I have several disks which contain files called READ.ME. My computer refuses to run them. What am I doing wrong?*

Such files are usually text files and contain information on how to run programs. Any file with the word READ in the file name is probably a text file. Such files **WILL NOT RUN when you just type the file name and press <ENTER>**. To see how to view these files on the screen, see the section starting on page 46. File extensions that indicate text files with instructions are: .DOC, .INF, .MAN, .PRN, .TXT, .ME and .1ST. These files can also be printed using your printer. For help on how to print these files, see the section starting on page 50. Be sure to read the section entitled Extensions—The Key to Computing Success which starts on page 39.

12. *I just got back from a software store, and most of the games that I bought won't run on my computer. I have an amber colored monitor. What do I need to know to buy software intelligently?*

You probably have a monochrome monitor. Trying to buy software without knowing what kind of system you have is like going into an auto parts store and announcing to the clerk, "I would like an oil filter for my car." The clerk responds with, "What kind of car do you have?" You reply, "I don't know." How can you possibly expect the auto parts clerk to give you the right oil filter?

Before you go out to buy software, you need to know the following:

- What kind of a machine do you have? What CPU does it have? Is it an XT clone, 286, 386, or 486 machine?
- How much RAM does it have?
- Do you have a hard drive? If so, what is its capacity?
- How many floppy drives do you have, and of what size and capacity?
- What kind of monitor do you have? If it is a monochrome monitor, is it Hercules compatible? If you have a color monitor, what kind is it? Is it CGA, EGA, VGA, or SUPER VGA. If you do have an EGA or VGA monitor, how much memory is on the graphics card.
- Do you have a Microsoft compatible mouse?
- What version of DOS are you running? You can find out by typing at the system prompt:

ver <ENTER>

If you don't know the answers to these questions, you need to consult your manuals or call up the people who sold you the computer. Write this information down. If you have DOS 6 or Windows 3.1, Microsoft has included a program called **MSD** (Microsoft Diagnostics). The MSD program will give you the information you need to know about your particular computer. To see how to use the MSD program, turn to the section starting on page 200. A company by the name of Qualitas, Inc., makes a shareware program called **ASQ** that will automatically analyze your computer, take a "snapshot" of your system, and save this "snapshot" in the form of a text file. ASQ will show you most of the information about your system that you will need to know to buy software. For the address of Qualitas, Inc., see page 258.

13. *I bought a used computer from an ad in the newspaper. It came with a popular spreadsheet program. However, the manual isn't any good. In fact, it is terrible! Do you have any suggestions?*

You can buy "third-party" manuals for most popular software programs. Sometimes a software program is excellent but the manual that came with the program isn't. You can obtain books on how to run all the popular software at bookstores. Usually, the bigger the bookstore the better the selection of computer books. To get a manual that is right for your software, you will need to know the version of the software you have. Try running the program. Often a program will display the version on the opening screen. Make a note of this version number. If the bookstore doesn't have a book in stock, ask the clerk to order it for you. If you try to operate a complicated program without a good book, you probably won't get very far. If the book you are considering doesn't have a good index, don't buy it. Often, by using the index, you can turn right to the task you have in mind; and you won't have to read the entire book.

14. *I have a computer with two floppy drives and a hard drive. I have both sizes of floppy disks, 3½" and 5¼". I have a friend who has only one floppy drive, a 3½" high-density. I wanted to copy some letters that were saved on a 5¼" disk to a 3½" disk, so I could give my friend a disk which her computer could read. I have not been having any luck, even though I have tried to use the DOS DISKCOPY command. What am I doing wrong?*

The DOS DISKCOPY command will not work between two different sizes of drives. Use the DOS XCOPY command. To see how to copy a 5¼" disk to a 3½" disk, see pages 80 - 81.

15. *How do I copy a floppy disk to my hard drive? I don't want to mess up the hard drive. What if I copy a program to the hard drive and I*

don't like it? What if I fill up my hard drive? Aagh!

See pages 118 - 122 in this book. You won't worry so much about your hard drive once you learn how to navigate it. **Work the examples in the section on Directories starting on page 96. That section was designed for readers to try the examples while they are reading.** If you copy a program to the hard drive and find you don't like it, you can simply delete it. The same DIRECTORIES section will show you how to delete files and directories that you no longer want. You will on occasion need to delete files and directories on the hard drive to make room for more useful software. If you just installed software without ever removing files, you would eventually fill up the hard drive. Deleting files and directories is a necessary part of hard drive management.

16.   *I have a 286 machine with a 40MB hard drive and 640K RAM. I have an EGA monitor, and I use XTREE to run everything. Sometimes I have trouble installing new programs. Do you have any suggestions?*

Yes! It is best to exit any shell or menu program when you want to install a new program on your hard drive. Sometimes programs will not work properly if installed from a shell. Also, some programs will not run properly from a shell. This does not reflect badly on the shell or menu program. This is simply the nature of shells and menus. For instance, often, if a set of programs have multiple files with .BAT extensions, they will not work if run from a shell or menu. You must exit to DOS to run these. The bottom line is this: **To be safe, install new programs from the DOS command line. See page 118 for installing programs. If you have trouble running a program from your shell, try exiting the shell and running it from the DOS prompt.** If you need help on how to exit a shell, see page 26.

17.   *I worked for seven hours typing a proposal using my computer. Apparently I got a power surge and lost all my work. How can I*

prevent something like this from happening in the future?

Whenever you are doing something important on your computer, you should save your work every fifteen minutes. That way you will probably not lose more than fifteen minutes of work.

Also, it is important to learn to back up your files on floppy disks. Back up your important work. See the section starting on page 130 and the one starting on page 172. If you have DOS 6, see the section starting on page 236. Hard drives do fail. And things can go very wrong. It is not a question of, "Will your hard drive ever fail?"; it is a question of, **"When will your hard drive fail?"** Protect yourself. Periodically back up your important files.

18.   *I accidently deleted an important file. Is there any way to get it back?*

Perhaps! If you are using DOS 5 or higher, there is an UNDELETE command. See the section starting on page 91 and the one starting on page 202.

If you have an earlier version of DOS, you can obtain the commercial program PC TOOLS which has an UNDELETE command. See page 172.

19.   *I have DOS version 6, and I am wondering if I can run a software program that has version 7.0?*

Your DOS version has nothing to do with the version number of other programs. You should be able to determine if you can run a program by checking out the system requirements on the software package. Also see question number 12 above.

20.   *I just bought a new game, and my computer gave me a message that I don't have enough memory to run the program. I am running DOS*

3.3. I thought I had a full 2MB of RAM. How can I squeeze more memory out of my machine so I can run this new program?

Try making a start-up disk as is shown on pages 67 - 69. Then start the computer with it in drive A. Memory-resident programs may be taking up some of your conventional memory. Booting from a floppy disk will bypass your normal start-up files. This may free up enough memory to run the game. You may want to make changes to your AUTOEXEC.BAT and CONFIG.SYS files. See pages 146 - 167.

Another option is to upgrade your DOS. If you have an 80286 or better machine with extended memory, DOS 5 or DOS 6 can give you more conventional memory. See pages 162 - 167 and 205 - 211. This means you will have more memory to run programs. DOS 6 has a program called MEMMAKER. This is for 80386 or better machines, and it will automatically optimize memory which usually results in more conventional memory for your computer. For more on MEMAKER see pages 215 - 219. If you are running DOS 6 on an 80386 or better machine and have DoubleSpace installed, make sure that DoubleSpace is loaded into upper memory. See page 224 on how to determine and fix such a problem. If DoubleSpace is loaded in conventional memory, it will take up more than 40K of memory.

21. *When I buy new programs, do I have to copy them to my hard drive? I would prefer to just run programs from my floppy drives.*

Software programs often must be installed or copied to the hard drive before you can run them. **Many new programs will not run from a floppy drive**. To see how to install new programs on your hard drive see pages 118 - 122.

22. *I bought a shareware program from an established dealer. When I got the disk home and ran the program, it said **EXPLODING...** on the screen. I wonder if it did any damage to my computer? Incidently,*

the program did not work.

What you described is a self-extracting file. A self-extracting file is a compressed file. The file contains a file or group of files that has been compressed to save space. When a self-extracting file is run, other files pop out (emerge) from it. You need to copy these to the hard drive (before you run them) where they will have plenty of room to expand. If you need help on copying a disk to your hard drive, see the section starting on page 118. Often, if you try to run a self-extracting file on a floppy disk, the disk fills up before all the files can pop out.

Part 3

DOS BASICS

IDENTIFYING THE EXECUTABLES

Starting DOS

To start your computer, try turning on your monitor and computer with no diskette in drive A. Drive A is usually the upper diskette drive, or the drive on the left. Get out your manuals if you can't find the power switches! Often, the power switch is located on the right side of the computer. The location of the monitor switch is often under the screen on the bottom right.

When you turn on your computer, DOS is loaded into memory. These days, many hard drive systems are set up with what is called a DOS "shell." A **SHELL** is a software program that provides a user interface, or menu, to the operating system. (DOS is the operating system.) DOS versions 4.0 and later give you a built-in shell.

For our purposes, we want to get to the DOS command line. When you are at the DOS command line, you can type in DOS commands. This is known as the **system prompt** or **C>**. The letter followed by the > symbol indicates which drive is the *active drive*. The active drive is also called the current drive. Usually drives A and B are floppy drives and drives C and greater are hard drives.

Getting Out of a Shell

These days, most PC's are set up with DOS shells of one type or another. You will need to find out how to exit the shell to DOS. Most of these programs have the command to exit to DOS showing on the opening screen or at least a help key. Read the entire screen carefully if you are having trouble getting out. If you are using the DOS shell (included with DOS 4.0 and later), you can escape to the command line by pressing <F3>. <F3> is the function key that is labeled F3. You might try pressing the function key labeled <F1>. This is often used as a help key. Sometimes the escape key labeled <ESC> is used to exit. If you can't figure out how to exit your

DOS shell, you might have to contact the people where you bought the computer. In any case, you want to get to the DOS command line.

You know you are at the command line when you see something like:

C> or **C:\DOS>**

By starting the computer and getting out of your DOS shell (if you have one), you get the C> which is the **system prompt**. If your prompt looks something like C:\DOS>, don't let it worry you. For simplicity, the C> will be used for the DOS command line prompt for many of the examples in this book. Later on, I will often say "At the system prompt..." The system prompt doesn't have to indicate the C drive. It may look like A>, B>, C>, D>, E>, etc. The system prompt can indicate any of your drives and tells which one is the *active drive*.

Now the fun begins. You are ready to type in some DOS commands.

Setting the Date and Time

The vast majority of computers sold these days have a built-in clock and calendar. If your system has a built-in clock and calendar, then you probably won't have to type in the time and date each time you start your computer. This will depend on how the AUTOEXEC.BAT file was set up in your root directory of your boot disk. However, the built-in clocks often get confused; and you will need to reset the time and date occasionally.

Any time you wish to change the date, at the system prompt type:

date <ENTER>

The computer will greet you with something like:

    CURRENT DATE IS TUE 1-01-1980
    ENTER NEW DATE (MM-DD-YY):_

The blinking character is called a **cursor** and is prompting you to enter the correct date. If the date shown is correct, just press <ENTER> and the date will not change. To change the date to June 2, 1994, you would type:

06-02-94 <ENTER>

You may use a forward slash (/) or a period (.) instead of a dash (-) to separate the date input characters. On many machines you are greeted with the date and time prompts upon starting DOS. If you want to change your computer's time, at the system prompt type:

time <ENTER>

You enter the time in a similar way that you entered the date, using a colon (:) to separate the numbers. Again, you can press the <ENTER> key to accept the time shown. All versions of DOS covered in this book can use 24 hour (or military) notation for time. EXAMPLE—4:20 pm is 16:20 in 24 hour notation. This can be entered as:

16:20:00 <ENTER>

Each time you create or save a file, DOS records the time and date for that particular file. This is why it is important to have the correct date and time.

Your DOS Version

You will need to know which version of DOS you are using. To show which version of DOS you have, you can use the VER command. At the system prompt type:

ver <ENTER>

DOS will then display your DOS version.

Clearing the Screen

To clear the screen, at the system prompt type:

cls <ENTER>

The screen will clear except for the system prompt C > in the top left corner of your screen. The CLS command can be issued from any drive.

Changing to a Different Drive

You will want to change to a different drive to use programs stored on another drive. Each disk drive is identified by a letter. If you have only one diskette drive, it will be the A drive. If you have two diskette drives, one will be called A and the other B. Drive C and greater usually designate hard drives. Your machine may have one or more hard drives. It depends on what hardware you have and how it is set up.

To change drives, give the drive letter followed by a colon; then press <ENTER>. Suppose you are working on the C drive and want to change to drive A. Place a disk with files on it in the A drive with the label facing up. If you have a 5¼" drive, you will want to close the little drive door. Then at the C> type:

a: <ENTER>

Be careful not to mistake the semicolon (;) for the colon (:). To make your C drive active again, at the A> type:

c: <ENTER>

If you are on your C drive and want to go to your B drive, place a disk that has been formatted in drive B and close the drive door. Then at the C> type:

b: <ENTER>

If only everything in DOS was this simple!

Turning the Computer Off

If you found the switch to turn the computer on, you probably already know how to turn the computer off. Most computers have drive lights which come on when a drive is being used. Do not turn the computer off while the computer is accessing a disk drive. Before you turn the machine off, save any file you happen to be working on. Then exit all programs so you have the DOS prompt, and turn the computer off. Be sure to turn the monitor off, too. If you are working on the computer and need to leave the room, at least turn the monitor off to avoid damage. Leaving the monitor on with the same screen showing for a long time can result in screen "burn-in" which means an image shows up on the screen even when the monitor is off! **If you are going to leave the room for more than 15 minutes, it is wise to turn the monitor off.** See page 258 for information about a shareware program called BLANK-IT that will blank the screen after a predetermined time.

CAUTION: Be careful not to turn the computer off when it is accessing a disk drive. Failure to heed this caution could result in a fragmented hard drive. Fragmentation means that the files are not stored in an efficient manner. This tends to slow down the hard drive, making tasks take longer than they would if the hard drive was not fragmented. See page 185 and page 195.

If you live in an area that has frequent lightning storms, it is best to unplug all your equipment when you are not using it. For example, I live in Florida. The summers in Florida have lightning storms often in the afternoons. In the summer, when I am not using the computer, I unplug everything. Even with good power surge protection, it is wise to **unplug all your computer equipment in a lightning storm**. If you have a modem, be sure to unplug both the electrical cord and the phone wire where it plugs into the wall.

Diskettes and Write Protection

These days, there are several types and sizes of diskettes. When you buy disks, you need to know what size disk drives you have and the capacity of each. The most popular sizes of disks are 5¼" and 3½". Even though the 3½" disks are hard, they are not called hard disks. Both 3½" and 5¼" diskettes are called "floppy disks."

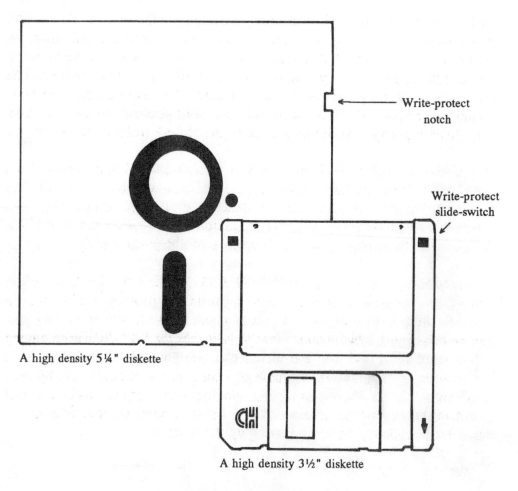

Write-protect notch

Write-protect slide-switch

A high density 5¼" diskette

A high density 3½" diskette

Figure 1. Diskettes.

5¼" Disks

There are two kinds of popular 5¼" disks, 360K (362,496 bytes) and 1.2MB (1,228,800 bytes) disks. Here, the K stands for kilobytes and MB stands for megabytes. The 5¼" 360K low-density disks are double-sided/double-density or DS/DD for short. These days, most 5¼" disks that are sold are the high-density type. The 5¼" high-density 1.2MB disks are known as DS/HD or double-sided/high-density.

Both 360K and 1.2MB 5¼" diskettes have a hole in the middle. On a 360K disk the hole will usually be reinforced with what is called a **hub ring**. A high-density 1.2MB 5¼" disk will usually not have a hub ring surrounding the hole in the middle. If you have a disk with files on it, you can determine the capacity by using the CHKDSK command. For more on the CHKDSK command see page 56. **You need to know what size disk drives you have and their capacity before you go out to buy blank disks or software.**

If you have a 1.2MB 5¼" drive, it will be able to read and write to both 360K and 1.2MB diskettes. However, a 360K drive will not read or write to a 1.2MB diskette. Be careful not to touch the magnetic surface of a disk. *There is an exposed oval section at the bottom of 5¼" disks that should not be touched.* Touching the magnetic surface of a disk can damage the disk.

It is important to know about **WRITE PROTECTION** for diskettes. Write protection does exactly what its name suggests. **It protects a disk so data can't be written to that disk.** In some situations writing over existing data can be disastrous! *One obtains write protect tabs for 5¼" disks* upon buying a box of blank disks; they are included in the box. They look like small pieces of tape. Don't ever use tape as a substitute as it could gum up your disk drive. To use a write protect tab, you put one over the small notch that is cut in the side of the diskette. Put it on so it overlaps both sides of the small notch equally, thereby covering up the notch.

3½" Disks

There are two kinds of 3½" disks that are readily available today, **double-density** and **high-density**. Both are double-sided. The double-density 3½" disks are the 720K. The **double-density 720K 3½" disks have only one small square hole in the top right corner**.

The 3½" disks that hold 1.44MB of data are called high-density disks and usually have HD stamped on them. High-density 3½" disks have two square holes in the disk. These holes are located in the top left and top right of the disk. If you have a 1.44MB 3½" drive, it can read and write data on both 720K as well as 1.44MB 3½" disks. A 720K 3½" drive will not read or write to a 1.44MB 3½" disk.

Yet another type of 3½" disk on the market is double-sided and holds 2.88MB of data. These are **extended-density diskettes and have ED stamped on them**. Extended-density diskettes are called DS/ED for short.

To **WRITE PROTECT** a 3½" disk, look for a small notch in the top left corner on the back side of the disk where there is a slide-switch like device. *By flipping that switch up and uncovering the hole, you get write protection.*

Write protection is used on a floppy disk when you do not want any data to be written to that disk. When you make backup copies of your important data or programs, you will probably want to write protect the disks. You write protect the disks *after* copying the data. If you try to save or copy information to a write protected disk, you will get a DOS error message.

Be careful not to expose your disks to magnets or electronic equipment that produces electromagnetism like: vacuum cleaners, etc. Such exposure could destroy the data on the disk. Disks can't take extreme heat or cold and should be kept clean, away from sand, dirt, and dust. Don't ever leave disks in a hot car in the summer months.

Displaying a Directory

If you have a floppy disk with programs on it, hold it in your right hand. If it is a 5¼" disk, be careful not to touch the exposed area at the bottom of the disk. Hold it up to the light being careful not to get it too close. Try as you might, you won't be able to see the files on the disk! **A DOS DIR command is used to list a directory of files on a disk.** This will be one of the most frequent tasks that you do while operating your computer. A DIR command is used to display a list of files in a particular directory or subdirectory. You will learn to change directories and navigate a directory structure starting on page 96.

Place a floppy disk that contains programs in your A drive with the label facing up. If your A drive is a 5¼" disk, the write protect notch should be on the left as you insert the disk. Close the little drive door. If you have a C>, you will want to change over to the A drive. At the C> type:

a: <ENTER>

Now you are ready to do a directory to see what files are on the disk. At the A> type:

dir <ENTER>

If you look at your computer's case where the A drive is mounted, you will notice that the drive light comes on when you issue the above command. Hopefully you did have a disk with programs on it. They should show up on the screen. Note that in the above example you did a directory on a floppy disk. However, *these DIR commands can be issued from any drive, whether it is a floppy drive or a hard drive, and from any directory or subdirectory.* If you did a directory and it contained more than 25 lines of directory information, then some of the information scrolled off the screen.

If that was the case, at the system prompt type:

dir /p <ENTER>

Here the /P was added to the DIR command. The forward slash followed by a letter is called a switch. Here, the /P "switch" tells DOS to display the directory until the screen fills up and then to pause. If the screen fills up, DOS will display the following message:

STRIKE ANY KEY WHEN READY....

This gives you time to look carefully at the directory before showing more. When you are ready to go on, press a key.

Yet another variation is the command:

dir /w <ENTER>

The /W "switch" tells DOS to display the directory in a wide version. The DIR /W command is very nice when you have a disk with lots of files on it. Maybe you have a disk with a hundred files on it. By using the DIR /W command, all the files will be shown on one screen. With the DIR /W command the directory is displayed showing the file names and extensions; however, other information about bytes, date, and time are not shown.

If you want to print a directory on paper, you can turn your printer on with paper in it and type:

dir > prn <ENTER>

The > symbol redirects the output of the DIR command from the screen to the device specified. The PRN represents the printer in DOS. All these different ways of showing a directory are very nice. However, if you don't understand the directory information, it will not do you much good. What shows up on the screen is probably very confusing to a new user. Making sense of this directory information is *essential*. The next section will help you understand this directory information.

Tips

- There is an excellent shareware program called **ZDIR** that will do a much better job of showing a directory than the DOS DIR command. It gives more information, too. ZDIR will display a directory with *color coding* of the extensions and can sort a directory in almost any way. It is very easy to use and should be copied to a directory that is in your computer's PATH. See pages 144 - 148 for more about PATHS.

  ZDIR is available from shareware vendors. See page 262 for more information on ZDIR.

- With DOS 5 or DOS 6 you can type the following at the system prompt:

  help dir <ENTER>

  This will give you more information about the DOS DIR command. Note that it has many optional switches.

Making Sense of a
Directory Listing

Please read this section and the one on extensions very carefully. Lack of knowledge in this area is perhaps the biggest stumbling block for the beginning PC user. When you give the DOS command—**DIR <ENTER>**, you will see five columns in the directory which appears on the screen. Going from left to right: the first column contains the file name, then that file's extension, the size of the file in bytes, the date the file was created, and the last column tells the time the file was created. An example of a single directory listing might look like:

CHKDSK EXE 16200 04-09-91 5:00a

The parts of a single directory listing are identified below.

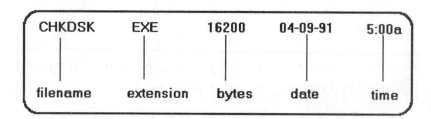

Figure 2. The parts of a directory listing.

The most important information for the new user to understand is the ***extension***. An extension is the up to three letter suffix that helps identify a file. The extension can be numbers and other characters instead of letters, or mixed with letters. **File extensions give valuable clues for identifying file types.** Occasionally, a file name does not have any extension at all.

Extensions

The Key to Computing Success

In my opinion, **this section on extensions is the most important for a beginner.** Extensions give valuable clues to help identify file types. A person, who is knowledgeable about DOS file name extensions, can take an unlabeled diskette and do a directory—**DIR <ENTER>**. From the directory, he (or she) can determine what programs are on the diskette and which files contain the manuals, and proceed to successfully run the software most of the time. *SO CAN YOU!* You will want to refer back to this chapter until you know this extension business *thoroughly*.

Please look at Figure 2 on page 38 showing the parts of a single directory listing. *Take a careful look at where the EXTENSION is located.* When you do a directory on a disk, there are no periods that appear before the extensions. However, DOS commands require a period to separate the file name from the extension. Therefore, when extensions are presented in this book, they will be preceded by a period as a *gentle reminder*.

The three types of extensions that identify the only files which you can run by simply typing the file name are:

.EXE
.COM
.BAT

A file with one of these extensions is sometimes called a "program" file or an "executable" file. If you see a file like CHKDSK.EXE, you can conclude that, since it has an .EXE extension, you can run that file. All you would have to do is type CHKDSK and then press the key marked <ENTER>. Suppose you did a directory on a disk—**DIR <ENTER>**, and your computer responded with the following screen:

```
        Volume in drive A is GA-014
        Directory of A:\

        WORDPLAY 000        11520 07-05-86   11:19a
        WORDPLAY COM        60407 07-05-86   11:19a
        WORDPLAY DOC        18503 07-04-86   12:31p
        WORDPLAY PUZ        14848 04-16-87   11:29p
        WORDPLAY PRM          110 10-25-87    2:09p
        ARCHERY  EXE        31616 07-26-86   11:46p
        ARCHERY  SCR          256 01-01-80   12:29a
                7 file(s)        137260 bytes
                                 221184 bytes free

        A>
```

Figure 3. A typical directory listing.

From looking at the above directory listing you should conclude that WORDPLAY.COM and ARCHERY.EXE will run by typing the file name. Remember, only files with **.EXE**, **.COM**, and **.BAT** extensions will run by simply typing the file name.

There are many types of files that you cannot run directly. For instance, a file with a **.SCR** extension may be a graphic screen file; and it is perhaps used by a main program with an .EXE extension. In other words, the .SCR file can only be used by another program. A file with a **.DAT** extension may be used to store data which is used by another file. **These kinds of files, which can only be used by another program, are sometimes called "data" files. You cannot run such files directly.**

40

Computer people call the manuals for software the **documentation**. The manuals on disk for programs can usually be recognized by the file's extension. When you do a directory on a disk, *look for the following EXTENSIONS when you want to find the instructions on how to run software. These usually indicate text files:*

.DOC
.INF
.MAN
.PRN
.TXT
.ME........The full name and extension would be **READ.ME**
.1ST.......The full name and extension would be **README.1ST**

Files with such extensions are usually **TEXT FILES,** sometimes called ASCII files (pronounced ASK-EE), and contain information on how to run programs. Take a look at Figure 3 on page 40. From glancing at the directory listing in Figure 3 you can conclude that WORDPLAY.DOC is probably the manual for the WORDPLAY.COM file. Shareware software and public domain software usually have manuals in the form of text files like these. You can read such files on the screen using most word processors and editors. You can also use the DOS **TYPE** command to view these files. **A file with an extension of .DOC, .INF, .MAN, .PRN, .TXT, .ME, or .1ST** *WILL NOT RUN* **when you type the file name and press <ENTER>.** These text files contain information and should be displayed on the screen, or better yet, printed out using your printer. See page 46 for instructions on how to display such text files on your screen using the **TYPE** command. See page 50 for information on how to print out text files using your printer. *A file with no extension at all is often a text file.* One should suspect a file with no extension as being a text file. If you are not sure, you can try to view the file on the screen using the DOS TYPE command or a better shareware viewing program. If you get unreadable characters that look like a communication from outer space, you can conclude that it isn't an ASCII text file. Get out fast before they come and get you!

Some **FILE NAMES** which may not have an extension and are likely **TEXT FILES** include:

READ
README
_README
READNOW
4U2READ
MANUAL
HELP
VENDOR

Any file with the word *READ* in the file name is probably a text file. When you do a directory on a disk and spot one of the above text files, you should make a note of the size of the file. You can get a good idea of how large the text file is by the number of bytes in the file. You can figure about one page for every 2500 bytes. So, if you see a text file with 7500 bytes, you can guess that it is about 3 pages of information. If the manual is more than a couple of pages long, you are well advised to print it out using your printer. People often ask me why they should print the manual when they can just view it on the screen. Unless you have a photographic memory, you probably won't remember what is on page 26. So, print the manual out, and have it beside your computer when you are attempting to run a program for the first time. See page 50 for information on how to print these text files on your printer.

The .BAT extension indicates a batch file which can be run by just typing the file name and then pressing <ENTER>. *Sometimes, when there are a group of .BAT files in a directory, they will not run properly from a shell or menu program.* You can try running a .BAT file from a shell; but, if you have problems, the solution is to get out of the shell. If you need help on getting out of a shell, see page 26. Then try running the .BAT file again from the system prompt. Sometimes, when you do a directory on a disk, you will see **FILE NAMES** like:

GO
START
RUNME
INSTALL
SETUP

If you see a file with a name like **GO**, **START**, or **RUNME** and it has an extension of .EXE, .COM, or .BAT, you can try just typing the file name to start the program. If you see a file with **INSTALL** or **SETUP** in the name, first look for any existing text file or manual. Such documentation may have special instructions for installing the program, and you should print these instructions. See page 50 for how to print these text files. When an INSTALL or SETUP program is present, you will most likely have to run the INSTALL or SETUP file *before* you can successfully run the main program.

When a program does use an INSTALL or SETUP file, first get out of any shell or menu program because it is best to install a new program from the system prompt. Sometimes a program will not install properly if the INSTALL or SETUP is run from a shell. For help on getting out of a shell, see page 26. If an INSTALL or a SETUP file has an extension of .EXE, .COM, or .BAT, you can often run it by just typing the file name and pressing the <ENTER> key. It is important to read any documentation *before* trying to install such a program.

There is an important type of file extension that identifies a program written in BASIC. It looks like:

.BAS

If a file has a .BAS extension, it indicates that the file is a BASIC file and requires you to load a special BASIC language, such as BASIC, GWBASIC,

BASICA, or QBASIC, before that program can be run. These are handled in a different fashion than other files and require you to run them in a special way. Information on how to run programs with a .BAS extension can be found on pages 181 - 184.

When you see a .ZIP, .ARC, .ARJ, .LZH, .PAK, or .ZOO extension, it indicates that the file is in a compressed archived format. An **archive file** is a file that has been compressed by a special program so that it will use less disk space. It is not unusual to get 900K of data on a 360K diskette by using these archival compression techniques. You will need to uncompress any of the above compressed file formats before they can be used. See the **Glossary of File Name Extensions** starting on page 281 for more specific information about .ZIP, .ARC, .ARJ, .LZH, .PAK, and .ZOO extensions. Also, see pages 177 - 180 for how to unzip files with a .ZIP extension.

When you do a directory on a disk, you see the number of bytes a program takes up. See Figure 3 on page 40. From the number of bytes, you can tell how large the program is and how much space it uses on a disk. When you do a directory, the bottom of the screen shows how many bytes are free on the disk. This important information informs you how much space is left on that disk.

This section on extensions seems to be very dry, but it is the most important section for the new user. Refer to it often! Also, *when you need to know more about extensions, see pages 281 - 287.* If you don't read the documentation, you won't be able to successfully run programs on a regular basis. It is important to learn how to view text files. **In the next section you will learn how to view text files on your screen.**

Summary

Extensions—The Key to Computing Success

1. To show the files in a disk directory, you issue a directory command— **DIR <ENTER>**.

2. When you want to identify files that will run directly, look for files with **.EXE, .COM,** and **.BAT** extensions. *To run these files, you can just type the file name and press <ENTER>.*

3. Often the **manuals** for shareware and public domain software are on the disk in the form of a text file. *Many commercial programs also contain important information in the form of text files.* **In fact, DOS 6 comes with a text file called README.TXT.** If you value your data, you should read this crucial text file. See pages 191 - 192. The following **extensions** indicate that the file is probably a text file with instructions on how to run the software: **.DOC, .INF, .MAN, .PRN, .TXT, .ME,** and **.1ST.** You can use the DOS TYPE command (see page 46) or one of the better viewing programs (LIST page 259) to read these files. See the section starting on page 50 for information on how to print these text files. You should always read the documentation before you try to run a program.

4. If you see a file with **INSTALL** or **SETUP** in the file name, it would be a good guess that you will have to run the INSTALL or SETUP program *before* you can successfully run the main program.

5. A file with a **.BAS** extension indicates the file is a BASIC program and requires a special BASIC language such as BASIC, GWBASIC, BASICA, or QBASIC. These are handled in a different fashion than other files and require you to run them in a special way. See pages 181 - 184 for information on how to run programs with a .BAS extension.

Viewing Text Files on the Screen

The manuals for software, called documentation, are sometimes found on disks in the form of text files. In the last section you learned how to recognize these files by their extensions. When you do a directory—**DIR <ENTER>**, you see file names and their extensions. See figure 2 on page 38 if you are uncertain about extensions. When looking for text files, check for the following **EXTENSIONS**:

.DOC
.INF
.MAN
.PRN
.TXT
.ME......The full name and extension may be **READ.ME**
.1ST.....The full name and extension may be **README.1ST**

These extensions indicate that the file is probably a text file. You can view text files using most word processing software and editor programs. You can also use the DOS TYPE command.

Using the DOS Type Command

Suppose you saw a file called WORDPLAY.DOC on a directory. Figure 3 on page 40 has a file by that name in the directory listing. Because the extension is .DOC, you can assume it is a text file. To view that text file on the screen, at the system prompt type:

type wordplay.doc <ENTER>

You *do* need to spell out the word TYPE. You will need to leave a space after the word TYPE. You *do* have to put the period after the file name to separate it from the extension. If you have a long text file and use the TYPE command, the text will continue to scroll off the screen. *To stop the scrolling,* you can on most computers press the key marked <PAUSE>. Press any *other* key to continue scrolling. Another alternative to stop the scrolling is to press <CTRL> S. That is, you hold down the key marked <CTRL>; and, while it is being held down, you press the S key. When you want to continue, you press any key; and the text will continue to scroll. The DOS TYPE command is an outdated command that should have been updated ten years ago. It is barbaric compared to LIST (see page 49).

If you are not sure whether a file is a text file or not, try viewing it on the screen using the DOS TYPE command. If you see unreadable characters that look like a communication from outer space, you will know that it is not a text file.

Occasionally, a text file will not have any extension at all. Suppose you saw a file on a disk called MANUAL with no extension at all. To view that file, you could issue the following command:

type manual ¦more <ENTER>

Here a ¦**MORE** "filter" was added to the end of the TYPE command which tells DOS to display the text one screen at a time. You can press any key to continue viewing. The (¦) character is on the same key as the backslash character (\). If the text file had an extension, such as .TXT, you could type: TYPE MANUAL.TXT ¦MORE <ENTER>. Sometimes, a software author gives a text file a name like _README.DOC. To view such a file, type:

type _readme.doc ¦more <ENTER>

If you forget the _ character, DOS will not recognize the file; and you will get an error message. Look out for those kinds of characters and also numbers.

Use EDIT with DOS 5 or Later

Starting with DOS 5, Microsoft has included a modern editor program. If you are using DOS 5 or DOS 6, there is a built-in editor called EDIT to view and print text files. Edit is much better for viewing text files than the DOS TYPE command. EDIT is easy to use. Earlier versions of DOS had a *dreadful* editor called EDLIN as the only editor. Don't bother to learn EDLIN. EDLIN is not at all "user friendly."

Suppose you did a directory on a disk and noticed a text file called CHECK.DOC. You can issue the following command at the system prompt:

edit check.doc <ENTER>

DOS will load EDIT and the document (CHECK.DOC) will appear on the screen. When viewing a file on the screen, press the <PG DN> key to go to the next page. Press <PG UP> to move up a page. With EDIT you can print any file you are viewing by pressing:

<ALT>

f

p

That is, press the key marked <ALT>, release the <ALT> key, and press the F key to bring down the files menu. Press the key marked P to print the file you are viewing. When you are in EDIT, you can press <F1> anytime you need help. To exit the EDIT program, press:

<ALT>

f

x

Editor programs are good for creating, editing, and printing text files.

48

Tips

- **LIST** is a marvelous small shareware program that replaces the DOS TYPE command. You can search for a key word or phrase. If you try LIST once, you will never want to use the DOS TYPE command again. You will really appreciate being able to search for a key word when you have a 400-page manual to go through! The search is exceptionally fast. You can <PgUp> or <PgDn> to look at text, and LIST will handle huge files. The DOS EDIT program will not handle large text files. LIST is menu driven with pop-up help. With LIST you can mark a section of text and send it to your printer or a file. Copy LIST to a subdirectory in your computer's path, and then it will be available from any drive or directory. For more about paths see page 144. When compared to LIST, the DOS TYPE command is absolutely *barbaric*. For more information on LIST, see the section starting on page 259.

- If you don't have DOS 5 or later, you should try to obtain a good editor for your editing needs. My favorite editor is a shareware program called **QEDIT**. It is menu driven. There are really only two commands you have to learn with QEDIT. Q starts it and <ESC> gives you pull down menus. See page 260 for more information on QEDIT. All editor programs can read text files.

- Most word processing programs can read text files, and you may find it easier to use your word processor to view them. You can look in the manual to see if your word processor can read text files. Look in the **INDEX** of your word processing manual under A for ASCII (an ASCII file is a text file) or T for TEXT.

Printing Text Files

In the last section you learned how to identify text files by their extensions and view these text files on the screen. The instructions for software are often on the disk in the form of text files. You should print out these manuals (and read them). Often, you can't successfully run software unless you follow the manual exactly. If you need a review of how to identify text files, see pages 40 - 42.

Suppose you did a directory on a diskette and noticed a file called QCHECK.DOC. Because it has a .DOC extension, you can surmise that it is the manual for the main program which might be called QCHECK.EXE. To print it out, **turn your printer on.** Make sure that paper is installed properly in your printer. You may have to read your printer manual if you are not familiar with your printer. Then at the system prompt type:

copy qcheck.doc prn <ENTER>

The PRN that you include after the file name and extension is what DOS uses to represent the printer. The text file should then start to print. On some printers you may have to take the printer off-line and then press the form feed button to eject the last page. With laser printers you often have to force a form feed to eject a page that isn't full. Below is a *secret* DOS command that will *eject the page* on those reluctant printers:

echo <CTRL> L > prn <ENTER>

With the above command you type the word ECHO, press the space bar, then hold down the key marked <CTRL>. While the <CTRL> key is being held down, press L; then hold down the shift key and press the key marked >. The > character is the greater-than symbol and redirects the output (in this case to the printer). When you finish the command by typing PRN and pressing <ENTER>, you will be rewarded with an ejected page. If you have a printer that occasionally needs this command for page ejection, you might want to make a batch file (see page 141) and keep the batch file in a directory that is located in your PATH. Then you can easily use a simple command from any drive or directory to eject a page.

Sometimes a text file doesn't have an extension. Any file with READ in the file name is probably a text file. Suppose you did a directory on a disk and noticed a file called README with no extension. To print out that file, you would type:

copy readme prn < ENTER >

Suppose you used the DIR command and noticed a file called README.1ST. You can redirect the output of the DOS TYPE command to the printer by issuing the following command:

type readme.1st > prn < ENTER >

Most word processors and editors can also load and print text files. If you have DOS 5 or DOS 6, turn to page 50 to learn how to print a text file using the editor called **EDIT**. Two excellent shareware programs for both viewing and printing out text files are LIST and QEDIT. See pages 259 - 260 for more information on LIST and QEDIT.

You can usually print whatever is showing on the screen (text, at least) by pressing the following key:

< PrtSc >

That key may be labeled < PRINT SCREEN >; it depends on your particular keyboard. On some older machines, to print text showing on the screen, you must press two keys:

< SHIFT > < PrtSc >

Printing Graphic Screens
with DOS 3.3 and Earlier

This section is for those who have DOS version 3.3 or earlier. You can print CGA graphics out on your printer, if you have a color graphics monitor, by first loading a DOS program called GRAPHICS.COM into the computer's memory (RAM). You should find this GRAPHICS.COM program in the directory that contains your DOS files (usually C:\DOS). At the system prompt type:

graphics <ENTER>

Then load the program that has the graphics that you want to print. When the graphic you want to print is showing on your screen, turn on your printer. Then press the following keys:

<SHIFT> <PrtSc>

This means to hold down the key marked <SHIFT> and, while that key is being held down, press the <PrtSc> key. The printer will then start to print. The DOS GRAPHICS command does not work properly on all printers. Remember that with DOS 3.3 and earlier the DOS GRAPHICS.COM program *only works with CGA graphics*. They have improved the performance with DOS 4.0 and later.

Printing Graphic Screens
with DOS 4.0 and Later

With DOS 4.0 and later, Microsoft improved the GRAPHICS.COM command. GRAPHICS.COM is part of DOS, and it should be in the directory that contains your DOS files. The newer version of this command will print out *CGA, EGA, and VGA graphics.* You should specify a printer parameter after the word GRAPHICS. In the below list of printers, which are listed alphabetically, HPDEFAULT through THINKJET are new parameters with DOS 5. This means they require DOS 5 or later.

Printer Parameter	Type of Printer
COLOR1	IBM Color Printer (black ribbon)
COLOR2	IBM Color Printer with 4 color RGB (red, green, blue, and black) ribbon
COLOR8	IBM Color Printer with CMY ribbon
DESKJET	Hewlett-Packard DeskJet Printer
GRAPHICS	Most Epson compatible, IBM Graphics Printer, IBM Proprinter and IBM Quietwriter.
GRAPHICSWIDE	Epson wide-carriage and IBM wide-carriage graphic printers
HPDEFAULT	Hewlett-Packard PCL printer
LASERJET	Hewlett-Packard LaserJet printer
LASERJETII	Hewlett-Packard LaserJet II and HP LaserJet III
PAINTJET	Hewlett-Packard PaintJet
QUIETJET	Hewlett-Packard QuietJet
QUIETJETPLUS	Hewlett-Packard QuietJet Plus
RUGGEDWRITER	Hewlett-Packard Rugged Writer
RUGGEDWRITERWIDE	Hewlett-Packard wide Rugged Writer
THERMAL	IBM PC Convertible thermal printer
THINKJET	Hewlett-Packard ThinkJet version 5

To use GRAPHICS.COM with DOS version 4.0 and later, you should specify one of the above printer parameters after the word GRAPHICS. For example, suppose you have DOS 6 and an HP LaserJet III printer. You would first look at the above table and see that LASERJETII is the printer parameter that will work with an HP LaserJet III printer. To print out graphics using the DOS GRAPHICS.COM command, you would first type:

graphics laserjetii <ENTER>

The GRAPHICS.COM program is then loaded into memory. Note that you load the GRAPHICS.COM program *before* you attempt to load the program that has the graphics you want to print. Then load the program that has the graphics you want to print, and turn the printer on. When the graphics that you want to print are on the screen, press:

<SHIFT> <Prt Sc>

The above means to press the key marked <SHIFT>; and, while that key is being held down, press <Prt Sc>. On newer computer keyboards you can just press the <Prt Sc> key which is sometimes labeled <Print Screen>. The graphics that were showing on the screen will then print out on your printer.

Suppose you had an Epson compatible printer, and you wanted to print some screen graphics. From looking at the above table you see that GRAPHICS is the correct printer parameter for both IBM graphics compatible and EPSON printers. **Most dot matrix printers on the market today are compatible with EPSON or IBM Proprinter printers.** For these printers type:

graphics graphics <ENTER>

Then you would load the program that had the graphics you wanted to print. When the screen was showing the graphics you wanted to print, you would turn your printer on by whispering sweet nothings near the ribbon. Then flip the power switch to "on." Next, press down the following keys together:

<SHIFT> <Prt Sc>

The printer may not start to print for quite some time. Be patient!

With DOS 4.0 and later you can reverse the white and black in the printed image if you use a /R at the end of the GRAPHICS command. For example:

graphics graphics /r <ENTER>

If you have a color printer, you can use a /B switch to print the background in color. That is, add a /B at the end of the GRAPHICS command. If you have an IBM PC Convertible, use a /LCD switch to help control the aspect ratio of the printed image. For example, suppose you had an IBM PC Convertible portable computer with an LCD display and an IBM Proprinter printer. To use the GRAPHIC command with such equipment, type:

graphics graphics /lcd <ENTER>

Then load the graphic program that you want to print. When it is showing on the screen the way you want it, turn your printer on and press the following keys simultaneously:

<SHIFT> <Prt Sc>

The CHKDSK Command

The CHKDSK command can give you a lot of important disk and memory information. *The CHKDSK command can be used on both hard drives and floppy disks.* Make the disk you want to check the *active drive* by changing to that drive. Then at the system prompt type:

chkdsk <ENTER>

You will see something like:

```
C>chkdsk
Volume Serial Number is 1421-0F0D

 65126400 bytes total disk space
    75776 bytes in 3 hidden files
   151552 bytes in 62 directories
 62035968 bytes in 2006 user files
  2863104 bytes available on disk

     2048 bytes in each allocation unit
    31800 total allocation units on disk
     1398 available allocation units on disk

   655360 total bytes memory
   632320 bytes free

C>
```

Figure 4.

The CHKDSK command will give you important information, and it is split into three sections. The first section includes: total disk space (in bytes), hidden files (if any), number of directories, number of bytes used by the files on the disk and total number of files, available bytes on the disk, and number of bad sectors (if any).

56

The section in the middle gives you information about how space is assigned.

The third section gives you information about the computer's memory (up to 640K) including: total bytes of memory and the number of bytes of memory that are free.

If DOS finds what it calls "LOST CLUSTERS," it will tell you. LOST CLUSTERS can happen when you turn the power off while a program has a file open. If you want DOS to fix errors, you can issue the command:

chkdsk /f <ENTER>

The /F switch tells DOS to fix errors. If you are asked:

CONVERT LOST CHAINS TO FILES (Y/N)?

You can answer yes by pressing:

y

DOS will name these files FILE0000.CHK, FILE0001.CHK, etc.; and it will write them to your root directory. You will probably want to delete such files to make room for more useful files. You will learn how to delete such files starting on page 87.

If you have DOS 5 or later, you can get more information about the CHKDSK (or any other DOS command) by typing HELP, a space, and then the DOS command. So, for help on CHKDSK, at the system prompt type:

help chkdsk <ENTER>

When you are learning any new DOS commands (and have DOS 5 or later), you can explore the command further by using this help system. DOS 6 has much better help than earlier versions. See page 192 for more information.

The MEM Command

With *DOS 4.0 and later* Microsoft has provided a command to give you more information about your computer's memory. At the system prompt type:

mem <ENTER>

If you are using *DOS 5 and later*, you can get a more detailed report by issuing the MEM command with a /C switch (for Classify) like this:

mem /c <ENTER>

This will provide you with a detailed report about your system's upper memory. If the information is more than one screen, you can issue the command with the |MORE "filter."

mem /c |more <ENTER>

The (|) character is located on the same key as your backslash characater (\). The |MORE portion of this command told DOS to display the screen until the screen fills. Press any other key to see the next page. You can also use |MORE in the same fashion (at the end of the command) when you issue a DOS TYPE command. See page 47.

With DOS 6 they got smart and provided you with a /P switch to pause the listing. So with DOS 6 you can issue the command like so:

mem /c /p <ENTER>

To obtain a printed copy, turn the printer on (with paper) and give the following command:

mem /c > prn <ENTER>

Formatting Diskettes

Before any disk can contain information, it must first be formatted or, as it is sometimes called, "initialized." Generally, when you buy blank disks in the store, they are not formatted. Anytime you format a disk, it will destroy any information that was previously on that disk. Be sure that when you format a disk, it is either a blank disk or one that you no longer consider of any value. This is very important.

WARNING: When you format a disk, all data on that disk will be destroyed! Be particularly careful not to format any hard drives by mistake. For example, most people reading this book have a hard drive called C; don't format it by mistake. Know which drives are your floppy drives, and only format disks in those drives. If you have to, look in the manual that came with your computer; or call the dealer where you bought the computer. Normally, your floppy drives are A and B (if you have two floppy drives).

You should know what size disk drives you have and what capacity they are before you try to format blank disks. The most popular sizes of disks are 5¼" and 3½". If you need help in identifying what kinds of diskettes you have, see pages 33 - 34. If you have DOS 6 or Windows 3.1, run the MSD program (see page 200). It will give you information on all your drives.

It is assumed that DOS is installed on your hard drive and that the directory that contains your DOS files (usually C:\DOS) is in the PATH statement in your AUTOEXEC.BAT file. These subjects will be covered starting on page 144. If DOS is not installed in the path of your hard drive, you may have to change over to the directory that contains DOS (Example: (CD \DOS <ENTER>) before you can issue some DOS commands. To set up your computer so that DOS is in your path, see pages 144 - 148. Once the directory that contains DOS is placed in your PATH, any of the DOS commands will be available from any directory or drive.

For the first example, make sure you place a blank disk in drive A that corresponds to the full capacity of your particular drive. If you have a 5¼" 1.2MB drive A, use a 1.2MB high-density (HD) floppy disk. If you have a 1.44MB 3½" drive A, use a 1.44MB high-density (HD) floppy disk. Be aware that *any data that is on the disk will be destroyed when it is formatted*. At the system prompt place a blank disk in drive A and type:

format a: <ENTER>

The above command will work with any version of DOS. For most people, this will be the format command that is used on a regular basis.

A high capacity drive will automatically try to format a disk for high capacity. Just follow the prompts, and your floppy disk in drive A will be formatted and ready to accept data. When DOS asks you for a *volume label*, you can make one up that will help you to identify the disk, using up to eleven characters. **It is not necessary that a volume label be given to each disk**; it is optional. If you don't want a volume label, just press <ENTER> when DOS prompts you for one.

If you have a high capacity 1.2MB 5¼" floppy drive for your A drive, you may on occasion want to format 360K disks in it. To format a 360K disk in a 1.2MB floppy drive A, issue the following command:

format a: /4 <ENTER>

You can also do it like this:

format a: /n:9 /t:40 <ENTER>

No wonder some people find DOS impossible! Don't forget any of the characters like (:) or (/). DOS is very unforgiving. To accomplish the same thing on your B drive (assuming it was also a 1.2MB floppy and you wanted to format a 360K disk), you would issue the same command with one exception. You would substitute B: where the above command has an A:.

A 1.2MB 5¼" drive will write data on a 360K disk; however, the data **may not** be readable on other 360K disk drives. This can sometimes be a problem when you want to make a copy of a program for a friend. One way to get around this problem is to format 360K disks on a 360K drive. Then a 1.2MB drive can write data on the disk, and it can be read by other 360K drives. So, if you have a friend with a 360K drive and you have a 5¼" 1.2MB drive, have your friend format some disks first before you try to make him copies. Another way around this problem is to use the commercial program called PC TOOLS by Central Point Software. This program works fine for formatting 360K disks in a 1.2MB drive. The resulting formatted disks work in all machines that use 360K disks (if you use the 360K option).

If you have two floppy drives, your second drive is called drive B. To format a disk in drive B, issue the following:

format b: <ENTER>

Again, a high capacity drive will attempt to format the disk for high capacity. Just follow the prompts, and watch for the little light that indicates your floppy drive is being used. If your drive B is a high capacity 1.44MB 3½" drive and you want to format a 720K disk, you can issue the following command:

format b: /n:9 /t:80 <ENTER>

61

If you have a 1.44MB drive for drive A and want to format a 720K disk in it, you would issue the same command with one exception. You would substitute A: where the above command has a B:.

Formatting Commands
with DOS 4.0 and Later

While the format commands previously covered will work with DOS 3.0 through 6, newer versions of DOS give you formatting commands that are easier to remember. **With DOS 4.0 and later, you can specify size after the /F: as in the following examples.** For a 360K disk you specify 360, for a 720K disk you use 720 for the size. 1.2MB disks are specified by 1200, and with 1.44MB disks you use 1440. DOS 5 and DOS 6 allow you to format 2.88MB extended-density disks by using 2880 for the size option if you have a 2.88MB drive.

Suppose you want to format a 360K disk in a 1.2MB 5¼" drive A. With DOS 4.0 through DOS 6 you can type:

format a: /f:360 <ENTER>

If you have a 1.44MB 3½" drive B and want to format a 720K disk in it, with DOS 4.0 or later you can do it as follows:

format b: /f:720 <ENTER>

With DOS 5 or later you can get help with the FORMAT command by typing:

help format <ENTER>

The Unconditional Format

Starting with DOS 5, there is an Unconditional format. This will destroy *all* the information that was on the disk as it prepares it for use. The unconditional format is great for used disks where you want to completely destroy the old data or when you have been having *trouble getting a used disk to format*. You can issue the unconditional format by adding a /U "switch" to a formatting command. To do an unconditional format on a disk that is the same capacity as your A drive, type:

format a: /u <ENTER>

Suppose you wanted to do an unconditional format on a 360K disk in your 1.2MB A drive. You could issue the following command:

format a: /f:360 /u <ENTER>

The Quick Format Command

Starting with DOS 5, Microsoft included a **Q**uick format command which is very fast. *This can only be used on disks that have already been formatted.* It wipes out the files that were previously on the disk. When you quick format a disk, *it does not check for bad sectors*. It does provide a quick way to clear all the data off a disk so you can use it for something else. You can issue a quick format command by adding a /**Q** "switch" to a format command. Suppose you had a disk that was already formatted and had data that you no longer needed. The below quick format procedure works for any type or size diskette that has been previously formatted. To quick format such a disk in drive A, issue a command like this:

format a: /q <ENTER>

If you want to format a used disk in the shortest possible time, type:

format a: /q /u <ENTER>

This will wipe the disk clean in just a couple of seconds. Here you are adding the Unconditional format "switch" to the **Q**uick format "switch."

The Unformat Command

With DOS 5, Microsoft implemented a MIRROR command to help keep track of deleted files. This feature will be mainly used on hard drives. MIRROR, combined with the DOS 5 UNFORMAT command, may help you restore a group of files on a disk that you have accidently formatted. Microsoft did away with the MIRROR command with DOS 6 and replaced it with a much improved UNDELETE command. To see how the DOS 6 UNDELETE command works, see the section starting on page 202.

Let's experiment with the UNFORMAT command on a floppy disk in drive A. To test it out, format a disk for drive A. Place it in your A drive, and at the A> type:

copy con test.doc <ENTER>
This is a test <ENTER>
<F6> <ENTER>

In the above example COPY CON tells DOS to copy from the **CON**sole (keyboard) and make a file called TEST.DOC. The second line is the contents of the file TEST.DOC. In the third line <F6> tells DOS that this is the end of the file. The <F6>, when used with COPY CON, functions the same as pressing <CTRL> Z. When you press <F6>, you will see ^Z on your screen. Then press the <ENTER> key, and the file TEST.DOC will be saved to disk.

Then you can show the directory of the disk by typing:

dir <ENTER>

You will see the text file TEST.DOC. If you have DOS 5, use the MIRROR command to save information to disk. This creates an image of the system area. You can UNFORMAT a disk without using the MIRROR command. However, with DOS 5, using the MIRROR command makes it more reliable. If you have DOS 6, just skip issuing this next MIRROR command:

mirror a: <ENTER>

This will create a file called MIRROR.FIL where DOS saves information about the disk.

Now format the disk again. Then show the directory by typing:

dir <ENTER>

You will see that the disk no longer has the file you created called TEST.DOC. However, you can bring it back with the UNFORMAT command. Type:

unformat a: <ENTER>

Show the directory of the disk by typing:

dir <ENTER>

You will see that UNFORMAT brought the information back! Please don't rely on UNFORMAT. It is not completely reliable but can save the day if you are lucky. For more information on the DOS 5 MIRROR command, see pages 91 - 92. See the section starting on page 202 for more information on the DOS 6 UNFORMAT command.

Tips

- If you have trouble remembering format commands, you might want to get the superb memory-resident shareware program called **CON > FORMAT** by a company called SYDEX. It will format all the different sizes of disks, including the low and high-density disks. It is completely reliable and is fast. It can format disks while you are using your word processor! Also, when you format a 360K disk in a 1.2MB drive, there is no compatibility problem with 360K drives. CON > FORMAT is all menu driven, so it is a joy to use. For more information on CON > FORMAT see page 258.

- If a disk refuses to format the first time you issue a formatting command, don't give up. **Try at least three times.** Make sure you are giving the command correctly. If you are trying to reformat a used disk and are having trouble, with DOS 5 and DOS 6 use the Unconditional switch. See page 63.

Formatting a Disk with
the System on it

Occasionally, one needs to format a disk with the system on it. A disk with the system on it has a file called COMMAND.COM and several hidden files. A disk with the system on it will automatically boot your computer when you start your computer with the disk in drive A. You can even use a diskette with the system on it with an AUTOEXEC.BAT file to start a particular program automatically. You will learn how to do that starting on page 154.

For the first example, make sure you place a blank disk in drive A that corresponds to the full capacity of your particular drive. If you have a 5¼" 1.2MB drive A, use a 1.2MB high-density (HD) floppy disk. If you have a 1.44MB 3½" drive A, use a 1.44MB high-density (HD) floppy disk. Be aware that *any data that was on the disk will be destroyed when it is formatted*.

To format a disk with the system on it, at the system prompt type:

format a: /s < ENTER >

Note that here you just added the /S "switch" to the standard format command. The computer will respond:

INSERT NEW DISKETTE FOR DRIVE A:
AND STRIKE ENTER WHEN READY

When you have a blank disk in drive A, press:

< ENTER >

The light on drive A will go on, indicating that the drive is being used. After a while the screen will read something like:

FORMAT COMPLETE
SYSTEM TRANSFERRED

Then it will tell you how many bytes of disk space you have, how many bytes are used by the system, and how many bytes are now available on the disk. The numbers will vary depending on the type of disk you are using. Then you will be asked:

FORMAT ANOTHER (Y/N)?

If you don't want to format any more disks, answer the question by pressing:

n

To format a low-density disk with the system in a high-density drive, you would *simply add the /S parameter to the commands found on pages 61 - 62.* For example, to format a 5¼" 360K disk with the system in a 1.2MB drive A, with DOS 4.0 and later you could type:

format a: /f:360 /s < ENTER >

Then just follow the prompts.

Tips

● *It is a good practice to safeguard a floppy disk with the system on it. Such a disk can be used to start your computer.* **You must use a disk that can be used in your A drive** *(the B drive will not work) and format a diskette with the system on it, as shown on page 67. Label it, write protect it, and keep it in a safe place. If your hard drive should ever fail to boot up, you can use this disk to start the computer.* Just for fun, you might want to try starting your computer this way now. Turn your computer off. Place a disk that has the system on it in drive A, and close the drive door. Turn on your computer. Instead of using your hard drive to boot up, your computer will use the floppy drive A. This is called "booting from a floppy." When you start your computer in this way, you will be greeted with the date and time prompts. See page 28 if you need instructions on how to put in the date or time.

● When your computer boots up from the hard drive, it may automatically run programs that take up precious memory. Booting from a floppy disk is sometimes a quick way to squeeze a little more memory out of your machine. Older versions of DOS did not make use of upper memory. Suppose you have an older version of DOS and bought a game that refused to run. Perhaps it reported that you did not have enough memory to run the program. You can use the CHKDSK command to check how much free memory you have. See page 56 for more on CHKDSK. Try booting from a *floppy disk with the system on it in Drive A.* Then try running the program again. If it works, after using the program, reboot without a disk in drive A; so your computer will work as usual.

For more information about your start-up files see the pages 146 - 167. If you have DOS 6, see pages 205 - 214. If you have DOS 6, you may wish to use MEMMAKER to squeeze more conventional memory out of your machine. See pages 215 - 219.

Copying a Disk

The DOS **DISKCOPY** command is used to make an exact copy of an entire diskette. If you only want to copy some of the files on a disk, you can use the DOS COPY command. You should make backup copies of your important disks. Make sure that you write protect any disk you want to copy. If you aren't sure about write protection, see pages 33 - 34. This prevents any accidental writing to the original disk.

When you want to copy a disk, **the one you want to copy is called the** SOURCE DISK. **The disk you want the files copied to is called the** TARGET DISK or DESTINATION DISK. The DISKCOPY command is used to copy a diskette, and *it formats the target disk as the copy is being made*. The DOS DISKCOPY command can be used only with diskettes and is not for fixed (hard) drives. Make sure you use the DISKCOPY command only when your target disk is a blank disk or is a disk that has information that is no longer valuable. When you use the DISKCOPY command, the data that was on your target disk gets destroyed. It is good practice to make sure your source disk has a label, so you don't confuse it with the target disk during the copying process.

Suppose you have a 5¼" drive A and a 3½" drive B. **You cannot use the DISKCOPY command to copy between two different sizes of diskettes.** If you want to do that, use the XCOPY command. See pages 80 - 86.

> When using the DISKCOPY command, you should use the same type and size disks for both the source and target disk. For example, if your source disk is a high density 5¼" disk, you must use a 5¼" high density disk as the target disk. Anytime you use the DISKCOPY command, the data that was on the target disk gets destroyed.

Suppose you want to copy a 5¼" disk in your drive A. At the system prompt type:

diskcopy a: a: <ENTER>

Be sure to put the colons (:) in the proper places. Make sure you put the spaces where they belong. DOS CAN BE VERY FUSSY ABOUT SPELLING AND SYNTAX. The computer will display the following:

INSERT SOURCE DISKETTE IN DRIVE A:
PRESS ANY KEY WHEN READY...

Place a 5¼" disk that you want to copy in drive A. Make sure it is write protected.

Then press:
<ENTER>

The disk will spin as it is being read. Your little drive light for drive A will come on, indicating that drive A is being used. Then a message will be displayed and finally:

INSERT TARGET DISKETTE IN DRIVE A:

PRESS ANY KEY TO CONTINUE

At this point place a blank 5¼" disk of the same type as the source disk in drive A. Then press:

<ENTER>

The computer responds with:

FORMATTING WHILE COPYING

71

This takes a while. When it is done, the screen will show:

COPY ANOTHER DISKETTE (Y/N)?

The Y/N stands for yes or no. This abbreviated form for yes and no is often used in computer software. Answer the question by pressing:

n

The computer will then give you the system prompt. If you do want to copy another disk, you would press Y; the procedure will start all over again. That wasn't too bad now, was it? If you are copying a high-density disk with lots of data, *you may have to switch between the source disk and the target disk a few times to get the job accomplished. Just follow the prompts on the screen.*

Suppose your drive B was a 3½" drive and you wanted to copy a 3½" disk. You would issue the following command:

diskcopy b: b: < ENTER >

Then just follow the prompts.

These days, if a computer has two floppy drives, they are usually two different types. That is, one is a 5¼" drive and the other is a 3½" drive. However, if you have a computer with *two floppy drives and both are the same type and size*, you can do a DISKCOPY using both of your drives. If that is the case, place the source disk in drive A and the target disk in drive B. Then type:

diskcopy a: b: < ENTER >

Tips

- If you try to copy a disk with DISKCOPY and get an error message, don't give up. Try using COPY *.* or XCOPY to copy the disk to a formatted target disk. See pages 77 - 79. COPY *.* and XCOPY can copy a source disk that is fragmented, and the new target disk will not be fragmented. Many DOS experts dislike the DISKCOPY command and prefer to use COPY or XCOPY to copy a diskette. They feel COPY and XCOPY are more reliable. See the last tip below for how to do it.

- There is a superior shareware program called **COPYQM** that can take the place of the DOS DISKCOPY command. The problem with the DOS DISKCOPY command is the absurd **DOS-E-DOE SHUFFLE**...that is, switching those blasted disks back and forth. By the time you are through copying a full high-density disk, you will think you were doing some kind of dance. Fortunately, the DOS-E-DOE SHUFFLE is altogether avoidable. COPYQM can copy a high-density disk and read the source disk in just one pass. For more on COPYQM see page 258.

- Suppose you want to copy the contents of a 5¼" 360K (low-density) disk and only have 1.2MB (high-density) 5¼" blank disks. You can accomplish this task by copying the source disk to the hard drive and then copying it back to a *formatted* target diskette. Do it like so:

  1. Copy the source disk to an empty or new directory on your hard drive. See pages 119 - 122.

  2. Copy the data you just copied to the hard drive to a *formatted* blank diskette as shown on pages 130 - 131.

You can use this same procedure to copy a 3½" 720K diskette to a 3½" 1.44MB diskette. *It also works with disks of the same size and capacity.*

Copying a File
with only One Floppy Drive

If you want to copy an entire diskette, you can use the DOS DISKCOPY command as shown on pages 70 - 73. If you want to copy a single file and have only one floppy drive, you can do it by bluffing DOS. You can instruct DOS to copy the file to a non-existing B drive. Suppose you want to copy a file called ASTRO.EXE. For this operation you will need to have a formatted disk which will be used as the target disk. If you need help with formatting a blank disk, see pages 59 - 62.

Place the disk with the file you want to copy in the A drive. This is called the source disk. Change to the A drive by typing:

a: <ENTER>

Even though you don't have a B drive, issue the copy command like this:

copy astro.exe b: <ENTER>

You will then get a message like:

INSERT DISKETTE FOR DRIVE B: AND STRIKE
ANY KEY WHEN READY

Remove the source disk from drive A. Since you don't have a B drive, you will place a formatted disk in the **A drive** which will be used as the target disk. Then press:

<ENTER>

The file ASTRO.EXE will be copied to the target disk in drive A. Do a directory—DIR <ENTER>—to confirm that the operation was a success.

You can use this same single floppy method to copy a number of files using wildcards. See pages 77 - 79 and 126 - 129 for information on how to use wildcards in DOS commands. You can also use this technique with the XCOPY command. See page 82. The advantage of XCOPY is that it will read more files into memory before wanting to write to the target disk. This makes the copying quicker. With the above procedure *you may have to switch disks to complete the copying task.* You will be prompted if you need to switch disks. Pay careful attention to the screen prompts to avoid a mix up.

Copying a File Between
Two Floppy Drives

Suppose you have a computer with two floppy drives, drive A and drive B. Perhaps you have a file named ASTRO.EXE on your diskette in drive A that you would like to copy to a diskette in drive B. If you want to copy the file to a disk that already has files on it, you can, provided that there is enough space on your target disk. You can confirm that there is enough room on the target disk by doing a directory or issuing the DOS CHKDSK command. For help with the CHKDSK command see page 56.

CAUTION: If you have a file on the target disk that has the same file name and extension as the file you want to copy, when you copy the new file to the target disk, the old file will be replaced by the new file. The old file will then be wiped out and lost forever.

Place the target disk in drive B. If this target disk is blank, it needs to be formatted. If you need help formatting a blank disk, see pages 59 - 62.

Make the A drive the *active drive* by changing over to that drive. If you were not already on the A drive, change to the A drive by typing at the system prompt:

a: <ENTER>

To confirm that the ASTRO.EXE file (our example file) is on the A drive, do a directory:

dir <ENTER>

Then at the A> type:

copy astro.exe b: <ENTER>

The example file ASTRO.EXE on the diskette in drive A will be copied to the diskette in drive B. To confirm that the file was copied to the B drive, you can change over to the B drive and do a directory on the disk. The above example will work on all types of drives. It doesn't matter that one drive is a 3½" and the other is a 5¼". You do have to have enough space left on the target disk to hold the file you want to copy.

If you want to copy a file from the B drive to the A drive, you would put a formatted disk in drive A and change over to the B drive to make it the *active drive* by typing:

b: <ENTER>

Then at the B> type:

copy filename.ext a: <ENTER>

In the above example, FILENAME is the **name** of any file you want to copy, and .EXT is that file's extension. If the file that you want to copy has no extension, you would leave off the period and the extension.

Copying Files Using Wildcards

You can use the DOS **COPY *.*** command to copy all the files in the current directory. The **current directory** is the *active directory* and is the one in which you are working. Most people do not make additional directories on floppy disks; usually, everything is stored in the root directory. The root directory is the first directory on a disk and was created when the disk was formatted. Directories are covered in detail starting on page 96.

You can determine if there are other directories on a disk by issuing the **DIR** command. You can recognize them by a <DIR> "thing" to the right of the directory name. See page 98 for an example. *The COPY *.* command can be used on floppy and hard drives*. It is often used for copying files between directories on a hard drive.

In the **COPY *.*** command, the asterisks (*) are wildcards. Yes, it is kind of like poker. However, if you know what you're doing, you will not be gambling! The first asterisk represents any file name. The period between the two asterisks delineates between the file name and the file's extension. The second asterisk represents any file extension. So, this tells DOS to copy all files with any or no extension. You can issue a **CHKDSK** command (see page 56) to check each disk to make sure that you have enough space on the target drive to hold all the files on the source disk. If you want to copy all the files in the current directory, **the target disk must have enough available space** to hold them. Otherwise, it will not copy all the files. If the source disk has more data than the target disk will hold, you can use XCOPY. See the section starting on page 83.

The **COPY *.*** command will not copy hidden files. A hidden file is a file whose attributes are set in such a fashion that they do not appear on the disk directory. Most diskettes do not contain hidden files. The DOS **CHKDSK** command will check for hidden files. See page 116 for more TIPS on how to deal with hidden files. If you have a diskette with hidden files (such as a DOS disk), you can use the DOS **DISKCOPY** command to copy the disk. See page 70.

Suppose you have a 5¼" drive A and a 3½" drive B. Place a blank formatted 3½" disk in drive B and a 5¼" disk you want to copy in drive A. Change to drive A by typing at the system prompt:

a: <ENTER>

Then issue the following command:

copy *.* b: <ENTER>

This will copy all files in the *active directory* of drive A to drive B.

Suppose you wanted to copy all the files on the disk in drive B to drive A. If you are not sure, use the **CHKDSK** command to check the source disk and target disk to determine if the target disk has enough space to hold all the files you want to copy. Then place a formatted disk in drive A. Place the disk that you want to copy in drive B. Then change to the B drive. At the B> type:

copy *.* a: <ENTER>

This tells DOS to copy all files with any or no extension in the *active directory* to the disk in drive A.

Let's explore another use for wildcard copying. Suppose you have a diskette in drive A that has many files with the extension .DOC. Perhaps you want to copy all the files with the extension .DOC to a formatted disk in drive B. Place the blank formatted disk in drive B. Make drive A the *active drive*:

a: <ENTER>

Then at the A> type:

copy *.doc b: <ENTER>

The asterisk represents a wildcard. The above command instructed DOS to copy all files in the active directory with *any file name having an extension of* **.DOC** to drive B. To learn more about wildcard copying, see pages 127 - 129.

Tips

● On the previous two pages you learned how to use the COPY *.* command. However, if you just hate typing in extra characters, *you can use a shortcut method*. This one may surprise even seasoned DOS users. To copy all the files from the current directory to the A drive, type:

copy . a: <ENTER>

The above command functions the same as COPY *.* A: <ENTER>. Here the period (.) represents the current directory. It will copy all the files in the current directory to drive A.

79

Copying a 5¼" Disk to a 3½" Disk

The XCOPY command can be used to copy files from any size disk to another. XCOPY is great for copying files to and from the hard drive, too. If you have both a 5¼" disk drive and a 3½" drive, you will at some time want to copy data from one to another. **The DOS DISKCOPY command will not copy between two different sizes of disk drives**.

The disk you want to copy is called the **source disk**. The disk that you want to copy the data to is called the **target disk**. You can use the DOS CHKDSK command to determine how much space the files on the source disk will require. Make sure that the target disk has enough space on it to hold all the data you want to copy.

Suppose you want to copy a 5¼" disk in drive A to a 3½" disk in drive B. Put the 5¼" disk you want to copy in drive A. At the system prompt type:

chkdsk a: <ENTER>

You will then be shown how much total disk space is on the disk and how much space is taken up by files on that disk. You should make a note of this information. With this information you can tell whether you will have enough room to copy data from drive A to drive B. You will then want to format a blank 3½" disk. For this example drive B is the 3½" drive. Place a blank 3½" disk in drive B (make sure it is the proper type for your particular drive). Type:

format b: <ENTER>

When it has finished formatting, you will want to leave the diskette in drive B. If you have any trouble formatting a disk, see pages 59 - 66. **Make sure you write protect the source disk**. With the write protected 5¼" source disk in drive A, at the system prompt type:

xcopy a: b: /s /e <ENTER>

All the files on drive A will then be copied to drive B. Note that the first drive mentioned in the above command is the source drive (in this case A), and the second drive mentioned is the target disk (B in this example). Do a directory on drive B to verify that the files were copied—DIR <ENTER>.

The XCOPY command was first introduced in DOS 3.2. It is significantly faster than the copy *.* command when you are dealing with a lot of files and copying between floppy disks. When you issued the command XCOPY A: B: /S /E you told DOS to copy all files on drive A to the target drive B. The /S portion of this command told DOS to copy any Subdirectories that might be on the source disk in drive A (that contain data). The /E portion of this command told DOS to copy subdirectories even if they are Empty. If there are no subdirectories on the source disk, the /S and /E switches will do no harm.

If your A drive is a 3½" drive and your B drive is a 5¼", then you would put a blank formatted 3½" disk in drive A and the 5¼" disk you want to copy in drive B. You would then issue the following command:

xcopy b: a: /s /e <ENTER>

CAUTION: It should be noted that the XCOPY command will not copy *hidden files*. A hidden file is a file whose attributes are set in such a fashion that they do not appear on the disk directory. You can check for hidden files on a diskette by issuing the DOS CHKDSK command. See page 56. The most common hidden files are those created by DOS when you format a disk with the system on it. See pages 116 - 117 for more on how to deal with hidden files.

Copying a 3½" Disk to a 5¼" Disk

If you want to copy a 3½" disk to a 5¼" disk, you need to know how much data is on the 3½" disk. You will also need to know the capacity of the 5¼" disk.

Let us assume you have a 1.2MB 5¼" drive A and a 1.44MB 3½" drive B. However, it should be noted that the below techniques will also work with 360K 5¼" disks and 720K 3½" disks. Often you want to share a disk with a friend. The friend may not have a 3½" drive but does have a 1.2MB 5¼" drive. To find out how much data is on the 3½" disk, you can use the DOS CHKDSK command. Place the 3½" disk you want to copy in drive B and type:

chkdsk b: <ENTER>

Let us assume the CHKDSK command told you there were 1,120,944 bytes in 12 user files. This means that a 1.2MB 5¼" disk should hold the information. Note that a formatted 1.2MB disk has 1,228,800 bytes free. So, you now know you can copy the data from the 3½" 1.44MB disk to the 1.2MB 5¼" disk. Next you would need to *format* a blank 5¼" 1.2MB disk. Place a blank 1.2MB disk in drive A and type:

format a: <ENTER>

If you have any trouble formatting a disk see pages 59 - 66. Place the 3½" disk that you want to copy in the drive B. Then type:

xcopy b: a: /s /e <ENTER>

The above command tells DOS to copy everything on the disk in drive B to the disk in drive A. However, it should be noted that XCOPY will not copy *hidden* files. See page 116 for how to deal with hidden files. The first drive mentioned in the above command is the source drive, and the second drive mentioned is the target drive. The /S in the above example tells DOS to copy to the A drive any Subdirectories that contain data. The /E portion of this command told DOS to copy subdirectories even if they are Empty.

If you have a 3½" drive A and a 5¼" drive B, you would adjust the DOS command for your particular drive configuration (XCOPY A: B: /S /E <ENTER>).

This was the best case scenario. If you had done a CHKDSK on the 3½" floppy disk and found that it contained more data then the 5¼" disk could hold, then keep reading. The next section will show you how to use XCOPY to copy all the files from a large capacity source disk to multiple smaller capacity target disks.

Copying a Group of Files to Multiple Diskettes

If you ran CHKDSK on the source disk and found that it contained more information than the target disk could hold, you can still use XCOPY to accomplish the task with one prerequisite. *No one file on the source disk may exceed the capacity of the target disk.* You need to do a directory on the source disk to make this determination.

The following procedure works with any type and capacity diskette; however, you will need *DOS 3.3 or later.* (The /S switch for the ATTRIB command was introduced with DOS 3.3.) You might not use this procedure often; but, when you need it, you will be glad to have it in your bag of tricks. First you will want to estimate how many target disks you will need. You can make this estimate with the information you get from running CHKDSK on the source disk. For example, if the source disk was a 3½" 720K floppy that contained 710K of data, you would need at least two 360K 5¼" diskettes. To be safe, you would **format at least three** 5¼" 360K disks. Let me repeat, for the below procedure to work, no one file can be larger than will fit on the target disk.

For the example let's assume that the source disk is a 720K 3½" disk in drive B and that the target disks are 360K 5¼" disks that can be used in drive A. Do a directory on the source disk and make sure that no one file is larger than 360K. Place the source disk in drive B, and change to the B drive by issuing the following command:

b: <ENTER>

In the next command the **A** in **+A *.*** has nothing to do with drives. It sets the archive bit to **on** for every file on the disk in drive B. Type:

attrib +a *.* /s <ENTER>

Place one of the three 5¼" formatted floppy disks in drive A and type:

xcopy *.* a: /m /s <ENTER>

After a while the files will begin to be copied to the A drive, and then you will get a message that may read something like:

INSUFFICIENT DISK SPACE
5 FILES COPIED

At this point you should remove the first 5¼" target disk in drive A and label it. Then put the second blank 5¼" formatted disk in the A drive. Then repeat the previous command:

xcopy *.* a: /m /s <ENTER>

On most machines (but not all), you can press the function key labeled <F3> to automatically repeat the previous command. You continue the above procedure until all the files are copied. If you continue this procedure with one more target disk than you need, you will finally get a response like:

0 FILE(S) COPIED

Then you will know that all files have been copied. Do a directory on the target disks to assure yourself that the files were copied.

When you gave the command **ATTRIB +A *.* /S <ENTER>**, it set what is called the archive bit on every file on the B drive. Because it was issued with the /S switch, it also set the archive bit on every file in any subdirectories. When you issued the command **XCOPY *.* A: /M /S <ENTER>**, the /M "switch" told DOS to copy only those files with the archive bit set. When you copy with XCOPY using the /M switch, it clears the archive bit after each file is copied. Therefore, XCOPY does not copy those files that have already been copied because those files that have been copied have the archive bit cleared. The /S "switch" in the XCOPY command told DOS to copy all subdirectories that contained files and to make any needed subdirectories on the target disk.

In the above example, XCOPY was used with a special archive attribute feature to copy a large capacity disk to a number of smaller capacity disks. You can also use the same procedure to copy files from your hard drive to multiple floppy disks. If you don't want to copy underlying subdirectories, just leave off the /S in the above commands.

Tips

- If you have DOS 6, you may be able to use DoubleSpace to almost double the capacity of a diskette. See pages 226 - 229.

- A shareware program by the name of **PCOPY**, by Norm Patriquin, is more powerful than the DOS copy commands. Like the DOS XCOPY command, PCOPY can copy subdirectories that might be on the source disk. However, PCOPY can copy a very large file and *split the file to multiple diskettes*. PCOPY will prompt you when you need to change disks. If the target disks are not formatted, it will do that too. If you want to acquire PCOPY, make sure you get version 9.0 or later to ensure that it is capable of splitting large files.

- There are other ways to solve space problems. **PKZIP** is a shareware program that compresses files so you can get more data into less space. The latest PKZIP program also has the ability to split a file across multiple diskettes. It is not unusual to compress a group of files to 70 percent or more by ZIPPING the data. You will also need **PKUNZIP** to uncompress the zipped files so they can be used. These programs are by PKWARE, INC., and are available from most shareware vendors. Also, there is an amazing shareware program by the same author called **PKLITE**. PKLITE will reduce the size of most .EXE files by 33 to 50 percent.

- A public domain program called **FDFORMAT** is available from some shareware vendors. It will format 360K disks to 410K, 1.2MB disks to 1.48MB, 720K disks to 820K, and 1.44MB disks to 1.72MB. You can also combine techniques. You could use PKZIP to compress the data on the source disk and use the FDFORMAT program to increase the capacity of the target disk. All these shareware and public domain programs come with manuals on the disks. See pages 256 - 263.

Deleting Files

In the examples below you will learn how to delete (erase) files on floppy disks. However, you delete files on a hard drive in the same way. Usually, you will want to change to the directory that has the files you want to delete, making that directory the *active directory*. You do this by using the CD command. That will be covered starting on page 102. There will be specific examples of deleting files on the hard drive starting on page 109.

Suppose you changed to the A drive by typing:

a: <ENTER>

Then you did a directory on a diskette—DIR <ENTER>—and found a file called RHINO.EXE that you wanted to erase. You could delete RHINO.EXE by issuing the following command at the A>:

del rhino.exe <ENTER>

Then to make sure that it is gone, you can do another directory on the disk by typing:

dir <ENTER>

Deleting with Wildcards

In the section on Copying Files Using Wildcards, starting on page 77, you found that wildcards can be very powerful. You can use wildcards to delete files in the same way you used them to copy files.

CAUTION: Because deleting with wildcards is so absolutely all inclusive, you will want to be very careful when you use it. You can erase all the files in the *active directory* in a flash. Most people, who have been computing for a while, have at some time accidentally deleted files they didn't mean to delete. It can be a very shocking experience! Be particularly careful when you delete with wildcards.

Suppose you did a directory on a disk in drive B and found that you no longer wanted any of the files. At the B >, with that disk in drive B, you could type the following command to delete all of the files:

del *.* <ENTER>

The above command instructed DOS to delete all files with any file name and any extension in the *active directory*. The asterisks (*) are wildcards. The first * in the above command represents any file name. The second * represents any extension. When you issue the above command, DOS will prompt you to confirm your intentions. Afterwards, doing a directory will verify that you have erased all the files.

Perhaps you did a directory of a diskette in drive A and found numerous files, and some of these were files with a .DOC extension that you wanted to delete. You can delete all the files with .DOC extension if you issue the following command:

del *.doc \<ENTER\>

In the above command the * represents any file name. So, this told DOS to delete *all the files that have a .DOC extension* and are in the *active directory*.

Suppose you did a directory on a disk and noticed a number of files with the same file name. In Figure 3 on page 40 there is a sample directory of a disk with five files that have WORDPLAY as the file name but have different extensions. To delete all the files with WORDPLAY as the file name, you can issue the following command:

del wordplay.* \<ENTER\>

This instructed DOS to delete all the files in the active directory with WORDPLAY as the file name. Here the asterisk (*) represents any extension.

For more information about using wildcards see pages 127 - 129.

Usually, people store everything in the root directory on a floppy disk. See the DIRECTORIES section starting on page 96 where you'll learn how to move around a directory structure. You can determine if there are other directories on a disk by issuing the **DIR** command. You can recognize them by a \<DIR\> "thing" to the right of the directory name. See page 98 for an example.

Tips

- If you want to delete all the files in the active directory and just hate typing in extra characters, *you can use a shortcut method.* This one may surprise even seasoned DOS users. To delete all the files in the *active directory*, type:

del . <ENTER>

This command functions the same as **DEL *.* <ENTER>**. *When you delete with wildcards, be very careful! Note the CAUTION on page 88.* Please be careful.

- To see what files are going to be deleted, you can issue a DIR command that will simulate the deletion. The advantage is that this will be a trial run that will not harm the files. For example, to see what files will be deleted when you type **DEL *.* <ENTER>**, you can issue the following command:

dir *.* /w <ENTER>

The files that show up on the screen would be deleted if you had issued the **DEL *.* <ENTER>** command instead. **When you delete with wildcard characters, you can't be too careful.**

Undeleting Files with DOS 5

With DOS 5, Microsoft included a command called MIRROR to keep track of disk information and an UNDELETE command. Microsoft improved the UNDELETE command with DOS 6 and did not include the MIRROR command. For how to use the DOS 6 UNDELETE command, see the section starting on page 202.

With DOS 5 you can use the MIRROR command to help recover deleted files. If you want MIRROR to keep track of information on drive C, you would type:

mirror /tc < ENTER >

The T in the above command told DOS to keep track of deleted files, and the C told DOS to track drive C. It saves information in your root directory in files called MIRROR.FIL and PCTRACK.DEL. You might want to include a line like the above in your AUTOEXEC.BAT file. Then DOS will automatically keep track of deleted files. For more on the AUTOEXEC.BAT file see pages 146 - 154.

If you want to unload MIRROR from the current drive, you can type:

mirror /u < ENTER >

Then DOS will stop tracking the deleted files. Let's experiment on a floppy drive with MIRROR. Place a formatted disk in drive A. Change over to that drive by typing:

a: < ENTER >
copy con test.doc < ENTER >
undelete test < ENTER >
< F6 > < ENTER >

You just made a file called TEST.DOC. The third line caused DOS to save the file to disk. To view this newly made text file, type:

type test.doc <ENTER>

Now you can use the MIRROR command on this diskette by typing:

mirror /ta <ENTER>

The /TA in the above MIRROR command told DOS to use deletion tracking for the files on drive A. Now type:

del test.doc <ENTER>

If you do a directory on the disk, you will see that it is gone:

dir <ENTER>

Next, you can use the UNDELETE command to try to bring it back. Type:

undelete <ENTER>

This tells DOS to try to bring back all files that have been deleted in the current directory. *The DOS UNDELETE command works best when you are using deletion tracking; however, it can recover files even if you are not using it.* Just follow the prompts and answer Y to bring back the file TEST.DOC. If you do a directory on the disk—DIR <ENTER>, you will find that the file TEST.DOC was recovered! For now, leave this file on the disk, and you can use it to do experiments in the next section. Unfortunately, you can not always recover a file with UNDELETE. When a file is deleted, DOS can use that space for saving other files. Once that space is filled with other data, you will not be able to recover the previously deleted file. *If you need to recover a file that you accidently deleted, you had better do it as soon as possible.* The longer you wait, the less your chance for success.

File Name Conventions

On occasion you will want to name or rename a file. A file name can't be more than eight characters long, and the extension can't be more than three characters in length. Each file in the current directory must have a unique file name. A period (.) is used to separate a file name from the extension. See the examples below. You can't have any spaces in a file name. Beginners often make that mistake. If you want to include a space, use the underscore character; for example: I_TOE_D.USO or BAD_DOG.BTE

DOS will not allow you to use the following special characters in a file name:

= \ + / [ ] " , ; : ? * < > |

This means you cannot use any of the above characters to name or rename a file.

CAUTION: Be careful when you name or rename a file. If the same file name and extension already exist in the current directory, the first file will be wiped out when you create the second version.

Renaming Files

On page 91 you learned how to make a file called TEST.DOC. If you wanted to change the name of TEST.DOC, you would first need to make the drive and directory that contains TEST.DOC the *active directory*. If you will recall, you made the file TEST.DOC on a diskette that would work in your A drive. Place the disk with TEST.DOC in the A drive, and change over to that drive by typing at the system prompt:

a: <ENTER>

Then do a directory to make sure that the file TEST.DOC exists. To change the name of TEST.DOC to FUN.TXT, type:

ren test.doc fun.txt <ENTER>

The above REN command changes the name of the file TEST.DOC to FUN.TXT. You can then do a directory on the disk to confirm that the file FUN.TXT is there and that the file TEST.DOC is not. Since the file TEST.DOC was a text file, you can confirm that the contents have not changed when you renamed it by using the TYPE command like:

type fun.txt <ENTER>

The contents of the newly named file will be displayed on the screen.

Part 4

HARD DRIVE FUNDAMENTALS

"I'VE WARNED PHIL **NOT** TO MESS AROUND WITH THAT **CONFU.SYS** FILE."

Directories

A hard disk holds much more data than a floppy disk. For that reason, it is necessary to organize a hard drive into sections. *These sections are called* **directories** *and* **subdirectories**. *A subdirectory is a file directory that is subordinate to another directory*. It may be helpful to think of these in genealogical terms. Think of the directory as a parent and the subdirectory as a child of that parent.

Usually, everything is stored on the root directory of a *floppy disk*. The root directory is the first directory on a disk and was created when the disk was formatted. People don't often put subdirectories on their floppy disks, but you certainly can if you want to. You make a directory on a floppy disk and navigate it in the same way you do for a hard disk. This information will be covered in this section. As technology improves and the capacity of floppy disks gets larger, the need increases for subdirectories on diskettes.

Computer people often refer to subdirectories as directories. Don't let such computer jargon throw you! If you want to be stuffy, the root directory is the only real directory. All other directories under the root directory are subdirectories because they are subordinate to the root. However, in this book, like other books on DOS, a subdirectory will also be called a directory.

This section on directories was designed for readers to try the examples as they are reading. If you try the examples as you go along, it will be easier to learn. *Once you learn to navigate the hard drive, you will enjoy your computer much more.*

Directory Structure

A simple hard drive directory structure might look like this:

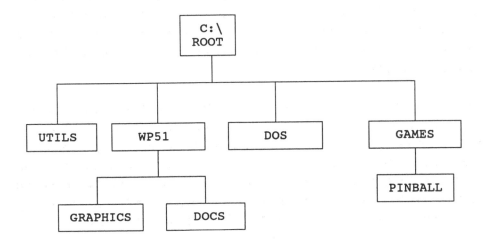

Figure 5. A hard drive directory structure.

Getting to the Root Directory

To get to the root directory of your C drive, at the C> type:

cd \ <ENTER>

The **CD** in the above command stands for **Change Directory**. The \ character is called a backslash. The \ character by itself stands for root directory, so this command instructed DOS to change to the root directory. This makes the root directory the current or *active directory*.

97

When you are on the root directory of the C drive, you can show the directory by typing:

dir < ENTER >

If your hard drive was set up like the example in figure 5 on page 97, you would see something similar to:

```
C>dir

 Volume in drive C has no label
 Directory of C:\

COMMAND  COM     25308   11-01-88    12:00a
DOS             <DIR>            1-16-92     8:23a
UTILS           <DIR>            1-16-92     8:35a
CONFIG   SYS        24   1-16-92     8:42a
AUTOEXEC BAT        51   1-16-92     8:39a
WP51            <DIR>            5-25-92     8:01a
GAMES           <DIR>           10-15-92     7:18a
        7 File (s)  16496640 bytes free

C>
```

In the above example, those files with the < DIR > "thing" to the right of the file name are really "1st generation" directories. Note that you do not see the subdirectories under WP51 or the subdirectory under GAMES. See Figure 5 on page 97. *You can tell if a directory has subdirectories under it by changing over to it; then issue the DIR command and look for "file" names with < DIR > to the right of them. For example, to see if there are subdirectories under GAMES, you would have to change to the C:\GAMES directory and then issue a DIR command.* Changing directories (CD) is covered on page 102.

Note that COMMAND.COM, CONFIG.SYS, and AUTOEXEC.BAT are the only real files in this example root directory. These files are used by the computer on start-up. You will learn about AUTOEXEC.BAT files and CONFIG.SYS files starting on page 146. Your computer's C drive root directory will probably have more files (and directories) than the example.

Root Directory Philosophy

Beginners often make the mistake of copying everything to the root directory of their hard drive. Usually, it is because they don't understand directories and don't know how to make or specify subdirectories. In this section you will learn how to make subdirectories and how to navigate your hard drive. You will learn how to copy files to your hard drive starting on page 118.

It is wise to keep the root directory of your hard drive as uncluttered as possible. Don't copy unnecessary files to your root directory. If you tried to store everything in the root directory of your hard drive, it would become very confusing. It would get to be a horrible mess. I have seen such computers and their bewildered owners.

The hard drive is similar to a file cabinet with drawers and files. The hard drive "file folders" are called directories. You will want to organize your files into logical groups called directories. You can have lots of directories *branching from the root directory,* but you should keep the number of actual files on the root directory to a minimum.

Copying everything to the root directory is like having a file cabinet and throwing all your papers into a single pile. You would have a hard time finding anything. You certainly don't want to *run* your computer like that. Just remember what Francis Bacon, the famous English philosopher, said in his delightful work, "Novum Organum."

"When a man runs the wrong way, the more active and swift he is, the further he will go astray."

The Tree Command

The DOS TREE command is used to show graphically the directory structure of your hard drive. To view the directory structure of your C drive, type:

cd \ <ENTER>
tree <ENTER>

If you have too many screens of information to get a clear picture, you can send the tree structure to the printer. First turn your printer on; and at the C>, with the root directory as the *active directory*, type:

tree > prn <ENTER>

The > PRN in the above command redirects the output to the printer. The output from such a command is not very pretty!

If you have DOS version 4.0 or later, you can issue the command like this; and it will give you a much better graphical representation:

tree /a > prn <ENTER>

If you want to show all the files in the directories, you can issue the command with the /F switch like this:

tree /f > prn <ENTER>

Make sure you have your printer turned on with plenty of paper ready. With DOS 4.0 or higher you can issue the command like this to get a better drawing:

tree /a /f > prn <ENTER>

By now you are probably thinking that this philosophy of root directories and the TREE command is about as much fun as a root canal. If you really want to frolic and have some good clean fun, make a directory! There are few computing tasks that are as intrinsically rewarding as creating a brand spanking new directory.

Making a Directory

The MD command is used to **Make** a **D**irectory on a hard drive or a floppy disk. The name you give your directory cannot be more than eight characters. For this example we will use GAMES. Don't worry about cluttering up your hard drive with useless directories because you will delete these a little later on. You can make a new directory (as shown below) from *any directory on your C drive.*

At the C > type:

md \games < ENTER >

Because the C drive is the active drive, the above command will make a directory called C:\GAMES. *When a backslash precedes the directory name (as in \GAMES), it means that the directory specified will be from the root directory.* Be aware of this when you issue other DOS commands.

Go to the root directory by typing:

cd \ < ENTER >

If you issue a DIR command, you will see that the GAMES directory is listed on the root directory. *If you try to make a directory and that same directory name exists on your current drive, DOS will give you an error message so you will not write over the original directory.*

Changing Directories

You will want to know how to change to other directories so you will be able to access files in those directories. The CD command is used to **C**hange **D**irectories. If you are working the examples in this section, you just made a directory called C:\GAMES. You might want to change over to that directory so that it will be the *active directory*. This can also be called "logging onto the GAMES directory." To change over to the C:\GAMES directory from *anywhere on the C drive*, type at the C prompt:

cd \games <ENTER>

If you had a subdirectory stemming from the C:\GAMES directory called C:\GAMES\PINBALL, you could change to it from *anywhere on the C drive* by typing at a C prompt:

cd \games\pinball <ENTER>

See Figure 5 on page 97 for a graphic representation of such a directory structure. There are shortcuts to get around a directory structure. Once you have mastered the above basic methods, you will be ready to undertake the shortcut methods. See the Tips starting on page 112 for shortcuts.

> The directory you are working in is called the current directory. This is the *active directory*. DOS keeps track of the last current directory that you were in for each drive. This includes floppy drives as well as hard drives. If you change drives, DOS will take you to the last directory you were working in for that drive. If you had not used that drive since turning on the computer, DOS will take you to the root directory.

Displaying the Current Directory

You made a directory called C:\GAMES on page 101. Change over to that directory by typing at the C>:

cd \games <ENTER>

You can use the CD command to assure yourself that you really are in the directory you think you are in.   Note that this time you do not include a backslash in the command. Type the following:

cd <ENTER>

The computer responds with:

C:\GAMES

This confirms that you are in the C:\GAMES directory and that it is the *active directory*.

Creating a Text File Using COPY CON

To make a file to place in the C:\GAMES directory, you can use COPY CON. After you are through with the example, you can delete the file. With C:\GAMES the *active directory* type:

copy con fun.txt <ENTER>
The fun starts here. <ENTER>
<F6> <ENTER>

In the first line, COPY CON tells DOS to **COPY** from the **CON**sole (which means the keyboard) and make a file called FUN.TXT. The second line is the contents of the file FUN.TXT. In the third line <F6> tells DOS that this is the end of the file. Notice when you press <F6>, you will see ^Z on your screen. Then press the <ENTER> key, and the file FUN.TXT will be saved to disk.

Since you are currently logged onto the C:\GAMES directory, you can do a directory by typing:

dir <ENTER>

Your computer will display something like:

```
Volume in drive C has no label
Directory of   C:\GAMES

.             <DIR>        8-28-92   10:56a
..            <DIR>        8-28-92   10:56a
FUN    TXT       22    8-28-92   12:02p
       3 File(s)   2705408 bytes free
```

There are three files showing. However, the "." and ".." can be ignored. These are at the top of any subdirectory. The single "." represents the current directory. The double dot entry ".." is an internal link to the parent directory. The parent directory in this case is the root directory. Some of the most effective DOS shortcuts involve using these "secret" dot entries. So really, there is only one file in this directory. It is the FUN.TXT file.

You can view the FUN.TXT file you just created by using the type command. At the system prompt type:

type fun.txt <ENTER>

The contents of the FUN.TXT file will appear on the screen. Let's make a subdirectory under the C:\GAMES directory. Perhaps you would want to put several games in the C:\GAMES directory. However, you might have a nice collection of pinball games that you want to have in a separate subdirectory. Note that you are still in the C:\GAMES directory at this time. To get back to the root directory, at the system prompt type:

cd \ <ENTER>

The CD \ <ENTER> command will take you to the root directory. Now at the system prompt type:

md \games\pinball <ENTER>

The above command told DOS to make a subdirectory called PINBALL subordinate to the C:\GAMES directory. Figure 5 on page 97 will graphically illustrate such a directory structure.

The current directory is C:\ which is the root directory. To change over to the PINBALL subdirectory, type:

cd \games\pinball <ENTER>

To confirm that you are in the PINBALL subdirectory, type:

cd <ENTER>

You should see:

C:\GAMES\PINBALL

This will assure you that C:\GAMES\PINBALL is the *active directory*.

Use the DIR command to get more information:

dir <ENTER>

You should see something like:

```
Volume in drive C has no label
 Directory of  C:\GAMES\PINBALL

.             <DIR>       8-29-92    4:47p
..            <DIR>       8-29-92    4:47p
        2 File(s)    3629056 bytes free
```

This shows you that you are in the C:\GAMES\PINBALL subdirectory, that PINBALL is a subdirectory of the C:\GAMES directory, and that the PINBALL subdirectory is empty (except for those "." and ".." entries). You can also see that you have about 3.5 megabytes left on the hard disk. That would be equivalent to about ten 360K floppy disks. Now change to the C:\GAMES directory. At the system prompt type the following:

cd \games <ENTER>

Do a directory of the C:\GAMES directory by typing:

dir <ENTER>

You should see something like:

```
 Volume in drive C has no label
 Directory of  C:\GAMES

.             <DIR>        8-28-92   10:56a
..            <DIR>        8-28-92   10:56a
FUN     TXT       22       8-28-92   12:02p
PINBALL       <DIR>        8-29-92    4:47p
        4 File(s)    3622912 bytes free
```

This shows you that you are in the C:\GAMES directory and that the GAMES directory has one file that you can access called FUN.TXT. The .TXT extension tells you that this is probably a text file (see section on extensions for further details). If you will recall, you did access that file using the DOS TYPE command. You can also see that there is a subdirectory under the GAMES directory called PINBALL. If you did not already know that PINBALL subdirectory was empty, you might want to explore it by changing over to it. You could change to the PINBALL subdirectory by typing CD \GAMES\PINBALL <ENTER>. Then you could use the DIR command to see what files it contained.

You should try to avoid making subdirectories too many layers deep as it can confuse the beginner and can make issuing commands more difficult. If you have subdirectories many layers deep and one is required in the PATH statement, it can really muddle it up. The number of characters are limited in the PATH statement. You will learn about the PATH statement starting on page 144.

By this time you might be saying to yourself, "This is all very interesting, but how do I get rid of an unwanted directory?"

Removing a Directory

Prior to DOS 6, if you wanted to remove a directory, you had to make sure the below procedures were followed.

- **All files in the directory must first be deleted.** *This means hidden files, too. Don't worry too much about hidden files as they are not very common.* See the TIPS section on page 116 for more about hidden files.

- **The directory must not contain subdirectories.** This means you have to remove any underlying subdirectories first. If the subdirectory has files, you have to delete them before you can remove the subdirectory.

- **Before you can remove a directory, you must change to a different directory.** You cannot delete a directory if it is the current directory.

In the previous example you made a directory called C:\GAMES containing one file and one subdirectory. Before you can remove the directory C:\GAMES, you must remove the subdirectory called C:\GAMES\PINBALL. Since there are no files in it, you can delete C:\GAMES\PINBALL by using the RD (**R**emove **D**irectory) command. To remove C:\GAMES\PINBALL, type:

cd \ < ENTER >

Then:

rd \games\pinball < ENTER >

Now the PINBALL subdirectory is gone. If C:\GAMES\PINBALL had files in it, you would first have to delete them before you could remove the PINBALL subdirectory. *As a safeguard, DOS through version 5 won't let you remove a directory if it has files in it or subdirectories below it. The RD command cannot be used to remove a root directory.* See page 197 for information on how to use the hazardous DELTREE command which comes with DOS 6.

Deleting Files on a Hard Drive

You will on occasion need to delete files and directories on the hard drive to make room for more useful software. If you just installed software without ever removing files, you would eventually fill up the hard drive. Deleting files and directories is a necessary part of hard drive management.

If you want to delete the GAMES directory, you need first to remove any files that are in it. Change over to the GAMES directory by typing the following at the C>.

cd \games <ENTER>

Now use the DIR command to see what is in that directory.

dir <ENTER>

You should see the file called FUN.TXT that you created earlier. Before you can delete the GAMES directory, you have to get rid of all files in the GAMES directory. The DOS DEL command is used to delete files. At the system prompt type:

del fun.txt <ENTER>

The FUN.TXT file will then be deleted. If there had been a bunch of files and you wanted to delete them all, you could have issued the following:

del *.* <ENTER>

This is called a wildcard delete. **It tells DOS to delete all the files in the active directory.** Because it is so powerful, you have to **be very careful** when using this command. DOS will ask you to confirm this type of delete. You do not want to make a mistake and delete an important file!

> **WARNING: The DEL *.* command tells DOS to delete everything in the active directory.** Make certain you are in the directory you think you are in before giving this command. Be particularly careful not to use this wildcard delete on the root directory of your C drive. **If you delete the file COMMAND.COM, your computer will no longer start from the C drive!** For more information on how to avoid such a disaster see pages 116 - 117 and 149 - 150.

Get back to the root directory by typing:

cd \ <ENTER>

To delete the C:\GAMES directory, at the C> type:

rd \games <ENTER>

You can do a directory on the disk to confirm that the C:\GAMES directory has been deleted. For more information on deleting files using wildcards see pages 88 - 90.

Summary

In this chapter you have learned the following DOS commands to deal with directories and subdirectories:

1. How to get a graphic representation of the directory structure — **TREE**

2. How to make a new directory — **MD**

3. How to change to the root directory — **CD **

4. How to change over to a particular directory to make it the *active directory* — **CD** example: CD \GAMES\PINBALL

5. How to determine if there are subdirectories under the *active directory* — **DIR**

6. How to remove a directory or a subdirectory — **RD**
    Before you can delete a directory, you need to delete all files in the directory and any subdirectories that are under it. Before you can remove a directory, you must change to a different directory. If you were in a tree, you wouldn't want to saw off the limb you were standing on, would you?

Tips and Shortcuts

- There is a shortcut for making a directory *subordinate to the current directory*. Suppose you were at the root directory of the C drive and wanted to make a subdirectory called C:\GAMES. You can at the system prompt type:

md games < ENTER >

Note you did not use a backslash before the directory name as was shown on page 101.

- A similar shortcut exists for changing directories. If you have a directory called C:\GAMES and you are at the root directory of the C drive, you can change to the C:\GAMES directory by typing:

cd games < ENTER >

Because the C:\ (the root directory) is immediately above the C:\GAMES, you don't need a backslash to precede the directory name.

Suppose the current directory is C:\GAMES and you wish to change to the C:\GAMES\PINBALL directory. Because the *active directory* is immediately above the directory to which you want to change, you can type:

cd pinball < ENTER >

See page 97 for a graphic representation of such a directory structure. Beginners often make the mistake of trying to issue the above command with a backslash before the file name like: CD \PINBALL < ENTER >. DOS then tries to locate a directory that is right below the root directory.

Tips and Shortcuts ...*continued*

- Suppose C:\GAMES\PINBALL was the current directory, and you wanted to remove it. First delete any files that are in the C:\GAMES\PINBALL directory by using a dot trick:

del . < ENTER >

The command DEL . is a shortcut for DEL *.* which deletes all the files in the *active directory*. Use the following two dot trick to move up one level:

cd.. < ENTER >

The CD.. command is a shortcut for moving up one level in a directory structure. To remove a directory, you must be in a different directory. The above command will take you to the C:\GAMES directory. Then to remove the C:\GAMES\PINBALL directory, type:

rd pinball < ENTER >

The above command allows you to remove the C:\GAMES\PINBALL directory. You do not have to give the full specifications because you are in the directory C:\GAMES which is one level above. See Figure 5 on page 97 for a graphic representation.

- Another shortcut that saves even more time is to change to the directory that is *one level above the directory that contains the files you want to delete* and issue the command DEL DIRECTORYNAME < ENTER >. For example, suppose you were in C:\GAMES and you wanted to delete all the files in C:\GAMES\PINBALL; at the system prompt type:

del pinball < ENTER >

Tips and Shortcuts ...*continued*

The computer will respond with:

ALL FILES IN DIRECTORY WILL BE DELETED!
ARE YOU SURE (Y/N) ?

To delete all the files in C:\GAMES\PINBALL, answer:

y

Note that you did not delete the directory C:\GAMES\PINBALL; however, you did delete all the files in it. Then to remove the directory C:\GAMES\PINBALL, type:

rd pinball < ENTER >

The advantage of this shortcut is that you can remove the files and delete the target directory, *all from the directory that is one level above the target directory*. See Figure 5 on page 97.

- A shareware program that makes it easier to change drives and directories is called **4DOS**. It can remove all the files and subdirectories with one command (even hidden files). 4DOS has many commands that are vastly superior. For more information on this and other shareware programs see the section starting on page 257.

- To change directories even more quickly, obtain a freeware program called **ACD**. See page 257 for more information. If you were working on the A drive and wanted to change to C:\GAMES\PINBALL, with ACD you could type:

acd pin < ENTER >

Tips and Shortcuts ...*continued*

- Here is a very useful trick to *find a lost file* that works with DOS 3.3 and later. It makes use of the DOS ATTRIB command. At the system prompt type:

attrib c:\ansi.sys /s <ENTER>

Try the above command to locate a file called ANSI.SYS. You will probably have the file ANSI.SYS in the directory where your DOS files are stored. This searches the drive starting from the root directory and all underlying subdirectories for the specified file. If it finds the file, it will display its location on your screen. You can also include wildcard characters in the file specifications. Try the command again, but this time with a wildcard like: ATTRIB C:\ANSI.* /S <ENTER>. This tells DOS to search for all files on the C drive with ANSI as the file name with any or no extension. If you have DOS 5 or later, see page 170 to learn how to make a macro to find lost files. Also, see page 261 for the description of the superb shareware program called **SST**.

- Suppose you want to *find a lost subdirectory* that you know is somewhere on your C drive. You will need DOS 5 or later for this command. In order for the command to work, **you must use UPPER CASE letters** when you type in the name of the directory for which you want to search. Let's say you want to find a directory called BIRD that you know is somewhere in the directory structure of your C drive. At the C prompt type:

dir \. /a:d /s |find "BIRD" <ENTER>

This command will search the *entire current drive* for a directory called BIRD. Who says you can't find a bird in the bush? The | character is on the same key as the backslash character (\).

115

Tips and Shortcuts ... *continued*

- If you have DOS 5 or later, you can *list just the subdirectories* of a directory with the following command:

dir /a:d < ENTER >

- If you have DOS 4.0 or later, you can produce a *list of subdirectories* of a directory using a beloved dot trick. GADZOOKS! A three dot trick! This one is fun to do:

dir... < ENTER >

The above command is DIR followed by three periods. The only subdirectories this command will not show are those that have an extention. Very unlikely! *It will also show files that do not have extensions.* If you run into that situation, you can add a /P switch to the end of the command to show one page at a time. Directories will have a < DIR > "thing" next to them.

- **Hidden files** do not show up when you type DIR < ENTER >. You cannot remove a directory if it has any files in it. This means that you cannot remove a directory if it contains hidden files. *If you have DOS 5 or later*, you can use a "switch" with DIR to show hidden files:

dir /a < ENTER >

This will show all the files in the *active directory*, including hidden and system files. If more files are revealed by issuing the above command, you can turn them into regular files *with DOS 5 or DOS 6* by typing:

attrib -h -s -r *.* < ENTER >

Tips and Shortcuts ...*continued*

This tells DOS to turn all files with **H**idden, **S**ystem, or **R**ead-only attributes into regular files. You can then delete the files. Once all the files are deleted, you can remove the directory.

WARNING: Do not delete the hidden files in the root directory of the start-up disk. These special files are named **IO.SYS** and **MSDOS.SYS**. These files are hidden for *your protection*. It makes them harder to delete. Also, be careful not to delete the file named **COMMAND.COM**. **If any of the above mentioned files are deleted from the root directory of the start-up disk, the computer will not start up! To prepare for such a disaster, see pages 149 - 150.**

If you are using DoubleSpace which comes with **DOS 6**, be careful not to delete the following hidden files: **IO.SYS, MSDOS.SYS, DBLSPACE.BIN, DBLSPACE.INI and DBLSPACE.000.** These will be on an uncompressed host drive; and if you move or delete them, it could result in the entire loss of the data on your C drive. For more on DoubleSpace see the section starting on page 220.

• The shareware program called **STEREO SHELL** will delete any type of file or directory. It will show all your files. See page 261 for more on STEREO SHELL. The commercial program **PC TOOLS** will also delete any type of file or directory. For more information on PC TOOLS see page 187. Both of the above mentioned programs will show hidden files and will make it easy for you to delete them.

Installing Software on a Hard Drive

When you buy software, you will often want to transfer it to your hard drive. Many programs will not run from floppy disks and must be transferred to the hard drive in order to work.

Let's assume you bought a calendar program, and you want to transfer it to your hard drive. If the program has printed instructions, you should read them. If you bought a shareware disk, you would need to do a directory on the disk(s) to find the manual. Many shareware programs have special instructions for installing the program. Look for any text file like: README or README.1ST and extensions such as .DOC, .INF, .MAN, .PRN, or .TXT. These would indicate text files with instructions on how to proceed. You should first print out any of these text files. See the section starting on page 50 for how to print text files.

If you do find a file like INSTALL or SETUP when you do a directory, it is best to *exit from any shell or menu program you might be in before you attempt to install or setup the program. Sometimes new programs will not install properly if done from a shell.* See page 26 for how to exit a shell. When you do a directory on a disk, look for files with names like: INSTALL.BAT, INSTALL.COM, INSTALL.EXE, SETUP.COM, or SETUP.EXE. If there are no special instructions for installation, it is often as simple as typing at the A>:

install <ENTER>

Then answer the prompts. If a program prompts you for the location or "PATH" for files, it is asking which drive and directory do you want to store the files. For example, you might want to keep a calendar program in a directory called C:\CAL. Then C:\CAL would be the PATH, or location, for those files. If the program has no INSTALL or SETUP file or special instructions, you can just copy it to your hard drive. See the next section.

118

Copying a Diskette to a Hard Drive

Change to the appropriate hard drive where you want to install the program. For this example we will assume you want to install a calendar program on drive C. At the system prompt type:

c: <ENTER>

Then at the C> type:

cd \ <ENTER>

The CD \ <ENTER> command will take you to the root directory on the C drive. The root directory is the main directory. You can then make a directory in which to store the new program. Of course, you could copy the diskette to an already existing directory on your hard drive. For this example we will make a new subdirectory. This is done using the MD (Make Directory) command. Think of a short name for this directory. It can be no more than eight characters long. For this example we will call the directory CAL. You should try to name a directory something that makes sense to you. At the C> type:

md \cal <ENTER>

This will make a directory called C:\CAL.

Next change over to the CAL subdirectory using the CD (change directory) command so that the CAL subdirectory is the *active directory*. At the C> type:

cd \cal <ENTER>

Note the backslash that precedes CAL. Make sure you *use a backslash* and not a forward slash. When you issued the CD \CAL <ENTER> command, you made CAL the *active directory*. This is important. You can check to make sure that C:\CAL is the active directory by typing:

cd <ENTER>

Place the disk that you want to copy in drive A. Then copy that disk to C:\CAL by issuing the following command:

xcopy a: /s /e <ENTER>

The above command will copy all the files on your A drive to the *active directory*. Note that **before** you issued this command, you made C:\CAL the *active directory*. The /S in the above command instructed DOS to copy any Subdirectories that contain data. The /E portion of this command told DOS to copy subdirectories even if they are Empty.

If you wanted to copy from drive B to the hard drive, you would substitute **B:** for the **A:** in the above example. **If you have more than one disk to copy, you can just repeat the above command.** On most computers (but not all) you can press <F3> to repeat the last command.

The XCOPY command was used to copy the disk to the hard drive instead of the COPY *.* command because XCOPY is usually faster. Also, the COPY *.* command will not copy subdirectories. The COPY and XCOPY commands will not copy hidden files. See pages 116 - 117 for more on how to deal with hidden files.

Below is a much faster way to copy a diskette to the hard drive. **If you have more than one disk to copy, just repeat the command.** Use the XCOPY command and give full path specifications for both the source and target drive and use the /S and /E switches. You can use this command from **any system prompt.** Place the diskette you want to copy in drive A and at any system prompt type:

xcopy a: c:\cal\ /s /e <ENTER>

Drive A is the source drive. The target directory is C:\CAL. **Note that a backslash immediately follows the target directory.** That backslash is important. Otherwise, DOS will stop and prompt you that the target directory does not exist. Since you issued the /S and /E switches, XCOPY will make the target directory and any needed Subdirectories. If you forget to use a backslash after the target directory and C:\CAL does not already exist, DOS will prompt you with:

DOES CAL SPECIFY A FILE NAME
OR DIRECTORY NAME ON THE TARGET
(F = FILE, D = DIRECTORY)>?

You would then have to press D for directory. Before DOS copies the files, it will automatically make the directory C:\CAL and any subdirectories—even Empty ones. Perhaps you want to run a file you just copied. Change to the C:\CAL directory by typing:

c: <ENTER>
cd c:\cal <ENTER>

Now that C:\CAL is the *active directory*, do a directory—**DIR <ENTER>**— to see the files. *If you are searching for a program to run directly, look for a file with an .EXE, .COM, or .BAT extension.* See pages 39 - 45 for more information about the importance of file name extensions.

Summary

In this section you learned how to install new software on the hard drive.

1. If the software didn't come with a printed manual, you should do a directory on the disk—**DIR** <**ENTER**>—and look for a file like README or an extension that would indicate a text file. For help with how to identify and view text files, see the section starting on page 46.

2. If the manual is in the form of a text file, print it using your printer. If you need help on printing text files, see pages 50 - 51.

3. When you do a directory, look for an INSTALL or SETUP file.

4. If the software has an INSTALL or SETUP program, you need to **exit any shell or menu program** and install the new program from the system prompt. Often it is as simple as typing: **INSTALL** <**ENTER**> from the A> and following the instructions on the screen.

If the software has no INSTALL or SETUP, you will need to do your own installation. The steps are outlined below:

A. Make a new directory on the hard drive using the MD command. You may wish to copy to a directory that already exists on your hard drive. In that case, you will not need to make a new directory.

B. Change over to the directory you just made (or the one you want to copy the program to) using the CD command. This makes it *active*.

C. After completing steps A and B above, you can copy a floppy disk from drive A to the *active directory* on the hard drive by typing:

xcopy a: /s /e <**ENTER**>

Copying a File to Your Hard Drive

Suppose you obtained a shareware program called LIST.COM. After testing it on your A drive, you decided to copy it from a diskette in drive A to a directory called C:\UTILS on your hard drive. Change to the drive that has the file you want to copy. For this example, you would change to the A drive by typing at the system prompt:

a: <ENTER>

Then type:

copy list.com c:\utils <ENTER>

The above commands will copy the file called LIST.COM in the *active directory* of drive A to the C:\UTILS directory on your hard drive. If you had wanted to copy a file from your B drive, you would have first changed to the B drive to start the procedure. If you didn't already have a directory on your hard drive that you wanted to use as a target directory, you would make a new one as is shown on page 119. You could also use wildcards to copy more than one file with a single command. See pages 127 - 129.

Change over to the C:\UTILS directory on the hard drive so the directory which contains the file LIST.COM is the *active directory*. Type:

c: <ENTER>
cd \utils <ENTER>

The above commands will make the C:\UTILS directory the *active directory*. Then you would run the file in the usual way. For instance, to run LIST.COM, type:

list <ENTER>

123

The Assign Command

The ASSIGN command is a trick command. It is used to reroute disk requests from one drive to another. DOS 6 does not include the ASSIGN command. If you upgraded from an earlier version of DOS and had the ASSIGN program in your C:\DOS directory, then DOS 6 will retain it when you install DOS 6. If you do not have the ASSIGN program and want it, you can order it, along with other utility programs that Microsoft cut from DOS 6, for $5.00. They call this package "supplemental disks." See their offer in the back of the DOS 6 manual.

The ASSIGN command is particularly useful when you obtain software that requires installation from a specific drive. For example, suppose you bought a software program on a 3½" diskette. You had intended to install it using your drive B which is a 3½" drive. Upon diligently reading the manual, you discover that the installation has to be done from the A drive. Perhaps your A drive is a 5¼" floppy. Your first instinct might be to try to cram the 3½" disk into your 5¼" A drive. Don't do it! Instead, you can cleverly fool the software into thinking your B drive is the A drive by using the ASSIGN command first. To make the computer go to drive B when drive A is called for, issue the following command:

assign a=b < ENTER >

This tells DOS, that every time drive A is called for, to go to drive B instead. Note that in the above command, the first drive mentioned is the original drive. The second drive mentioned is the drive that you want to reassign to the original drive.

For fun, you can test this sneaky command. Place a diskette with files in your B drive. Change to the A drive by typing:

a: < ENTER >

Then do a directory:

dir <ENTER>

Note that your B drive light comes on as the directory of the diskette in drive B is being read.

To cancel the ASSIGN command, type:

assign <ENTER>

Now your drives will be back to normal. You can also undo the ASSIGN command by *turning the computer off*. The assign command should only be used in those few instances when you really need it. Avoid trouble by immediately canceling the ASSIGN command after completing the task that required this command.

WARNING: When you are using ASSIGN, do not use BACKUP, RESTORE, JOIN, LABEL, and SUBST commands. DISKCOPY and FORMAT ignore the ASSIGN command. Be particularly careful when using the ASSIGN command. As soon as you complete the needed task, cancel ASSIGN.

When you are attempting to install new software, pay attention to your drive lights. The drive lights indicate which drive the installation program is using to look for files. There may be times when you will need to fool software by using the DOS ASSIGN command.

Copying Files From Your Hard Drive to Floppy Disks

When you want to copy files from your hard drive to a diskette, you should first have one or more formatted floppy disks on hand. If you need help on formatting blank disks, see pages 59 - 66.

Suppose you had written a number of letters to a fellow named Sam and had saved them on the C:\WP51 directory. If you have the word processing program WordPerfect 5.1, you might very well have a directory like this on your hard drive. You might have named these files SAM1, SAM2, etc. Suppose you wanted to copy some files to a floppy disk. You would need to **change over** to the directory that has the files that you want to copy **to make it the** *active directory*. To make C:\WP51 the *active directory,* at the C> type:

cd \wp51 <ENTER>

The CD\ command (change directory) gets you to the directory that you want to be in and makes it the *active directory*. Now you will want to **issue a DIR command to see what files are in that directory**.

At the C:\WP51 system prompt type:

dir /p

Here the /P was added to the DIR command. By adding the /P, you told DOS to display the directory until the screen fills up and then pause. Press another key to continue reading the directory.

Look for the file or files you wish to copy to the floppy drive. Next you will learn how to copy a single file to a floppy disk; then you'll learn how to copy groups of files.

Copying File by File

Suppose you do a directory, and there is a file called SAM1.LET on C:\WP51 directory. To copy SAM1.LET to the A drive, put a blank formatted disk in drive A. If you need help with formatting a disk, see page 59. With C:\WP51 still the *active directory* type:

copy sam1.let a: <ENTER>

The file would then be copied to the floppy in the A drive. In this way you can copy one file at a time to a diskette.

Copying Using Wildcards

Perhaps you have a directory called C:\MOUSE on your hard drive which you would like to copy to a diskette in drive B. Change to that directory by typing at the C prompt:

cd \mouse <ENTER>

This makes C:\MOUSE the *active directory*. Do a directory by typing—DIR <ENTER>. Make sure that the target floppy disk has the capacity to hold all the files. If the files won't fit on one diskette, see pages 131 - 133. If everything looks good, place a blank formatted disk in drive B and type:

copy *.* b: <ENTER>

The asterisks (*) represent wildcards for any number of characters. This told DOS to *copy all the files* in the current directory *with any file name* and *any or no file extension* to the diskette in drive B.

Suppose you want to copy a number of files from your hard drive that have

SAM as part of the filename. You might have written a number of letters to Sam and named them SAM1.LET, SAM2, SAMPOOL, and BIGSAM.TXT. Place a formatted floppy disk in drive A. Make the directory that contains the files you want to copy the *active directory* by changing over to it using the **CD** command. In this example the files you want to copy are on the C:\WP51 directory. If that is the *active directory*, type:

copy sam*.* a: < ENTER >

This told DOS to copy to drive A all files with SAM in the **first part** of the file name and with any or no extension. The above command would copy all the example files with SAM in the first part of the file name. These include: SAM1.LET, SAM2, and SAMPOOL; however, BIGSAM.TXT would not be copied.

The question mark (?) represents a wildcard for a single character. Using the above examples, if you were in the C:\WP51 directory, you might issue the following command:

copy sam?.* a: < ENTER >

Since the question mark represents a wildcard for a single character, you would only copy the files SAM1.LET and SAM2 to the disk in the A drive. In the above command the asterisk (*) is a wildcard that represents any or no file extension. The question mark (?) wildcard is not used nearly as often as the asterisk (*).

Suppose you wanted to copy all files with an extension of .TXT from a directory on your hard drive to a floppy disk in drive A. After changing to the directory that has the files you want to copy, type:

copy *.txt a: < ENTER >

This would copy all files in the *active directory* with an extension of .TXT to the disk in the A drive.

128

Tips

● If you intend to copy (or delete) with wildcards and are not quite sure of what the results will be, you can first do a trial run. Use the DIR command with the same file specifications to see which files will be handled. The DIR command will do no harm because it will only list the files on the screen. For example, you could first issue a command like:

dir sam*.* <ENTER>

Then you can see the list of files that fit your wildcard specifications before issuing the command that will actually copy the files:

copy sam*.* a: <ENTER>

Copying an Entire Directory to a Floppy Disk

Use the change directory command (CD) and go to the directory that you want to copy. Then show the directory by typing—DIR <ENTER>. This will list your files in that directory and how many bytes the files use. With this information you will be able to determine if the files will fit on a single target disk. Format a blank floppy disk that you can use as the target disk. When you format the disk, you will be informed of how many bytes are free on the disk. If the files will fit on a single target disk, use the techniques shown next. If they will require more than one floppy disk, see the section starting on page 131.

If you have determined that the directory you want to copy from your hard drive will fit on a single floppy disk, you can use XCOPY as is shown in the next example. First make the directory that you want to copy the *active directory*. Suppose you wanted to copy all the files in the C:\GAMES directory to a diskette in drive B. To change to C:\GAMES directory, you would at the C> type:

cd \games <ENTER>

Once you change to the directory you want to copy, which makes it the *active directory*, you can type:

xcopy c: b: <ENTER>

This will copy all the files from the current directory in drive C to drive B, provided there is enough room on the floppy in drive B.

If you want to copy all the files in the C:\GAMES directory to a diskette in drive A and don't want to first change to the directory that you want to copy, you can issue the XCOPY command like this:

xcopy c:\games a: < ENTER >

This will only copy the files from the directory C:\GAMES to drive A. It will not copy any subdirectories that might be under the C:\GAMES directory. This also assumes that you have enough room on your floppy disk in drive A to hold all the files in the C:\GAMES directory. If you don't have room on a floppy disk to hold all the files, you can use the technique shown in the next section.

Copying a Directory
Requiring Multiple Target Disks

If the files you want to copy won't fit on a single target diskette, you can use the following technique. First you will need to estimate how many target disks you will need. Change to the directory that you want to copy using the CD command. Then show the directory—DIR < ENTER >. This will show you how many bytes the files will require. *The following procedure only works when the source disk does not contain a file larger than the target disk can hold.* Format a few more blank disks than you think you will need. It is always good to have a few extra formatted disks handy and ready to use.

Change to the directory that has the files you want to copy. If you want to copy C:\GAMES, you would change to that directory. To make certain that you are in the directory you want to copy, type:

dir < ENTER >

In the next command the **A** in **+A *.*** has nothing to do with the A drive. What it does is sets the archive bit to on for every file in the active directory. Type:

attrib +a *.* < ENTER >

Place one of the blank formatted disks in drive A and type:

xcopy *.* a: /m < ENTER >

If you had wanted to copy the files to the B drive, you would adjust the above command by substituting B: where you see the A:. The files will begin to be copied, and then you will get a message that may look something like:

INSUFFICIENT DISK SPACE
    17 FILES COPIED

At this point you should remove the first target disk from drive A and label it. Then put the next formatted diskette in the A drive and repeat your last command by typing:

xcopy *.* a: /m < ENTER >

On most machines (but not all), you can press the function key labeled < F3 > to repeat the previous command. You continue the above procedure until all the files are copied. If you continue this procedure with one more target disk than you need, you will eventually get a response like:

0 FILE(S) COPIED

Then you will know that all files have been copied. Do a directory on the target disks to assure yourself that the files were copied.

The **ATTRIB +A *.* < ENTER >** command sets what is called the archive bit on every file in the active directory. In other words, it marks every file in the active directory. When you issued the command **XCOPY *.* A: /M < ENTER >**, the /M told DOS to copy only those files with the archive bit set. When you copy with XCOPY using the /M switch, it clears the archive bit after each file is copied. Therefore, XCOPY does not copy those files that have already been copied because they have the archive bit cleared.

If you had wanted to copy any subdirectories that the source directory might have below it (that contain files), you would add the /S switch to the end of both the ATTRIB command and the XCOPY command. Look on pages 84 - 85 where the /S switch is used for a similar copying task. *When you want to copy the resulting floppy disks back to a hard drive, you can use the command shown in the section starting on page 121.*

You can also use the BACKUP or the DOS 6 MSBACKUP command to copy a directory from your hard drive to diskettes. See the section on Making Partial Backups starting on page 175. See the section starting on page 245 for MSBACKUP. These backup programs have no trouble copying a file that is too big to fit on a single diskette. They automatically split a large file over multiple diskettes.

You may wish to look at the Tips section starting on page 86. This includes information about shareware programs called PCOPY and PKZIP. These will split a large file over multiple floppy disks.

Copying Files Between Directories

This section will show you two ways to copy a single file from one directory to another. In this example you will be copying a file to the root directory of your C drive. The first way is copying with *full path specifications*. The second approach is a much simpler way.

Copying with Full Path Specifications

To copy the file ANSI.SYS (which should be in your C:\DOS directory) to the root directory of your hard drive, type at *any system prompt*:

copy c:\dos\ansi.sys c:\ <ENTER>

The first drive mentioned is the source drive and the second drive mentioned is the target drive. The C:\ with nothing after the backslash is what DOS uses to represent the root directory of the C drive. When you copy like this, it is called copying with *full path specifications*. It means you are telling DOS where you want to copy the files from; and you are specifying the drive, the directory and, in this case, the particular file. You are also telling DOS where you want the file copied to. Here you are specifying the target drive and directory. *The beauty of copying with full path specifications is that you can do it from any drive or directory.* If you had wanted to copy the file to another directory, you would have specified it as your target directory. Since we wanted to copy ANSI.SYS to the root directory of the C drive, the target drive was just C:\.

Merely *looking* at an example with full path specifications can cause headaches. However, on occasion you will need to know about them. Full path specifications are quite common in those fat DOS books.

134

A Much Simpler Way

A simpler way to copy the file ANSI.SYS to the root directory of the C drive is to *first change to the directory that has the file you want to copy*. In the above case it was C:\DOS. You could do that by typing at the C>:

cd \dos <ENTER>

This makes C:\DOS the *active directory*. Then issue the following command:

copy ansi.sys c:\ <ENTER>

The above commands will copy the file ANSI.SYS to C:\. The root directory of your drive C is called C:\. In fact, if you wanted to shorten the above command even more, you could type:

copy ansi.sys \ <ENTER>

DOS knows you are on the C drive and \ stands for the root directory.

Let's try another example. Perhaps you have a file called BATTLE.EXE on your C drive in a subdirectory called C:\MISC. To copy this file to an already existing directory on your D drive called D:\GAMES, change to the directory that has the file you want to copy. In this case it is C:\MISC. At the C> type:

cd \misc <ENTER>

Do a directory to make sure that the file you want to copy is in the *active directory*. Then copy the file to the drive and directory you desire, such as:

copy battle.exe d:\games <ENTER>

Copying Entire Subdirectories to Other Subdirectories and Drives

Suppose you have numerous files on your C drive in a directory called C:\MISC, and you want to copy all of them to your D drive to a directory called D:\GAMES. If the D:\GAMES directory didn't already exist, you could make it. If you need help on how to make a directory (MD command), see page 101. *This section shows three ways to accomplish the same copying task*. There are often many ways to accomplish the same task in DOS. The destination drive for the three examples below all use the D drive, and it is assumed that a directory called D:\GAMES exists on that drive. In this section you will also be shown how to copy the files in one directory to another directory on the same drive.

1ST EXAMPLE:

The first step is to change to the D:\GAMES directory to make it the *active directory*. If you were working on the C drive and wanted to change to the D drive, you would type at the C>:

d: <ENTER>

Then to change to the D:\GAMES directory, type:

cd \games <ENTER>

DOS keeps track of the last *active directory* for each drive. As you will see, this feature can be quite useful. Next, change to the directory on drive C that you want to copy.

c: <ENTER>
cd \misc <ENTER>

136

This would make C:\MISC the *active directory*. *Because DOS keeps track of the last directory that was active on the D drive, you can copy the files like this:*

copy *.* d: <ENTER>

The above commands will copy all the files in C:\MISC (the active directory) to D:\GAMES (the last directory that was used on D drive). When you change drives and then return back to a drive you were working on, DOS returns you to the last directory that you were using on that drive.

2ND EXAMPLE:

To accomplish the same copying task as was shown in the first example, change to the directory you want to copy. For this example it is C:\MISC; therefore, at the C> type:

cd \misc <ENTER>

This makes C:\MISC the *active directory*. Then use the COPY *.* command and give full path specifications for the target drive. For this example the target drive is D:\GAMES which already exists on the D drive. Issue the command like this:

copy *.* d:\games <ENTER>

That will also copy all the files in C:\MISC to D:\GAMES. If you had wanted to copy the files to C:\GAMES, you would substitute C: where you see the D: in the above example; however, this assumes that the C:\GAMES subdirectory already exists. If it didn't exist, you would first make it using the MD command. See page 101.

These commands work for copying to floppy drives too. See pages 77 - 79.

3RD EXAMPLE:

A third way to accomplish the same copying task is to use the XCOPY command. First change to the directory you want to copy which makes it the *active directory*. In these examples it is assumed that C:\MISC is the directory that has the files you want to copy. Type:

cd \misc <ENTER>

Make certain that you are in the directory you want to copy by issuing the **CD <ENTER>** command. Then use the DOS XCOPY command and specify the target drive and directory. For the example below, the target drive and directory is D:\GAMES which already exists on the D drive. At the system prompt type:

xcopy c: d:\games <ENTER>

The above command will result in copying all the files in the *active directory* on the C drive to D:\GAMES.

Suppose you had wanted to copy all the files in the *active directory* to another directory on the *same drive*. Perhaps the desired target drive and directory is C:\PLAY. If the C:\PLAY directory already exists and you want to copy all the files in the *active directory* on the C drive to C:\PLAY, type:

xcopy c: c:\play <ENTER>

In the above examples, if the target directory did not exist, you would have had to create it. You can use the MD command to make a directory. See page 101. The next section will show how to use XCOPY to automatically make any necessary subdirectories on the target drive.

Copying a Directory with Subdirectories to Another Drive

The following procedure will use XCOPY to actually create the target directory as well as copy the entire source directory (including all its underlying subdirectories and files). Before you attempt this copying task, make sure you have enough room on the target disk. You can use the DOS CHKDSK or DIR command to check the disk space.

Perhaps you have a subdirectory called C:\AVERY, and this directory has many files *and several subdirectories with files under it*. You would like to create a new directory on the D drive called D:\LAB and then copy C:\AVERY (with all its subdirectories and underlying files) to D:\LAB. At any system prompt type:

xcopy c:\avery d:\lab\ /s /e < ENTER >

Note that the first drive mentioned is the source drive and the second drive mentioned is the target drive. **The above command automatically creates the directory D:\LAB (if it doesn't already exist) and reproduces the entire directory structure of the directory C:\AVERY and copies it to D:\LAB.** *By adding the backslash* (\) after the target directory (D:\LAB) you avoid DOS prompting you and asking if LAB is a file or a directory. The /S in the above command tells DOS to copy all Subdirectories that contain files. The /E tells DOS to copy all the subdirectories even if they are Empty. **XCOPY is a very powerful DOS command!**

Tips:

- If you are copying the current directory to another directory on the same drive, you can use an even shorter notation. *Suppose you are currently in C:\MISC,* and you want to copy all the files in C:\MISC to C:\GAMES. Try copying like this:

  copy *.* \games <ENTER>

  DOS knows you are on the C drive; and if you give the \ symbol (which stands for the root directory), DOS assumes the directory named after the leading backslash stems from the root directory. So, this would copy all the files from the C:\MISC subdirectory to the C:\GAMES subdirectory. If you wanted to really keep the keystrokes to a minimum, you could also accomplish the same task with:

  copy . \games <ENTER>

  Here the two asterisks were left out. See pages 79 and 90 for similar dot tricks.

- When you are using XCOPY and other DOS commands, it is imperative that you know where you are on the directory structure. You can make your system display this information with very little effort on your part. Set up your AUTOEXEC.BAT file with a separate line that reads:

  prompt pg

  Then DOS will display a system prompt that will tell you which drive and directory is *active.* See pages 146 - 153 for details on how to put this line in your AUTOEXEC.BAT file. It is best to know where you are and where you are going!

How to Make Simple Batch Files

A batch file is a file with the extension .BAT. Batch files are used to automate tasks that you perform often. **A batch file is simply a text file that contains a DOS command or series of DOS commands** and has the telltale extension .BAT. Batch files can do almost anything. Entire books have been written on batch files. We will keep it very simple here. It is important to remember that **a batch file can be run by just typing the filename and then pressing the key marked <ENTER>**.

Suppose you have a file on your C drive called PINBALL.EXE that resided in a subdirectory called C:\GAMES. To start this file, you have been changing to the C:\GAMES subdirectory and typing: PINBALL <ENTER>. Because you are finding yourself playing that game on a regular basis, you want to automate the task by making a batch file. Change to the C:\GAMES subdirectory to make it the *active directory* by typing:

cd\games <ENTER>

Then to make a batch file called P.BAT, type:

copy con p.bat <ENTER>
pinball <ENTER>
<F6> <ENTER>

The first line told DOS to make a file called P.BAT. COPY CON tells DOS to **COPY** from the **CON**sole (keyboard). Note that there is a space between COPY and CON. The second line is the contents of the file P.BAT which, in this example, only contains one word PINBALL. This is the command that starts the program. On the third line <F6> <ENTER> told DOS that this is the end of the file and to write the file to disk.

Once PINBALL.EXE and P.BAT are in the same directory, you can start the pinball game by making that directory the *active directory* and then typing:

p <ENTER>

If you wanted to make starting the pinball game even easier, you could put the directory C:\GAMES in the PATH statement of your AUTOEXEC.BAT file. (See pages 146 - 153.) Then you could type P <ENTER> to start the pinball game from any directory or drive without first having to change to the C:\GAMES directory.

If you have a program that has a long sequence of keystrokes to start it up, you can make a batch file to do it for you. You merely put in the batch file the keystrokes that are used to start that program. Keep the batch file name short to save yourself keystrokes. Make sure that the batch file you create is saved as a text file and that it has an extension of .BAT. If you want, you can make batch files to start programs for children or adults who don't use the computer often.

In the above example you used a batch file on a hard drive. It should be noted that batch files work just as well on floppy disks. If you want to make a special batch file that will automatically start up a program from a floppy disk, see pages 154 - 155 and page 184.

You will learn how to make a special batch file called AUTOEXEC.BAT starting on page 146, but first you need to know about DOS PATHS.

Tips

• If you are writing a longer batch file, you might find it more convenient to use an editor or a word processor instead of using the DOS COPY CON command. If you had used an editor or word processor, you would have typed in only one word **PINBALL** and saved the file under the name of P.BAT. If you make the file with a word processor, you want to make sure that you save the file as a text file, or ASCII file as it is called. Most word processors can save a file as an ASCII file. You may have to look in the **INDEX** of the manual for your word processor to find out how to do it. You would look under T for text, or A for ASCII, or S for save. Editors use ASCII format to save files. Most people find that an editor is perfect for writing batch files. *If you have DOS 5 or DOS 6, see page 48 and pages 162 - 163 for more on how to use* **EDIT**. EDIT is an easy to use editor which comes with DOS 5 and later. See the section on shareware starting on page 256 if you don't already own an easy to use editor program.

The PATH Command

If the PATH of your system is set up properly, it can make life at your computer a lot easier. **DOS uses the PATH command to tell it where to look for software.** The PATH command specifies which directories DOS must search to find files with .EXE, .COM, or .BAT extensions. When you issue a command, DOS first searches the **active** or current directory. If DOS can't find the file in the current directory, it then searches for files in the directories that are specified in the PATH statement. **If no PATH has been specified, then DOS searches only the current directory.**

The term PATH can also mean **the full directory name where a particular file is stored.** Suppose you keep a pinball game in C:\GAMES\PINBALL. The path for that pinball game would be C:\GAMES\PINBALL.

To see what your computer's PATH looks like, type:

path <ENTER>

If no path has been specified, you will see:

NO PATH

If your computer usually starts up on the C drive, the directory that contains your DOS files should be in your PATH statement. For most people, this will be a directory called **C:\DOS**. Then the directory called **C:\DOS should be in your PATH statement.** Some people use a directory called C:\SYSTEM to keep their DOS files. The directory that contains the DOS files should be in your computer's PATH statement. Most computers will also have other directories defined in the PATH statement. Your PATH might look like:

PATH=C:\DOS;C:\UTILS

With the above PATH statement DOS would search in the directories of C:\DOS and C:\UTILS for files. The PATH statement can be up to 127 characters long. Note that the directories are separated by a semicolon (;).

Setting Your Path

You can set your PATH at the command line by just typing it in. For instance, if you tried to issue DOS commands and got a "Bad command or file name" error, it was probably because DOS was not set up in your computer's PATH. The other possibility is that the DOS files had not been copied to your hard drive. Let's assume you do have a directory called DOS on your C drive; but when you typed PATH <ENTER>, you got a response of "NO PATH." Then at the system prompt type:

path=c:\dos <ENTER>

After typing in the above PATH statement, DOS should be able to find any of your DOS files from any drive or directory that you happen to be on. However, when you turn your computer off and then start a new session, you would have to type your PATH in again. There is a better way, and this is to put the PATH statement in your AUTOEXEC.BAT file. The computer automatically reads the AUTOEXEC.BAT file each time you start your computer; so it will also automatically read your PATH statement, too. Next you will learn how to make an AUTOEXEC.BAT file which will include a PATH statement.

The AUTOEXEC.BAT File

> **CAUTION:** Before you attempt experiments with changing your AUTOEXEC.BAT file or CONFIG.SYS file, it is essential that you have a bootable floppy disk on hand. See pages 149 - 150.

An AUTOEXEC.BAT file is a special kind of batch file. Remember that a batch file is simply a text file. *Whenever you start your computer, DOS looks for files called AUTOEXEC.BAT and CONFIG.SYS in the root directory of the start-up disk.* The file called AUTOEXEC.BAT contains DOS commands that the computer automatically executes on start-up. The CONFIG.SYS file contains configuration information that DOS reads on start-up. You will learn about the CONFIG.SYS files a little later in this book. Both the AUTOEXEC.BAT file and the CONFIG.SYS file can be defined by the user. If the people who set up your computer did it properly, you will have an AUTOEXEC.BAT file; and the DOS directory will be in the PATH statement in the AUTOEXEC.BAT file on your hard drive. To see if you have an AUTOEXEC.BAT file, at the C> type:

cd \ < ENTER >

This will take you to your root directory. You can do a directory to look for a file called AUTOEXEC.BAT. Type the following:

dir /w < ENTER >

If you see a file called AUTOEXEC.BAT, you can view it on the screen by issuing the following command:

type autoexec.bat < ENTER >

The AUTOEXEC.BAT file will then be displayed on the screen. A *minimum* AUTOEXEC.BAT file might look like this:

@ECHO OFF
PATH C:\DOS;C:\UTILS
PROMPT PG

The first line (@ECHO OFF) told DOS not to display the batch file on the screen as it is processed. The second line is the very important *PATH statement*. This is the line that sets your computer's PATH and tells DOS where to look for files with .EXE, .COM, and .BAT extensions. When you issue a command, DOS first searches the *active* or current directory. If DOS can't find the file in the current directory, it then searches for files in the directories that are specified in the PATH statement. If no PATH has been specified, then DOS searches only the current directory. The above example assumes that you have directories called C:\DOS and C:\UTILS. Notice that in the second line (PATH C:\DOS;C:\UTILS) there is a **semicolon (;) that separates the directories. DOS is very fussy about such punctuation**, and you have to be very careful when you are making an AUTOEXEC.BAT file that you have the backslashes (\), colons (:) and the semicolons (;) in the proper places. You also have to be very careful that the directories you specify actually exist and that they have the correct drive specifications. Incidently, in the above example C:\UTILS might be the name of a directory to keep often used utility programs (for instance, the LIST program; see pages 123 and 259). Once it is put in your PATH, you can execute the programs in that directory from any directory or drive.

The DOS directory should contain your DOS files. The DOS directory should be in your PATH so that you will not have to change to the C:\DOS directory to issue DOS commands. When the directory that contains all your DOS files is in your PATH, you can issue DOS commands from any drive or directory. The newer versions of DOS (4.0 and later) automatically set up your computer with the DOS directory in your PATH and DOS files in the DOS directory.

The third line (PROMPT PG) in the above example AUTOEXEC.BAT file customizes the system prompt so that, when DOS displays a system prompt, it tells you which drive is the *active drive* and which directory is the *active directory*. This is optional and a matter of personal taste, but most people seem to like being reminded.

In addition to the list of (1st generation) directories, the root directory of your hard drive C will probably contain the following files: AUTOEXEC.BAT, CONFIG.SYS, COMMAND.COM, and several hidden files. You should not clutter up your root directory with unnecessary files. You might have a few more files in the root directory, but it is important to keep the root directory as simple as possible. Beginners often make the mistake of copying all kinds of files to the root directory. Don't *YOU* make that mistake.

CAUTION: Before you try to experiment with changing your AUTOEXEC.BAT file or your CONFIG.SYS file, it is essential to make a bootable floppy disk. The next section shows how. You should also make a backup of your AUTOEXEC.BAT and CONFIG.SYS files.

Making a Bootable Floppy Disk

Format a disk **with the system on it** that will fit in the **A drive**. Place a blank floppy disk in drive A and type:

format a: /s < ENTER >

If you need help with formatting a blank disk with the system on it, see pages 67 - 68. After completing this task, you will have a **start-up disk** which is sometimes called a **boot-disk**. Label this disk as a start-up disk and keep it in a safe place. Should your computer fail to start-up from the hard drive, you can use this floppy disk to start the computer. To start your computer with this disk, you would put it in drive A and then turn on the computer. You will be prompted for the date and time. After answering the prompts, you will get an A > .

> *CAUTION: Before you attempt experiments with changing your AUTOEXEC.BAT file or CONFIG.SYS file, it is essential that you have a bootable floppy disk on hand.*

Backing Up the Root Directory
of Your C Drive

People often accidently delete all the files in their root directory. When that happens, the computer will not start from the hard drive. To restore the root directory, you must have a start-up disk to start the computer and a backup of your root directory. To make a backup of the root directory of your hard drive, place a blank formatted disk in drive A and at the system prompt type:

copy c:*.* a: < ENTER >

This will copy all the files on your root directory of your C drive to the floppy disk in drive A. You can do a directory on drive A to verify the copying was a success. You should have plenty of room on your floppy disk to hold all the files that were on the root directory of the C drive.

If you didn't have room, it means that your root directory has been cluttered up with unnecessary files. If that is the case, at least copy your AUTOEXEC.BAT file and the CONFIG.SYS file to a blank floppy disk. Now you will have a floppy disk that contains a backup of your AUTOEXEC.BAT file and your CONFIG.SYS file. Please carefully label this disk and store it where you can find it.

Whenever you make changes to your AUTOEXEC.BAT or CONFIG.SYS files, you should make a new backup as was shown above. It is also good to have a printed copy of both the AUTOEXEC.BAT and CONFIG.SYS files. Remember, these are text files and you can print them. See page 50.

If *you* accidently delete all the files in the root directory, the computer will not start from the hard drive. I have made this mistake myself! It is a really shocking experience. Should that ever happen, you can use the start-up disk you made on page 149 to start your computer. Then when you have an A >, you can remove the start-up disk and place the disk in drive A that contains backup of your root directory. At the A > type:

copy *.* c:\\ < ENTER >

The above command will restore the root directory to the C drive. Remove the diskette from drive A. Then restart your computer with no diskette in drive A. Your computer should start from the C drive and be back to normal.

Modifying an Existing AUTOEXEC.BAT File

From time to time you may want to modify your AUTOEXEC.BAT file. **First make a backup as shown on page 150 before you do any modifications.** It is best to use an editor or a word processor to edit the AUTOEXEC.BAT file. If you have DOS 5 or later, you can use the built-in editor called EDIT. If you don't have a good editor, I would highly recommend a shareware program called QEDIT by SemWare. Editors automatically save files in the necessary ASCII (text) format. If you want to use a word processor to modify your AUTOEXEC.BAT file, look in the manual to make sure that it can save files in the needed ASCII format. Use the **INDEX** and look under A for ASCII, T for text, or S for saving files. Remember that a text file is an ASCII file and that the AUTOEXEC.BAT file must be saved in ASCII format.

Suppose your current AUTOEXEC.BAT file looks like:

@ECHO OFF
PATH C:\;C:\DOS
PROMPT PG

Perhaps you would like to add a couple of directories called C:\GAMES and C:\UTILS to your PATH statement to make it easier to run programs in those directories. When a program is located in a directory that is in your PATH, you can run that program from any directory or drive. Perhaps you would also like to load a ram resident program called CONFMT.COM when your computer starts up. Since you keep CONFMT.COM in your C:\UTILS directory, you want this directory to be in your PATH so DOS will find it on start-up. **The first thing to do is to REName your existing AUTOEXEC.BAT file so you will have a backup.**

Get to the root directory of your C drive by typing at the C>:

cd\ <ENTER>

Then type:

ren autoexec.bat autoexec.bak <ENTER>

AUTOEXEC.BAK will then be the new name for the AUTOEXEC.BAT file. Use your editor or word processor to modify the file AUTOEXEC.BAK. (See page 48 if you need help with loading a file using the DOS 5 or DOS 6 EDIT program.) The modified file should look like:

@ECHO OFF
PATH C:\;C:\DOS;C:\GAMES;C:\UTILS
PROMPT PG
CONFMT

Now save this modified AUTOEXEC.BAK file under the new name of AUTOEXEC.**BAT**. If you are using EDIT (DOS 5 and later), use *SAVE AS* in the *FILE* menu. It is best to keep the PATH statement one of the beginning lines in the AUTOEXEC.BAT file. Then, if you have other programs that you want to start from the AUTOEXEC.BAT file, DOS will find them if they are located in a directory that is in the PATH. Note that there is a semicolon (;) that separates each directory in the PATH statement. Be careful! When it comes to syntax, DOS is fussier than a teased polecat. The PATH statement can be up to 127 characters long. If you make the AUTOEXEC.BAT file in a different directory, make sure you copy it to your root directory. *In order for the AUTOEXEC.BAT file to take effect, you must restart your computer.* If you want to, "cold boot" your machine by turning off the machine and then turning it back on again. Once you restart your computer, DOS will search all the directories in your PATH statement when it searches for files to run. If you want to use a shell or menu program, the last line in the AUTOEXEC.BAT file should contain the command to start your shell or menu. If this is the case, make sure that you put the directory that contains the shell or menu program in the PATH statement.

Making a New AUTOEXEC.BAT File

If you don't already have an AUTOEXEC.BAT file in your root directory, you can make one using the DOS COPY CON command. It is assumed that you do have a DOS directory called C:\DOS and that all your DOS files are stored in that directory. At the C> type:

cd \ <ENTER>

This will take you to the root directory of your C drive. The AUTOEXEC.BAT file must be in the root directory of your start-up disk. Then type:

copy con autoexec.bat <ENTER>
@echo off <ENTER>
path c:\;c:\dos;c:\utils <ENTER>
prompt pg <ENTER>
<F6> <ENTER>

The last line <F6> <ENTER> tells DOS (when you are using COPY CON) that this is the end of the file and to save the AUTOEXEC.BAT file to disk. You may want to have other directories in your PATH statement. Note that here the PATH statement has C:\ (which is the root directory), C:\DOS (which is where the DOS files are stored), and C:\UTILS (a directory where utility programs are kept). Also, you might want to include other lines so that additional programs will load upon start-up. If your AUTOEXEC.BAT file gets much more complex than the above example, you will probably want to use an editor or word processor to create it. With COPY CON you can't easily edit the file except with the backspace key. To view a sample DOS 6 AUTOEXEC.BAT file, look at page 205.

Removing a Menu or Shell from the AUTOEXEC.BAT File

Someone may have set up your computer with a menu or shell program that you don't like. Perhaps Microsoft Windows is coming up when you start your computer and you would prefer that it didn't. To modify your system so the menu or shell does not come up automatically, **first make a bootable floppy disk and then a backup of your root directory.** See pages 149 - 150. Next, use an editor or word processor and load the AUTOEXEC.BAT file which is located in the root directory of the start-up disk. **The statement that loads the menu or shell will usually be on the last line of the AUTOEXEC.BAT file.** You can then remove the statement. Then save the modified AUTOEXEC.BAT file. If you use a word processor, make certain that you save the AUTOEXEC.BAT file as an ASCII file. All editors save files in the needed ASCII format. Turn to page 161 and page 208 where you will learn how to use a REM statement to disable a line in the AUTOEXEC.BAT or CONFIG.SYS file. The change does not take effect until you restart your computer.

How to Make a Program Start Automatically from a Diskette

You may wish to make a particular program start automatically from a floppy disk. Suppose you have a child who loves to play a particular game called PINBALL.EXE. Perhaps you don't want to have him fooling around on your hard drive but don't mind if he uses his own programs on floppy disks. The example program is PINBALL.EXE, but you can substitute your favorite program.

To make an auto-booting disk, follow the steps outlined below:

1. Format a blank disk **with the system on it in drive A (format a: /s
    <ENTER>).** It must be your A drive. The B drive will not do. If
    you need help, see pages 67 - 68.

2. Copy the program that you want to auto-boot to the just formatted disk.
    Some programs need more than one file. The example in this case is
    PINBALL.EXE. The formatted disk with the system on it should now
    contain PINBALL.EXE.

3. Put that disk in drive A and type:

    > **copy con autoexec.bat <ENTER>**
    > **pinball <ENTER>**
    > **<F6> <ENTER>**

The first line in the above example told DOS to copy from the **console** (the
keyboard) to make a file and to name it AUTOEXEC.BAT. The second line
contains the name of the program that you want to automatically start up. It
is entered just like you would to start the program from the system prompt.
In the third line <F6> tells DOS that this is the end of the file. The
<F6>, when used with COPY CON, functions the same as pressing
<CTRL> Z. When you press <F6>, you will see ^Z on your screen.
Then press the <ENTER> key, and the file AUTOEXEC.BAT will be
saved to disk.

Now when you turn the computer on with this disk in drive A, the PINBALL
game will start automatically! Instead of booting from the C drive, the
computer boots from the A drive.

The CONFIG.SYS File

CAUTION: Before you attempt experiments with changing your AUTOEXEC.BAT file or CONFIG.SYS file, it is essential that you have a bootable floppy disk on hand. See pages 149 - 150. However, if you have DOS 6, you can perform a "clean boot" or an "interactive boot." See the section starting on page 213.

The CONFIG.SYS file is a special file that, if it exists, resides on the root directory of your disk which contains DOS. For most people it will be in the root directory of drive C. *The CONFIG.SYS file is simply a text file named CONFIG.SYS. When DOS starts up, it reads the CONFIG.SYS file and follows the configuration commands in that file.* You can create or edit a CONFIG.SYS file with an editor or a word processor. Sometimes, when you buy software, you will have to place special lines in the CONFIG.SYS file in order for the software to work properly.

Viewing a CONFIG.SYS File

First let's look for a CONFIG.SYS file on the root directory of your hard drive. At the C> type:

cd \ <ENTER>

This takes you to the root directory. Now do a directory—DIR <ENTER>. If you see a file called CONFIG.SYS, you can view it on the screen by typing:

type config.sys <ENTER>

156

Making a New CONFIG.SYS File
with COPY CON

> **CAUTION:** If you have a CONFIG.SYS file, it is important to keep a backup of this file and other files in your root directory. **Don't attempt to modify or make a new CONFIG.SYS file without first following the special instructions starting on page 149.** Do not attempt to modify your CONFIG.SYS or AUTOEXEC.BAT if you do not have a bootable floppy disk on hand.

If you found no CONFIG.SYS file in your root directory, you can make one with an editor, a word processor (see page 159), or the DOS COPY CON command. Below is an example of making a CONFIG.SYS file using the DOS COPY CON command. Perhaps you bought a new software program that requires two statements in the CONFIG.SYS file: *FILES=20* and *BUFFERS=30*. The following is a *bare bones* CONFIG.SYS file. First change to the root directory where the CONFIG.SYS file belongs. At the C> type:

cd \ <ENTER>

Then to make the CONFIG.SYS file, type:

copy con config.sys <ENTER>
files=20 <ENTER>
buffers=30 <ENTER>
<F6> <ENTER>

In the above example, the DOS COPY CON was used to make a text file called CONFIG.SYS. The first line told DOS to **COPY** from the **CON**sole (keyboard) and make a file called CONFIG.SYS. The second line containing

FILES=20 told DOS to allow 20 files to be open at one time. The third line, BUFFERS=30, allocates a portion of memory that will be used to store data that is retrieved from the disk drive. The second and third lines are the contents of this CONFIG.SYS file. The last line of <F6> <ENTER> tells DOS (when you are using COPY CON) to write the file to disk. Since the CONFIG.SYS file is read by DOS upon start-up, **the new CONFIG.SYS file will not take effect until you restart your computer**. You can restart your computer by pressing:

<CTRL> <ALT> <DEL>

That is, press all three of the above keys at the same time. When you restart your computer like this, it is called a **"warm boot."** A **"cold boot"** is turning the computer on using the power switch. There are two new methods of booting your computer with DOS 6. These are the **"clean boot"** and the **"interactive boot."** See the section starting on page 213.

DOS BOOTS

Making a CONFIG.SYS File with an Editor or Word Processor

Writing CONFIG.SYS files with COPY CON can be a bit difficult due to the lack of editing features. A better choice would be to use an editor. If you use a word processor to make a CONFIG.SYS file, it needs to be able to save the file in ASCII format. For instance, if you were using a DOS version of WordPerfect, you would have to press <CTRL> <F5> to start the process of saving the file as a text file. Look in the manual to make sure that your word processor can save files in ASCII format. Use the **INDEX** and look under A for ASCII, T for text, or S for save. Remember that a text file is an ASCII file. If you had constructed the example CONFIG.SYS file shown on page 157 using an editor or a word processor, you would name the file CONFIG.SYS; and you would type the following lines:

> **files=20**
> **buffers=30**

Remember to *save the file with the name CONFIG.SYS*. (It does not matter if you use upper case or lower case letters.) You might want to make the file using an editor on some other directory of your hard drive. You would then need to **copy the file to the root directory.** See page 135 if you need help with copying a file to your root directory.

The above example would be a *minimal* CONFIG.SYS file. *Some software will require a larger number of files and a larger number of buffers in order for it to work properly.* If a program has special CONFIG.SYS needs, it will be in the manual that came with the software. Some programs will automatically try to modify your CONFIG.SYS file. *Sometimes they will not do it properly*, and you will have to fix their mistakes. Therefore, every once in a while it is wise to view your CONFIG.SYS file. You can view it with the TYPE command, an editor, or a word processor.

Modifying a CONFIG.SYS File

Sometimes a software program requires special device drivers. *Device drivers usually have an extension of .SYS.* These are placed on a separate line in the CONFIG.SYS file. Consult the program's manual for details.

For example, you might buy a mouse; and the instructions say to add to your CONFIG.SYS file a line like:

DEVICE=C:\MOUSE\MOUSE.SYS

The MOUSE.SYS file would be on the disk that came with the mouse. You would want to make a directory called C:\MOUSE to store this MOUSE.SYS file. Then you would copy the MOUSE.SYS file to the directory called C:\MOUSE.

Before attempting to edit your existing CONFIG.SYS file, you should have a bootable floppy disk that will work in your A drive and make a backup of your root directory. See pages 149 - 150. It is also a good idea to have a printed copy of the CONFIG.SYS file. You could load your CONFIG.SYS file into an editor or a word processor and add the line DEVICE=C:\MOUSE\MOUSE.SYS. You would save the file again, making sure you called it CONFIG.SYS. The CONFIG.SYS file might look like this:

FILES=20
BUFFERS=30
DEVICE=C:\MOUSE\MOUSE.SYS

You might buy another software program that requires ANSI.SYS to be installed in your CONFIG.SYS file. ANSI.SYS is a file that comes with DOS, and this file should be located in the C:\DOS directory or another directory that contains your DOS files. The ANSI.SYS file is a device driver that enhances the graphics display and keyboard input. You would want to make a modification to the existing CONFIG.SYS file so that it contains a DEVICE=C:\DOS\ANSI.SYS line. Note that this line specifies where the ANSI.SYS file can be found. The new CONFIG.SYS file might contain a number of device drivers including ANSI.SYS. It might look like:

FILES=20
BUFFERS=30
DEVICE=C:\MOUSE\MOUSE.SYS
DEVICE=C:\DOS\ANSI.SYS

Remember that, when you make a new CONFIG.SYS file, it does not take effect until you reboot your machine.

One technique that is quite useful when trying to fine-tune a **CONFIG.SYS** *or* **AUTOEXEC.BAT file** is to place **REM** at the beginning of a line statement. Any line that begins with REM is ignored by DOS. You can then reboot your computer and that line will not execute. For example, if you wanted to see how the above CONFIG.SYS file would operate with the line DEVICE=C:\MOUSE\MOUSE.SYS disabled, you could modify the CONFIG.SYS file to read:

FILES=20
BUFFERS=30
REM DEVICE=C:\MOUSE\MOUSE.SYS
DEVICE=C:\DOS\ANSI.SYS

Then you can restart the computer to activate the new CONFIG.SYS file and observe how the machine functions with REM disabling your selected line statement.

NOTE: You can also use REM at the beginning of a line to make a **REMark** or note to yourself.

DOS 5 and the CONFIG.SYS File

If you install DOS 5 or DOS 6, the installation program will automatically analyze your computer. It will try to load DOS into what is known as **High Memory Area (HMA)** if it is available on your computer. The DOS 5 and DOS 6 upgrades will very likely make modifications to your existing CONFIG.SYS and AUTOEXEC.BAT files. To view a sample DOS 6 AUTOEXEC.BAT or CONFIG.SYS file, see the section starting on page 205. **However, DOS 6 users will benefit from reading this section on the DOS 5 CONFIG.SYS file.**

You can make more modifications to the DOS 5 CONFIG.SYS file, and DOS will perform much better. **You can use the EDIT program (which comes with DOS 5 and DOS 6) to edit the CONFIG.SYS file.**

- **Below is a typical CONFIG.SYS file for an *80286 machine with one megabyte of memory* using DOS 5.** See page 209 if you have DOS 6.

```
DEVICE=C:\DOS\SETVER.EXE
DEVICE=C:\DOS\HIMEM.SYS
DOS=HIGH
DEVICE=C:\DOS\SMARTDRV.SYS 256 128
FILES=30
BUFFERS=20
STACKS=9,256
```

Be sure to follow the special instructions on pages 149 - 150 before you attempt to modify the CONFIG.SYS file. To load the CONFIG.SYS file into EDIT, at the DOS prompt type:

edit c:\config.sys <ENTER>

After you are through editing, don't forget to save the file before you exit by typing:

<ALT>

f

s

Anytime you are in EDIT you can press <F1> for help. To exit EDIT, type:

<ALT>

f

x

The first line in the sample CONFIG.SYS file on page 162 loads the DOS version table which some programs might need in order to report a different DOS version. The next line refers to HIMEM.SYS. This HIMEM.SYS file is an extended memory manager that comes with DOS 5 and later and allows 80286 and 80386 computers to use the High Memory Area (HMA). The third line, DOS=HIGH, instructs DOS to load into High Memory Area. The fourth line, DEVICE=C:\DOS\SMARTDRV.SYS 256 128, tells DOS to use the disk cache that comes with DOS 5 called SMARTDRV.SYS. A disk cache uses a portion of memory to store information that DOS reads from disk. *DOS can read the information from the disk cache much faster than it can read information from a drive. Therefore, you will get a big performance boost.* The first number is the maximum size for the disk cache which in this case is 256. The second number is the minimum size for the disk cache which in this case is 128. If only one number is given after SMARTDRV.SYS, it is for the maximum disk cache size and the minimum size will be 0. With DOS 5, SMARTDRIVE is loaded using a device command in the CONFIG.SYS file. If you have an 80286 or higher machine and installed **Windows 3.1 or DOS 6**, a new and improved SMARTDRIVE will most likely be installed automatically in your AUTOEXEC.BAT file. Windows 3.1 or DOS 6 will remove your old SMARTDRIVE. If that is the case, don't try to modify your CONFIG.SYS file to look like the above sample or the one shown on page 164. Leave the SMARTDRIVE line in your AUTOEXEC.BAT file. If you have DOS 6 see page 209.

If you have an 80286 machine with two megabytes or more of memory, you can get a larger disk cache by changing the above DEVICE line to read:

DEVICE=C:\DOS\SMARTDRV.SYS 1024 256

The FILES line and the BUFFERS line were discussed on page 158. The last line is STACKS=9,256. This told DOS to create 9 stacks and have each one to contain 256 bytes. A STACK is memory area where an interrupt handler stores information. If you leave the STACKS line out, 80286 machines and greater will default to STACKS=9,128. Also, see the Tips on page 211.

DOS 5 and DOS 6 include a memory manager called EMM386.EXE for 80386 and 80486 machines, but it will not work on 80286 machines. If you have an 80286 or an 8088 machine, you should consider third-party memory management software to get the most out of your machine. See page 167.

- **Below is a typical DOS 5 CONFIG.SYS file for an *80386 or an 80486 machine with one megabyte of memory*.** For DOS 6 see page 209.

DEVICE=C:\DOS\SETVER.EXE
DEVICE=C:\DOS\HIMEM.SYS
DOS=HIGH,UMB
DEVICE=C:\DOS\EMM386.EXE NOEMS
DEVICEHIGH=C:\DOS\SMARTDRV.SYS 256 128
FILES=30
BUFFERS=20
STACKS=9,256

The first line tells DOS to load the DOS version table which some programs might need in order to report a different version of DOS. The second line in the CONFIG.SYS file refers to HIMEM.SYS. This HIMEM.SYS file comes with DOS 5 and DOS 6 and allows 80286 and 80386 computers to use the High Memory Area (HMA). In the third line of the CONFIG.SYS file DOS=HIGH,UMB tells DOS to load high on 80386 and greater machines.

The UMB stands for **Upper Memory Blocks.** *You need an 80386 machine or higher to use this UMB specification.* The fourth line refers to EMM386.EXE which is used to simulate expanded memory on an 80386 machine. The NOEMS tells DOS to use all the extended memory to load programs and device drivers and not to use it to simulate expanded memory. **If you have programs that require expanded memory, you can use the DOS EDIT program to edit the EMM386 line in the CONFIG.SYS file. Substitute the word RAM for NOEMS.** You can determine if a program needs expanded memory by reading the manual. To provide expanded memory, the EMM386 line in the CONFIG.SYS file can be changed to look like:

DEVICE = C:\DOS\EMM386.EXE RAM.

The EMM386.EXE works with HIGHMEM.SYS device driver to provide memory management for 80386 and 80486 machines. Note that the fifth line in the above CONFIG.SYS file has a DEVICEHIGH statement. That tells DOS to load it into high memory. *The DEVICEHIGH statement can be used only on 80386 and higher machines.* If you had other device drivers, you could use the DEVICEHIGH statement to load them, too. FILES, BUFFERS, and STACKS are discussed on pages 161 and 164. If you want to squeeze out an extra 2K of RAM, see page 211 for the tip on STACKS.

If you have an 80386 or an 80486 machine with two megabytes or more of memory, you might increase the numbers following the SMARTDRV.SYS line to:

DEVICEHIGH = C:\DOS\SMARTDRV.SYS 1024 256

If you have Windows or DOS 6, see page 163 and pages 205 - 207.

With an 80386 or higher machine and the above example CONFIG.SYS file (or the one for DOS 6 shown on page 209), you can use the LOADHIGH command in your **AUTOEXEC.BAT** file to load programs into high memory. For example, suppose you had a memory-resident utility program called CONFMT.COM that resided in the directory called C:\UTILS. To load CONFMT.COM into high memory, you could add a line to your **AUTOEXEC.BAT** file like:

LOADHIGH C:\UTILS\CONFMT

Instead of spelling out the entire word LOADHIGH, you can use the abbreviation of LH.
Example:

LH C:\UTILS\CONFMT

The LOADHIGH command will only work with 80386 and higher machines because the **UMB (Upper Memory Blocks)** option in the CONFIG.SYS file will not work on 80286 or 8088 machines. However, *you can buy software from other vendors that will help with upper memory on 80286 and 8088 computers.*

Third-Party Memory Management Software

The DOS 5 CONFIG.SYS file can be a bit difficult to get just right. If you want to know more about memory management, I would highly recommend Jeff Prosise's excellent book, PC MAGAZINE DOS 6 MEMORY MANAGEMENT WITH UTILITIES. See page 275 for more information. Prosise's book covers DOS 5 and DOS 6. **If you want to get the most out of DOS 5 or DOS 6 and your machine has extended or expanded memory, you will want to consider third-party memory management software.** With some memory management programs, you might get as much as 800K or more of useable memory. The software is always being improved and new versions come out often. These third-party memory management programs will perform better than the DOS 6 memory management program called MEMMAKER. See page 215 for more on the DOS 6 MEMMAKER program.

- Quarterdeck makes **QEMM 386** for 80386 and 80486 machines and **QRAM** for 8088 and 80286 PC's. Their address is: Quarterdeck, 150 Pico Boulevard, Santa Monica, CA 90405.

- Qualitas, Inc., makes **386MAX** for 80386 and 80486 computers and **MOVE'EM** for 80286 computers that use the NEAT CHIPSet, or any PC computer with an EMS 4.0 hardware memory board. The address for Qualitas, Inc., is: 7101 Wisconsin Avenue, Bethesda, MD 20814.

These products will *automatically analyze your system and then create your CONFIG.SYS and AUTOEXEC.BAT file for you.* They do a good job. The software may consider hundreds of possible solutions before configuring your system! When you add new programs, you can use the above mentioned memory management software to re-configure your system. You can still make any desired modifications manually.

Summary

In this chapter you learned the following about the CONFIG.SYS file:

1. The CONFIG.SYS file is simply a text file that is named CONFIG.SYS.

2. When DOS starts up, it looks for a file called CONFIG.SYS in the root directory of the start-up disk and follows the commands in that file.

3. Sometimes software requires special lines to be placed in the CONFIG.SYS file in order for the software to work.

4. Before attempting to modify a CONFIG.SYS file, make a bootable floppy disk that will work in your A drive (FORMAT A: /S <ENTER>); and make a backup copy of the CONFIG.SYS file and other important files in the root directory.

5. If you need to make or modify a CONFIG.SYS file, you can use an editor or word processor program. The only requirement is that it must be able to save files in ASCII format. If you have nothing better, you can use the DOS COPY CON command to make a CONFIG.SYS file.

6. When you modify or make a new CONFIG.SYS file, the changes don't take effect until you re-boot your computer.

7. To get the most out of your computer if your system has extended or expanded memory, you should consider third-party memory management software. Many of these third-party programs will automatically optimize your AUTOEXEC.BAT and CONFIG.SYS files for you.

DOSKEY—A Quick Tour

DOSKEY is a nice command line editor and macro recorder which comes with DOS 5 and DOS 6. Even if you don't have DOS 5 or later, you probably will want to read this section to evaluate some of the features of DOSKEY.

The DOSKEY program keeps a log of the commands that you have typed. You can recall them by pressing the <F7> function key. DOSKEY can also record macros. A MACRO is simply a set of keystrokes that you can assign to a key or sequence of keys. The DOSKEY macro recorder will allow you to assign keystrokes to a macro name. It is best to keep the assigned macro name short so that you will save a lot of keystrokes. Anytime you find yourself typing in a long command, you may wish to make a DOSKEY macro to make your work easier. With DOSKEY a macro cannot be more than 127 characters in length. Because the macro is stored in RAM, you will lose it when you turn your machine off. However, *you can make a batch file as is shown on page 141 to store one or more macros.* You could insert lines into the AUTOEXEC.BAT file so the macros would be available when you start your computer.

DOSKEY Macro Recording

Let's briefly explore the DOSKEY macro recording features. Suppose you have trouble remembering how to format 720K 3½" disks in your 1.44MB 3½" drive B. You can use DOSKEY to assign the regular keystrokes to a shorter name like FL (for Format Low capacity). At the C> type:

doskey fl=format b: /f:720 <ENTER>

Now type:

fl <ENTER>

The screen will show:

FORMAT B:/F:720

Just press <ENTER> to complete the command. The macro you just created is stored in RAM, so it can be quickly executed from any drive or directory.

Perhaps you would like to make a macro to find lost files on your hard drive. You could issue the following command:

doskey ff=dir $2\$1 /s /b /p <ENTER>

Don't worry about how it works, just type it in. This creates a macro named FF (for find file) that will search any of your drives for files. Perhaps you lost a file on your D drive called RAMKEY.DOC. To find it, type:

ff ramkey.doc d: <ENTER>

If it exists on the D drive, your new macro FF will find it and show you where the file is located. Try using the above FF macro to find some of your files. To find the file called ANSI.SYS, at the C> type:

ff ansi.* <ENTER>

Note the use of the asterisk which is a wildcard character. This should find your ANSI.SYS file located on the C:\DOS subdirectory since C is your current drive.

The DOSKEY Command Line Editor

With DOS 5 or greater you can run DOSKEY, and then you can recall your previous DOS commands by pressing <F7>. To experiment, type the following commands:

> **doskey <ENTER>**
> **cls <ENTER>**
> **dir /w <ENTER>**
> **dir /w /p <ENTER>**
> **dir *.doc <ENTER>**
> **dir... <ENTER>**

Now press:

> **<F7>**

Here you pressed the <F7> function key without pressing <ENTER>. You will see that the commands that you entered appear on the left side of your screen. You can use your **up arrow** key to move up the list and the **down arrow** key to move down the list. Notice that the commands at the DOS prompt change as you move up and down the list of previous commands. To run a previous command, just press **<ENTER>** when the one you desire is showing on the screen. If you want to edit a command, just press the **<HOME>** key. When you press the <HOME> key, the curser goes to the beginning of the command that is showing at the DOS prompt. You can move the cursor by using the right and left arrow keys. You can toggle the **<INS>** key to insert mode to do editing. When you have the command the way you want it, execute it by pressing the **<ENTER>** key. DOSKEY is useful and fun.

Backing Up Your Hard Drive

Until DOS 6 and MSBACKUP, the BACKUP program that came with DOS was rather primitive. However, the DOS BACKUP program is in some respects easier. If you want information on the DOS 6 MSBACKUP program, see the section starting on page 236.

DOS 6 does not include the old BACKUP program. If you upgraded from an earlier version of DOS and had the BACKUP program in your C:\DOS directory, then DOS 6 will retain it and copy the new MSBACKUP program when you install DOS 6. If you have DOS 6 and do not have the old DOS BACKUP program and want it, you can order it along with other utility programs that Microsoft cut from DOS 6 for $5.00. They call this package "supplemental disks." See their offer in the back of the DOS 6 manual.

Many people feel that they don't need to back up their entire hard drive because they have their original programs on diskettes. However, most people do need to back up parts of their hard drive, especially those directories which contain important data files. To back up a full 120MB hard drive might require as many as 100 high-density (1.2MB) diskettes using the DOS BACKUP program. When compared to other backup programs on the market, the DOS BACKUP doesn't do very well. **The DOS BACKUP program does not use file compression and is slow.** (The DOS 6 MSBACKUP program does use file compression. See pages 236 - 252.) With the DOS BACKUP program, if you want to restore your backup to a different computer and that other computer has a lower version of DOS (version 3.2 or earlier), it will not work.

There are plenty of third-party backup programs that are much better and faster than the DOS BACKUP. The commercial program called **PC TOOLS**, by Central Point Software, has an excellent hard drive backup program. The address of Central Point Software is 15220 N.W. Greenbriar Parkway #200, Beaverton, OR 97006.

Backing Up Your Entire Hard Drive

If you have DOS 6, see the section on MSBACKUP starting on page 236.

Make sure you have plenty of disks on hand **before you start** backing up your hard drive. It is best that you use the disks that are designated for your particular floppy drive. If your A drive is 1.2MB, use 1.2MB high-density disks. If your A drive is 1.44MB, use high-density 1.44MB disks. The following procedure assumes that you are using disks that have the same capacity as your floppy drive.

If you have the C:\DOS subdirectory in your path, you can issue the following command to back up your entire hard drive C. Place a blank disk in drive A and at the system prompt type:

backup c:\ a: /f /s <ENTER>

This tells DOS to back up the entire C drive and to copy the data to drive A. If you want to backup drive D instead of drive C, you can substitute D: for the C:. If you want to backup the hard drive to the floppy drive B, you can substitute B: where the above command has an A:. The /F instructs DOS to format the blank floppies. With DOS 4.0 through DOS 5, you do not have to use /F to format disks, because DOS will determine if the target disks need formatting. The /S in the above command instructs DOS to back up all the data in all the subdirectories. You should label each backup disk carefully. Write something on the label like "BACKUP DISK #1—11/14/94." When your first disk gets full, you will be prompted to put in the second disk. Make sure you assign a number to each disk and carefully label it. If you want to abort the backup at any time, you can press <CTRL> C. Then you would have to start the entire procedure over again.

If you want to use *low capacity disks* and you have a *high-density floppy drive*, you must **format plenty of disks before you begin**. See the section on formatting disks for details, pages 60 - 62. Then issue the following command to back up your entire drive C.

backup c:\ a: /s < ENTER >

Notice that in this example the /F was left out. If you issue the command like this, make sure you have more floppy disks formatted than you are going to need.

Restoring Your Backup

The RESTORE command is included with DOS. Microsoft even includes it with DOS 6; so that if you want to transfer files from one computer using an older DOS to one using DOS 6, you can. If you have DOS 6, see the section on MSBACKUP starting on page 236.

To copy disks that were backed up with the DOS BACKUP command to your C hard drive, place the first disk of the set in drive A and type:

restore a: c: /s < ENTER >

After the first disk is copied, you will be prompted to put in the second disk, etc., until all the backup disks are restored.

Making Partial Backups

You can use the DOS BACKUP command to make a partial backup of your hard drive. For example, you might want to back up a directory and all it's subdirectories. You can also use it to back up a single file that exceeds the capacity of a target disk. That is, it can split a very large file to multiple diskettes.

Suppose you wanted to back up a directory on drive C called C:\WP51. To backup C:\WP51 and any subdirectories that might be under it, using diskettes that have the same capacity as your A drive, place the first blank disk in drive A and type:

backup c:\wp51 a: /f /s < ENTER >

If you wanted to backup the directory but not any subdirectories under it, you would issue the above command and leave off the /S.

To restore C:\WP51 and all the directories under it, you would place the first diskette of the partial backup in drive A and type:

restore a: c: /s < ENTER >

Then follow the prompts on your screen. If the subdirectories do not exist on the target disk, don't worry. The /S instructed DOS to make any needed subdirectories on the C drive. If you want to make a partial backup using the DOS 6 MSBACKUP program, see the section starting on page 245.

Tips

- The commercial program **PC TOOLS** has a backup program that is superior to DOS's BACKUP. See page 172 for their address. It uses file compression and is more reliable, substantially more flexible, and significantly faster than DOS's BACKUP.

- If you back up a large hard drive, you will want to investigate tape backup systems. These come in many sizes and are a better media than diskettes for doing backup work. They are much faster and require less supervision. Instead of having to shuffle as many as 100 floppy disks, you just put in one tape! These tape backup systems usually come with their own backup software.

- The shareware program **POINT & SHOOT BACKUP/RESTORE** is better and faster than DOS's BACKUP. It is very easy to use. Many people don't make backups, because they feel it would be too complicated. This program eliminates that excuse. It is menu driven and works with DOS 2.0 and later. See page 260 for more details.

How to Unzip Zipped Files

A zipped file is a file or a collection of files compressed into a smaller space. So, a zipped file is a compressed file. Files that have a .ZIP extension are usually zipped using a program called PKZIP. Files with the .ZIP extension are unusable until you unzip them with a shareware program called PKUNZIP.EXE. In other words, *you can't get to the goodies unless you unzip'em.* It is usually best to unzip zipped files on the hard drive where they will have plenty of room to expand. It is not unusual for a zipped file to be one-half to one-third the size of the original file. If you intend to use a modem, you will find that most **B**ulletin **B**oard **S**ystems (BBSs) store their files in zipped format. For more information on PKZIP and PKUNZIP see page 260.

If you obtain the unzipping program from a shareware vendor, it may be in the form of a self-extracting file. *A self-extracting file is also a compressed file. When a self-extracting file is run, other files pop out (or emerge) from it. It is best to run a self-extracting file from the hard drive, so it will have plenty of space to expand. Sometimes, if you try to run a self-extracting file from a floppy disk, the disk fills up before all the files can pop out.* **New computer users often make this mistake.** If *you* make this mistake and do a directory on the disk, you will see that there is not enough space left on the floppy disk.

If you order PKUNZIP from a shareware vendor and do a directory on the disk, you may see only one file called PKZ204G.EXE. **The version number changes periodically. You will want the latest version to insure compatibility.** This is a self-extracting file, so you will want to copy it to your hard drive before you run it. If you need help on how to copy a file to your hard drive, see page 123. When you run the self-extracting program PKZ204G.EXE, a file called PKUNZIP.EXE will pop out of it, and other files, too. For our example you will want to have a copy of PKUNZIP.EXE on a floppy disk. If you need to know how to copy a file from your hard drive to a floppy disk, see page 127. For this example make a temporary directory on your hard drive called C:\TEMP. At the C> type:

cd \ <ENTER>

This takes you to the root directory of the C drive. Then make a directory using the MD command:

md \temp <ENTER>

Now place a disk that contains PKUNZIP.EXE in the floppy drive A and type:

copy a:pkunzip.exe c:\temp <ENTER>

PKUNZIP.EXE will be copied from the A drive to the TEMP subdirectory on the C drive. Next, copy the file or files that need to be unzipped to that directory. Put the disk which has the zipped file that you want to unzip in drive A and type:

copy a:filename.zip c:\temp <ENTER>

In the above example *filename is the **name** of the zipped file*, and ZIP will be the extension. If there are numerous zipped files on the A drive that you wanted to unzip, you could copy them all to C:\TEMP by issuing the following command: COPY A:*.ZIP C:\TEMP <ENTER>. Note that PKUNZIP.EXE and the file or files that need to be unzipped are now in the same subdirectory (C:\TEMP) on the hard drive. Now switch over to C:\TEMP to unzip the file(s) with a .ZIP extension.

At the C> type:

cd \temp <ENTER>

dir <ENTER>

When you issue the DIR command, you should see PKUNZIP.EXE and the file or files with the ZIP extension that you are going to unzip. Then type:

pkunzip filename <ENTER>

In this example, *filename is the **name** of the zipped file*. If the file was named PINBALL.ZIP, you would have typed: **PKUNZIP PINBALL <ENTER>**. A file or files will pop out of the zipped file. ZIP-ITY-DO-DA! It's like popcorn. Those files *explode* out of the original file! Don't be alarmed if you see EXPLODING... or INFLATING... on your screen when you unzip. This is normal. You can then run the files that appear in the usual manner. You will not have to unzip them again. If you have room, you can copy the files to a floppy disk or somewhere else on your hard drive. You may want to delete the file with the .ZIP extension in C:\TEMP at this time to save room on your hard drive.

Summary

How to Unzip Zipped Files

1. Make a directory on your hard drive using the MD command.

2. Copy the file with the .ZIP extension (the file you want to unzip) to the directory you just made in Step 1.

3. Copy PKUNZIP.EXE to the directory you made in Step 1.

4. Change to the directory you made in Step 1 using the CD command. This makes it the *active directory*. It should now contain PKUNZIP.EXE and the file you want to unzip.

5. Type:
    ### pkunzip filename < ENTER >

    Note that *filename* is the name of the file that you want to unzip. This file will have a .ZIP extension. For example, if you had a file called CHESS.ZIP, you would type: PKUNZIP CHESS < ENTER >

Tips

You can unzip zipped files from any directory when PKUNZIP.EXE is in a directory that is in your computer's PATH. Then you can eliminate Step 3 above. Why not make a directory called C:\UTILS and copy PKUNZIP.EXE to it? To see how to place C:\UTILS in your PATH, see pages 152 - 153.

Running Programs Written in BASIC

BASIC programs can usually be identified by their **.BAS** extension. Before you can run a basic program, you need to have a copy of the BASIC language which is a software program. Some computers do not come with BASIC on a diskette or on the hard drive, so you might have to obtain a copy. Your BASIC may be known as **BASIC**, **BASICA**, or **GWBASIC**. All of these BASICS are made by Microsoft Corporation.

DOS 5 and later come with a version of BASIC called **QBASIC**. *Unfortunately, QBASIC is not directly compatible with older BASIC programs. Normally, older BASIC programs were saved in a special binary format.* In the future, programmers may write a new batch of programs using QBASIC. However, as of this writing, there are very few programs written to take advantage of the new QBASIC. So, if you have only QBASIC, you will probably want to obtain BASIC or GWBASIC.

However, if you have GWBASIC, you can save older BASIC programs in ASCII format like so: SAVE "FILENAME.BAS",A <ENTER>. Then many (but not all) of those GWBASIC programs can be loaded and run in the new QBASIC without any modifications!

The best way to set up your computer to run BASIC programs is to make sure that BASIC is in your computer's path. Since the DOS subdirectory should be in your path, you can copy your version of BASIC to the C:\DOS subdirectory. To see if the DOS subdirectory is in your path, type:

path <ENTER>

If C:\DOS is not in your path, see pages 152 - 153 for instructions on how to put the path statement in your AUTOEXEC.BAT file.

Suppose you have a version of BASIC on disk called GWBASIC.EXE. Place this disk in drive A. To copy it to your C:\DOS subdirectory, at the system prompt type:

copy a:gwbasic.exe c:\dos < ENTER >

If your version of BASIC is called BASIC or BASICA, you would modify the above command accordingly.   Now that BASIC is installed in your computer's path, you can run BASIC programs from any drive or directory. Suppose you did a directory on a disk and found a program called TEACHER.BAS. To run that program, you would place the disk with the program TEACHER.BAS in drive A and at the A prompt type:

gwbasic teacher < ENTER >

If your version of BASIC is called BASIC or BASICA, then you would modify the above command accordingly. If you had BASIC, you would type: BASIC TEACHER < ENTER >.   Once your version of BASIC is in your computer's path, you will be able to run BASIC programs from any drive or directory as shown in the above example.

If you are using DOS 5 or DOS 6 and would like to run a QBASIC program, you do it in a different manner. For example, to run GORILLA.BAS which is a nice game that comes with DOS 5, you would first change to the directory that contains GORILLA.BAS (most likely, C:\DOS) and at the system prompt type:

qbasic /run gorilla < ENTER >

There are a few things you should know about BASIC programs.

If a BASIC program does not respond properly, try putting the **< CAPS LOCK > on** and try again. For many BASIC programs you need to use capital letters to respond to questions.

182

You can often halt a BASIC program by pressing two keys. First press the key marked <CTRL> and, while holding <CTRL> down, press C.

<CTRL> c

If you want to see a directory of a disk while in BASIC, you can first halt it by pressing <CTRL> C. Then type:

files <ENTER>

If you want to see the BASIC program source code, first halt it with <CTRL> C and then type:

list <ENTER>

To stop the list from scrolling, you can press the key marked:

<PAUSE>

Getting Out of BASIC

You can exit most BASIC programs to get back to DOS by pressing <CTRL> and, while holding <CTRL> down, press the key marked C.

<CTRL> c

Then typing:

system <ENTER>

This will return you to the system prompt.

Tips

You may want to have a BASIC program start up automatically from a floppy disk. Suppose you have a program called CHECKERS.BAS that you want to automatically start up from a floppy disk.

1. Format a blank disk **with the system on it in drive A (format a:/s <ENTER>)**. See pages 67 - 69 if you need help.

2. Copy your version of BASIC to the just formatted floppy. For the following example it is assumed that your BASIC is called GWBASIC.EXE.

3. Copy the file CHECKERS.BAS to that same floppy. You should now have a formatted disk *with the system on it* which contains the files GWBASIC.EXE and CHECKERS.BAS.

4. Put this disk in drive A. At the A> type:

> **copy con autoexec.bat <ENTER>**
> **gwbasic checkers <ENTER>**
> **<F6> <ENTER>**

Note that the second line, GWBASIC CHECKERS <ENTER>, is the command that starts the CHECKERS.BAS program. Now if you turn on your computer with this disk in your A drive, the CHECKERS.BAS program will run automatically!

Hard Drive Defragmenting

With active use, a hard drive becomes fragmented which means the files are not stored in an efficient manner. This tends to slow down the hard drive, making tasks take longer than they would if the hard drive were not fragmented. A badly fragmented hard drive can greatly benefit from being defragmented. This is done with a software program. Hard drive performance can be boosted as much as 400 percent. It should be noted that *defragmentation is also called disk optimization.*

Unfortunately, until DOS 6, Microsoft did not provide a defragmentation program. If you have DOS 6, see the section on DEFRAG starting on page 195.

If you have an older version of DOS, you can purchase a commercial defragmentation program. The software package called **PC TOOLS**, by Central Point Software, contains an excellent defragmentation program called **COMPRESS**. If you have DOS 6, you should read the README.TXT file in the C:\DOS directory before you run any third-party utility programs. Some defragmenting programs are not compatible with DOS 6.

WARNING: Do not use any defragmenting program unless you are certain that it is compatible with your operating system. If you have DOS 6, make sure that it is designed to work with DOS 6.

PC TOOLS comes with a set of good manuals, and COMPRESS is not hard to use. When you consider all the other excellent utility programs that come with PC TOOLS, I think you will find that it is very attractively priced. The address of Central Point Software is 15220 N.W. Greenbriar Parkway #200, Beaverton, OR 97006.

Hard Drive Parking

Newer model hard drives will automatically park the heads of the hard drive when the computer is turned off. Older models, using a stepper motor, will not. To avoid a hard drive head crash on older hard drives, it is wise to park the heads before the computer is to be turned off. This is especially true if the computer is going to be moved. If you do not know if your drive automatically parks the heads, you can first contact the people where you bought the computer. If they don't know, contact the manufacturer. Most hard drive manufacturers have toll free numbers.

The commercial program **PC TOOLS**, by Central Point Software, includes a hard drive head parking program. You can also find excellent hard drive head parking programs in shareware.

DOS Shells and Menus

A shell is a program that *attempts* to make DOS easier to use. A shell surrounds DOS, insulating the user from the austere DOS command environment. That is why it is called a "shell." A shell often allows you to perform common DOS functions by moving a cursor to highlight a file, or group of files, and then pressing a couple of keys. Thus, a shell can be a very attractive piece of software for a beginner.

There are hundreds of shell and menu programs on the market. Shells provide an easy way to do file management tasks like copying, moving, and running files. They often provide a simple way to do things like making and changing directories and changing drives. A shell usually has a way to view and edit text files. Usually you just place the cursor on the file that you want to view and then press a function key. DOS 4.0 and later have a built in shell. The shells that come with DOS are not very attractive when compared to other shells on the market. The commercial program PC TOOLS includes a good shell. PC TOOLS is made by Central Point Software. Their address is 15220 N.W. Greenbriar Parkway #200, Beaverton, OR 97006. XTREE GOLD is another commercial shell that is very popular. XTREE GOLD is by EXECUTIVE SYSTEMS, INC., 4330 Sante Fe Road, San Luis Obispo, CA 93401.

My current favorite DOS shell is a shareware program called STEREO SHELL. It is very fast and has plenty of features. See page 261 for the address. Since there are hundreds of excellent DOS shells on the market, you might wonder which one is best for you. If you ask twenty DOS computer professionals, "What is the best DOS shell on the market?" you are likely to get 12 or more different answers. Some of these people would tell you not to use any DOS shell or menu. It is really a matter of personal taste.

A DOS menu program allows the user to make a choice—often by choosing a number or letter. A software menu is kind of like a restaurant menu;

except, instead of listing food items, it lists specific programs or functions. These days many DOS menu programs do more than just make programs easier to use. They often will perform basic DOS functions, too. In other words, the DOS menus are becoming more like DOS shells. An excellent shareware DOS menu program is QUIKMENU. The latest version of QUIKMENU is very slick. Always try to obtain the latest version of these programs. Many shareware programs are updated three or four times a year! Usually the changes they make in the programs are improvements. For more information, see the section on SHAREWARE SOFTWARE starting on page 256.

Tips

- I would recommend that new users get used to issuing commands from the DOS command line before they start relying on any shell or menu program. If you know DOS, you will be a better computer user. Knowing your way around DOS will make any shell or menu a lot easier to understand.

- Some software programs won't run properly from a shell or menu. Also, some software will not install properly from a shell or menu. That is when you must go to the DOS command line. If you decide to use a shell or menu program, have a DOS book handy for reference and know how to use the **INDEX**.

Part 5

DOS 6 SECTION

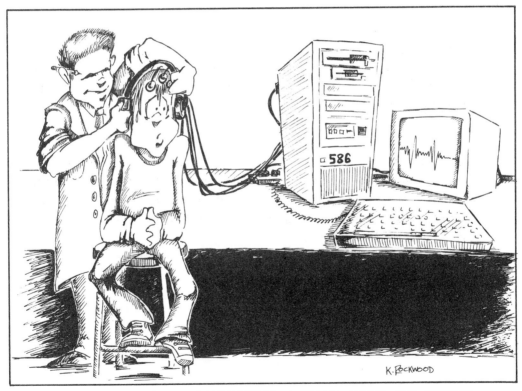

DR. CMOS PEROT ADMINISTERS A SMALL DOSE OF SODIUM PENTIUM FOR A QUICK DIAGNOSTIC TRUTH TEST.

New DOS 6 Commands

MS DOS 6 has plenty of new commands that can replace many third-party utility programs. Some of the more outstanding features include:

1. **HELP** — A much improved on-line help.

2. **DOUBLESPACE** — Increases the capacity of your hard drive by using disk compression. The program is called DBLSPACE.

3. **DEFRAGMENTATION** — A long overdue disk defragmenting program called DEFRAG. Defragmentation has always been a necessary part of hard drive maintenance.

4. **MEMORY MANAGEMENT** — An automatic memory management program called MEMMAKER.

5. **MSBACKUP** — Microsoft's first attempt to include a modern backup program.

6. **VIRUS PROTECTION** — A virus protection and removal program called MSAV.

7. **UNDELETE** — An improved program that can increase your chances of recovering accidentally deleted files.

The last three programs mentioned have both DOS and Windows versions of each program (MSBACKUP, MSAV, and UNDELETE). If you had Windows installed prior to updating to DOS 6, you may find that the DOS versions of MSBACKUP, MSAV, and UNDELETE did not get installed.

Also, if you did not have Windows on your machine when you installed DOS 6, then the Windows versions of these programs would not have been installed. If you find that your system does not have the DOS or Windows versions of these programs installed, you can do it now. You will have the option of installing the DOS or Windows versions or both. Get out your DOS 6 diskettes and place the first diskette in the appropriate drive. Change over to that drive. For example, if you used your A drive, you would place the first DOS 6 diskette in drive A and type:

a: <ENTER>
setup /e <ENTER>

Read the screen information carefully and follow the prompts. You will need to have the Windows program installed before DOS can install the Windows versions. The Windows versions of these three programs are accessed by double clicking on the Microsoft Tools group found in the Program Manager, and they operate much like the DOS versions.

CAUTION: Before you work with DOS 6, you should read the file called README.TXT in the C:\DOS directory. The SETUP program places this file there when you install DOS 6. It contains important notes on DOS 6 and should be compulsory reading as the information may help you avoid a disaster!

To load the README.TXT file into the DOS EDIT program, at the system prompt type:

edit c:\dos\readme.txt <ENTER>

To scroll through the file while you are in EDIT, you can use your arrow keys or <PG UP>, <PG DN> keys. If you want to print the file, press:

<ALT>
f
p
<ENTER>

The DOS 6 HELP

To get a short explanation and overview of DOS commands, at the DOS prompt type:

fasthelp <ENTER>

If you want to access a table of contents for DOS HELP, at the DOS prompt type:

help <ENTER>

Then press the first letter of the command on which you would like more information. Use your arrow keys to make your selection. When the cursor is on the command where you want help, press:

<ENTER>

To get detailed information on any particular DOS command, at the system prompt type HELP followed by a space and the command that you want information on. For example, if you want help on the DIR command, type:

help dir <ENTER>

A screen of information is shown with Notes and Examples at the top. Press N for Notes or E for Examples. The cursor will then go to the one you selected. Then press:

<ENTER>

You can use your arrow keys to scroll through the text. You can also press <PGDN> or <PGUP> to scroll one page at a time. If you select E for Examples, you are shown actual examples of how to use the command. If you want to search for a key word or phrase, you can start the search process by pressing:

<ALT>
s

Then just follow the screen prompts.

Printing HELP Information

You can print the HELP information you are viewing by pressing:

<ALT>
f
p
<ENTER>

I recommend printing the help information, so you can have a copy to use beside your computer. If you do this for all the DOS commands, you can print your own personalized DOS manual!

HELP with Other Commands

While you are using the DOS HELP, you can get a table of contents of all the covered commands by pressing:

< ALT >

c

Anytime you are using DOS HELP and want assistance on how to get around in HELP, press the function key labeled:

< F1 >

Getting Out of HELP

To get out of HELP and return to the DOS prompt, type:

< ALT >

f

x

Defragmentation

A drive becomes fragmented with active use. A drive is fragmented when files are not stored in an efficient manner. This tends to slow down the drive and makes tasks take longer than they would if the drive were not fragmented. It should be noted that defragmentation is also called disk optimization.

Finally, with DOS 6, Microsoft provides a defragmentation program called DEFRAG.EXE. It reorganizes files to optimize disk performance. You should defragment your hard drive(s) at least once a month. **Defragmenting should be considered routine hard drive maintenance.**

> **CAUTION:** Before you use the DEFRAG or DBLSPACE commands, be sure to read the text file called README.TXT in the C:\DOS directory. See page 191 for how to do that. **Do not use third-party optimizing programs unless you are certain they are designed to work with DOS 6.** If you use DBLSPACE, you will want to use the special commands shown on page 225 to defragment a DoubleSpaced drive.

You should not try to run the DEFRAG program from within Windows or use it on network drives. It should also be noted that defragmenting a large hard drive can take a very long time.

Before you defragment a drive, you should run the DOS CHKDSK program and have DOS fix any errors. For more information about the DOS CHKDSK program, see page 56. At the C prompt type:

chkdsk /f   < ENTER >

The /F tells DOS to fix errors. If DOS finds what it calls "LOST

CLUSTERS," it will tell you and ask:

CONVERT LOST CHAINS TO FILES (Y/N)?

You can answer yes by pressing:

y

DOS will name these files FILE0000.CHK, FILE0001.CHK, etc.; and it will write them to your root directory. You will probably want to delete these .CHK files to make room for more useful files.

Then, to start the DOS 6 DEFRAG program, type:

defrag <ENTER>

Next, select the drive you want to defragment. In this example it is the C drive, so you would select drive C by using the up arrow or the down arrow. When you have the C drive selected, press:

<ENTER>

The program will recommend a defragmentation option. If you want to learn more about your options, press the function key labeled <F1>. To start the defragmentation process, press:

<ENTER>

It may take quite a while to defragment a drive. Be patient and don't interrupt the process. When it is done, your drive should work faster. If you need more help with using the DEFRAG command, at the DOS prompt type:

help defrag <ENTER>

DELTREE—The Ultimate Wipe-Out

Watch Out! This new and dangerous command can wipe out an entire directory, its subdirectories, and all files contained therein in one command. Needless to say, you have to be very sure when you use the DELTREE command; or it could result in bad things happening! However, it is fast.

CAUTION: If you use DELTREE to delete a directory, you will not be able to use UNDELETE to bring any of the deleted files back. Be very careful with the DELTREE command.

Suppose you had a directory called C:\GAMES, and it had some files in it and a subdirectory called C:\GAMES\PINBALL which also contained files. To wipe out C:\GAMES and C:\GAMES\PINBALL and all the files contained in those directories, first move to the root directory by typing:

cd\ <ENTER>

Then type:

deltree c:\games <ENTER>

The computer will respond with:

DELETE DIRECTORY "C:\GAMES" AND ALL ITS SUBDIRECTORIES? [YN]

Think about it very carefully before answering. Make sure you have typed the correct directory name. If you want to delete the entire directory with its files and subdirectories, press:

y

Faster than you can say "Pentium," they will be gone.

Tips

The shareware program called 4DOS has a delete command that will delete a directory and all its subdirectories and files. So, even if you have an earlier version of DOS, you can obtain a program that will accomplish this task. See page 257 for more information on 4DOS.

The MOVE Command

The DOS 6 MOVE command is used to perform two tasks:

1. To rename directories.

2. To move files.

Suppose you have a directory called C:\TEMP, and you would like to **rename** it C:\PERM. At the system prompt type:

move c:\temp c:\perm < ENTER >

Note that the above command did not actually move any files. The above command simply renamed the C:\TEMP directory to C:\PERM. Any files that were in the directory were not changed.

Now suppose you want to **move** a file. You have a directory called C:\PERM, and it contains a file called SPAM.TXT. You decide that you really like this file and that it is time to move it to your directory called C:\FOOD. To move this file, type:

move c:\perm\spam.txt c:\food < ENTER >

This results in DOS copying the SPAM.TXT file to the C:\FOOD directory and then deleting the SPAM.TXT file in the C:\PERM directory. Before DOS 6, you would have had to use the COPY command to copy the file to the desired new location and then use the DEL command to delete the file in the old location. More than likely, you might have forgotten to delete the file in the old location and wound up with the same file in two locations.

Three shareware programs that have even more powerful move utilities are 4DOS (page 257), PCOPY (page 259), and STEREO SHELL (page 261).

The Microsoft Diagnostic Utility (MSD)

New with DOS 6 is an MSD (Microsoft Diagnostics Utility) program that will give you plenty of technical information about your computer. To run this program, at the DOS prompt type:

msd <ENTER>

Press a highlighted letter for information. You will see a lot of interesting information, including what kind of computer you are using (80286, 80386, 80486, etc.), what kind of monitor and video card, how much memory, and more. You can save this information on disk. Here is how to do it. Place a formatted diskette in drive A, and at the DOS prompt type:

msd /p a:computer.inf <ENTER>

The above command will save the diagnostic information about your computer in a text file called COMPUTER.INF on the A drive. Label this disk and put it in a safe place. It will even contain a copy of your current AUTOEXEC.BAT and CONFIG.SYS files. To view the COMPUTER.INF file, use the DOS EDIT program by typing at the DOS prompt:

edit a:computer.inf <ENTER>

If you want to print the file, press:

<ALT>
f
p
<ENTER>

Store the printed output in a safe place where you can find it. See the Tips below.

200

Tips

- If you have Windows 3.1, then you have the MSD program. The MSD program also comes with Windows 3.1. When you install Windows 3.1, the setup program places MSD.EXE in your Windows directory. Just go to the system prompt and run the program as shown on page 200.

- If you don't have Windows 3.1 or DOS 6, you can obtain a shareware program that is very similar to MSD. This shareware program is called ASQ. It will analyze your computer system and save the results as a text file. For more about ASQ see page 258 in the section on shareware.

- If the battery in your computer goes dead, you will lose your computer's CMOS (Complementary Metal Oxide Semiconductor) SETUP information. This is generally refered to as SETUP information. Sometimes computers lose the SETUP for unknown reasons. Then your hard drive will not work until you get this SETUP information back. *Save the MSD information as a text file on a diskette as was shown on page 200. Label this disk and keep it in a safe place. It contains a lot of the SETUP information and could really save the day.*

> **WARNING:** Do not change the information in your CMOS SETUP unless you know exactly what you are doing. Be careful if you go into CMOS SETUP on your computer. Exit the program without making changes. Changing the information could result in your computer's hard drive not working. If you do go into it, take the time to write down all the information so you will be able to restore it in an emergency. Running SETUP is best left to an experienced computer person. If you lost your SETUP and don't have the information, **don't panic!** Computer dealers are quite familiar with this problem, and most will know how to fix it.

Undeleting Files with DOS 6

The UNDELETE program recovers deleted files. You have a choice of three levels of protection with DOS 6. They are:

Standard — lowest level of protection.
Delete Tracker — middle level of protection.
Delete Sentry — highest level of protection.

Delete Sentry offers the highest level of protection and comes at the expense of using a small amount of memory and disk space. Delete Tracker is the middle level of protection. It uses just as much memory as Delete Sentry protection but does not use any disk space. The Standard level of protection offers the lowest level of protection but does not require any memory or disk space.

NOTE: When DOS 6 was originally installed, there were three programs that could be installed in DOS, Windows, or both. These programs are the MS Anti-Virus, MS Backup, and MS Undelete. If you had Windows already on your computer, the default was to install only the Windows versions of these programs. So, if you type the below UNDELETE command and get a "FILE NOT FOUND" error message, you can correct the problem. See page 191.

To use UNDELETE, change to the directory where you want to try to recover deleted files; and at the system prompt type:

undelete <ENTER>

The above command tells DOS to try to recover all deleted files in the current directory. It will list them on the screen and prompt the user for confirmation of each file. Answer Y for yes if you want to recover a file. You will also be prompted for the first letter of the file you want to recover. With the above command, DOS will try to use the highest level of deletion tracking available. *If you have not installed Delete Tracker or Delete Sentry, DOS will use the Standard level. You should try to recover any deleted files as soon as you can. The longer you wait, the less your chance for success.*

You can use wildcards in the UNDELETE command. For example:

undelete *.txt < ENTER >

This command tells DOS to try to recover all files with a .TXT extension.

Installing Delete Tracker

To install Delete Tracker on drive C, at the system prompt type:

undelete /tc < ENTER >

The /TC tells DOS to use Delete Tracker on drive C. The T is for Tracker and the C is for drive C. This will use some memory. *If you are going to use some memory anyway, you might as well skip the Delete Tracker and go to the Delete Sentry which offers much better protection.* The UNDELETE /TC command installs Delete Tracker. This command can be added to your AUTOEXEC.BAT file so that DOS installs it on start-up. See pages 151 - 152 for how to install an additional line in the AUTOEXEC.BAT file. You will probably want to use the DOS EDIT program to make such a modification. For help on using EDIT, see page 48.

Installing Delete Sentry

Delete Sentry is the best level of file deletion protection. To install it on drive C, at the system prompt type:

undelete /sc <ENTER>

The /SC in the above command tells DOS what kind of UNDELETE protection to use and on which drive. The S is for Delete Sentry, and the C stands for drive **C**. If you wanted to use Delete Sentry for both your C drive and D drive, you could issue the following command:

undelete /sc /sd <ENTER>

As with the Delete Tracker on page 203, *you would probably want to add a line to your AUTOEXEC.BAT file so that your computer would automatically install it on start-up.* Remember, if you want to recover files, you need to change to the drive and the directory where the files you want to recover are located and type:

undelete <ENTER>

To learn more about the DOS 6 UNDELETE command, type:

help undelete <ENTER>

DOS 6 and the AUTOEXEC.BAT File

Below is a typical DOS 6 AUTOEXEC.BAT file for an 80286, an 80386, or an 80486 machine.

```
@ECHO OFF
PATH C:\DOS;C:\WINDOWS;C:\UTILS
PROMPT $P$G
SET TEMP=C:\DOS
SMARTDRV
WIN
```

You can use EDIT, the built-in DOS editor, to make or modify the AUTOEXEC.BAT file or the CONFIG.SYS file. Both of these files reside on the root directory of your start-up disk. Remember, the changes you make when you modify an existing AUTOEXEC.BAT or CONFIG.SYS file will not take effect until you restart your computer. *Never make a modification to either the AUTOEXEC.BAT file or the CONFIG.SYS file without first making a backup of these important files on diskette.* See pages 149 - 150. If your start-up disk is drive C, you can load the AUTOEXEC.BAT file into EDIT by typing:

edit c:\autoexec.bat <ENTER>

For more on using DOS EDIT see pages 162 - 163. When you are in EDIT, you can press <F1> for more help. In the above AUTOEXEC.BAT file, the first three lines are very similar to the sample AUTOEXEC.BAT file for DOS 5 shown on page 147. It is explained there what these three lines do.

The fourth line in the above AUTOEXEC.BAT sample file is SET TEMP=C:\DOS. This SET line creates an environmental variable called TEMP and sets it to equal the directory C:\DOS. This environmental variable is used by programs to store temporary files. If you want to use another directory to store this environment variable, you can. The only criteria is that the directory you specify must exist. For example, you might decide to change the SET line to SET TEMP=C:\TEMP. Then you would need to make the directory C:\TEMP (use the MD command).

The next line is SMARTDRV. *SMARTDRV is a disk cache that works with computers that have extended memory. If you have an 80286 or greater machine with at least 1 megabyte of memory, then you can probably use SMARTDRV. A disk cache uses a portion of memory to store information that DOS reads from disk. DOS can read information from the disk cache much faster than it can read information from a drive. The result is that you will get a big performance boost if you use a disk cache.*

The DOS 6 SMARTDRV will cache both floppy and hard drives and is faster than the DOS 5 SMARTDRV. The SMARTDRV that came with DOS 5 would only cache hard drives and had to be loaded in the CONFIG.SYS file using a device command. See page 164. The DOS 6 SMARTDRV is very similar to the one that is included with WINDOWS 3.1 and can be loaded in the AUTOEXEC.BAT file. The DOS 6 version of SMARTDRV will automatically calculate values by determining how much upper memory exists in your machine. *It will also automatically load itself into high memory if it is available.* The DOS 6 SMARTDRV will do read caching and write caching for hard drives and read caching for floppies. With write caching, you could lose data if you turn your computer off immediately after quitting a program. **It is best to wait at least five seconds after you quit an application before you turn the machine off.** On drives that are write cached, SMARTDRV waits until the cache is about full, or until there has been about 5 seconds of idle time, before writing the data to your hard drive. If you want to force the write cache to immediately write the data to the hard drive, type:

smartdrv /c <ENTER>

> **To avoid potential write caching problems, you may want to disable the SmartDrive write caching feature.**

You can disable write caching by following the SMARTDRV command with the letters of your hard drives. Suppose you had hard drives C, D, E, and you wanted to disable write caching on these drives. Use the DOS EDIT program to change the SMARTDRV line in the AUTOEXEC.BAT file to read the following:

SMARTDRV C D E

The above line tells DOS to allow read caching while disabling write caching for drives C, D, and E. Don't try to cache a DoubleSpaced drive. Smart-Drive will not cache compressed drives (DoubleSpaced drives), CD-ROM drives, network drives, or RAM drives. If you are running DoubleSpace, you can get information on all your drives by typing:

dblspace /info <ENTER>

If you want to see which drives SMARTDRV is caching, at the system prompt type:

smartdrv <ENTER>

For more information on the DOS 6 SMARTDRV command, type:

help smartdrv <ENTER>

The last line in our sample AUTOEXEC.BAT file is WIN. This tells DOS to run the Windows program on start-up. *The last line in the AUTOEXEC.BAT file is where the command that starts any desired shell or menu is placed. Then the computer loads your desired shell or menu program on start-up.*

Tips

- Suppose you want to stop Windows from starting when you boot your computer. If that is the case, you can delete the last line in the sample AUTOEXEC.BAT file or use a REM statement like so:

  REM WIN

  Note that this is REM and then a space. By placing a REM statement in front of any line in the AUTOEXEC.BAT or the CONFIG.SYS file, you are telling DOS to skip processing that line. If you should later change your mind to have Windows run on start-up, you can just delete the REM portion of the line. For more about REMing out a line in your CONFIG.SYS file, see page 161.

- If you have an 80386 or an 80486 machine, see pages 165 - 166 for how to use the LOADHIGH command in the AUTOEXEC.BAT FILE to load memory-resident programs into high memory. Loading a program high will give you more conventional memory.

The DOS 6 CONFIG.SYS File

Below is a typical DOS 6 CONFIG.SYS file for an 80386 or an 80486 machine with two or more megabytes of memory:

```
DEVICE=C:\DOS\SETVER.EXE
DEVICE=C:\DOS\HIMEM.SYS
DOS=HIGH,UMB
DEVICE=C:\DOS\EMM386.EXE NOEMS
DEVICEHIGH=C:\MOUSE\MOUSE.SYS
FILES=30
BUFFERS=20
STACKS=9,256
NUMLOCK=OFF
```

The CONFIG.SYS file resides on the root directory of the start-up disk. *Never make a modification to either the AUTOEXEC.BAT file or the CONFIG.SYS file without first making a backup of these important files on diskette.* See pages 149 - 150 for more information on how to back up these important files. If your start-up disk is drive C, you can load the CONFIG.SYS file into EDIT by typing at the DOS prompt:

edit c:\config.sys <ENTER>

When you are in EDIT, you can press <F1> to obtain help on using EDIT. Don't forget to save your changes if you modify the CONFIG.SYS file. When using DOS EDIT, you can save the file you are working on by pressing:

**<ALT>
f
s**

In the above CONFIG.SYS file, DEVICE=C:\DOS\SETVER.EXE is the first line. This command loads the DOS version table which some programs might need in order to report a different DOS version. For more information on SETVER, type:

help setver < ENTER >

The next three lines of the sample DOS 6 CONFIG.SYS file are the same as are used in the sample for DOS 5 explained on page 164 - 165. *If you have programs that require expanded memory, you should substitute the word* **RAM** *for* **NOEMS** *in the EMM386 line.* The RAM parameter tells DOS to simulate expanded memory. So, if you need to provide expanded memory, change the fourth line in the sample CONFIG.SYS file to:

DEVICE=C:\DOS\EMM386.EXE RAM

The fifth line is DEVICEHIGH=C:\MOUSE\MOUSE.SYS. *DEVICEHIGH tells DOS to load it into high memory. The DEVICEHIGH statement can be used only on 80386 and higher machines.* This line loads a mouse driver that resides in the directory C:\MOUSE. Some mice have mouse drivers that are loaded using a CONFIG.SYS file, and other mice use programs that are loaded in the AUTOEXEC.BAT file. A mouse driver is normally included on the diskette which comes with the mouse. One should read the instructions that come with the mouse to see how to make it work.

Lines six and seven of the sample CONFIG.SYS file concern FILES and BUFFERS which are discussed on page 158.

The eighth line of the CONFIG.SYS file is STACKS=9,256. If you do not use a STACKS statement, DOS automatically defaults to STACKS=9,128 on 80286 and greater machines.

The ninth line of the sample CONFIG.SYS file is NUMLOCK=OFF. This NUMLOCK command is new with DOS 6. It allows you to set your

<NUMLOCK> key to the off position. You can also set it to on by changing the line to read NUMLOCK=ON.

Below is a typical CONFIG.SYS file for an 80286 machine with at least one megabyte of memory using DOS 6.

```
DEVICE=C:\DOS\SETVER.EXE
DEVICE=C:\DOS\HIMEM.SYS
DOS=HIGH
DEVICE=C:\MOUSE\MOUSE.SYS
FILES=30
BUFFERS=20
STACKS=9,256
NUMLOCK=OFF
```

Note, that in the DOS 5 sample CONFIG.SYS file on page 162 there is a SMARTDRIVE line. With DOS 6 the SMARTDRIVE line is simplified and is usually placed in the AUTOEXEC.BAT file. See pages 205 and 206.

Tips

- The changes you make when you modify an existing AUTOEXEC.BAT or CONFIG.SYS file will not take effect until you restart your computer.

- You can try placing a STACKS=0,0 line in the CONFIG.SYS file. This will squeeze out almost 2K of extra memory which you can use to run programs. If you get an error message saying "INTERNAL STACK OVERFLOW SYSTEM HALTED," you should take out the STACKS=0,0 line. Don't try to install Windows with a STACKS=0,0 in the CONFIG.SYS file. Use STACKS=9,256. After you have Windows installed, you can try making the STACKS statement STACKS=0,0.

Tips ... *continued*

- If you need to test a line in your CONFIG.SYS file to see if it is interfering with your system, use the DOS 6 "interactive boot" shown on page 214. Then answer N for no when you want to skip processing a line that might be giving trouble.

- If you want to stop a line from processing in your CONFIG.SYS file, you can REM it out as was shown on pages 161 and 208. With DOS 6 you can use a semicolon (;) to take the place of REM in the CONFIG.SYS file to skip processing a line. This semicolon trick does not work for the AUTOEXEC.BAT file. For example, to stop the last line in the sample CONFIG.SYS file from processing, you could use DOS EDIT to edit the CONFIG.SYS file and insert a semicolon and a space in front of the last line:

  ; NUMLOCK=OFF

- Take a look at the section starting on page 215. It shows how to use the DOS 6 memory management program called MEMMAKER. MEMMAKER can often squeeze a little more conventional memory out of your system. Also, see the section on Third-Party Memory Management Software on page 167.

- You can check to see which programs were loaded into high memory or conventional memory by using the following command at the system prompt:

  mem /c /p <ENTER>

The DOS 6 "Clean Boot"

When DOS 6 is starting up, you can press the function key labeled <F5>; and DOS will start without executing the CONFIG.SYS file or the AUTOEXEC.BAT file as it usually does on start-up. Wait until you see on your screen:

STARTING MS-DOS...

Then press your function key labeled:

<F5>

Then release the <F5> key. Instead of pressing the <F5> key, you could hold down a <SHIFT> key to get the same results. If you are having trouble starting your computer and if the trouble is related to the AUTOEXEC.BAT or the CONFIG.SYS file, then this "clean boot" will allow your computer to start without processing the AUTOEXEC.BAT or the CONFIG.SYS file. Since this "clean boot" does not process the AUTOEXEC.BAT file which contains your PATH statement, your computer will not work as it usually does. DOS will set the PATH to **C:\DOS**. This means that you will need to change to the appropriate directory when you want to use programs that are not in the C:\DOS directory. For more on PATHS see pages 144 - 153.

The DOS 6 "Interactive Boot"

If you are having trouble with your CONFIG.SYS file, DOS 6 provides a way of testing and confirming each command in the CONFIG.SYS file. If you want to test this capability, restart your computer. Wait until you see on your screen:

STARTING MS-DOS...

Then press the function key labeled:

<F8>

Then release the <F8> key. DOS will ask you to confirm each line in the CONFIG.SYS file. For example, if you had a CONFIG.SYS file that looked like the sample shown on page 209, DOS would show the following on the screen:

DEVICE=C:\DOS\SETVER.EXE [Y,N]?

DOS is asking if you want it to process the first line of the CONFIG.SYS file. If you want it to process this line, answer YES by pressing:

Y

You continue the process, carefully watching to see the effect of each line in the CONFIG.SYS file. After going through the CONFIG.SYS file, DOS will give you the following prompt:

PROCESS AUTOEXEC.BAT [Y,N]?

Then answer the question by pressing Y for yes or N for no. You may want to do another "interactive boot" for more testing.

MEMMAKER to Optimize Memory

If you have an 80386, an 80486, or a Pentium (586) computer with extended memory, you will probably be able to free some conventional memory by running the DOS 6 MEMMAKER program. **MEMMAKER requires at least an 80386 machine with extended memory.** It will modify your AUTOEXEC.BAT and CONFIG.SYS files. These reside on the root directory of your start-up disk (usually drive C). MEMMAKER attempts to load device drivers and memory-resident programs into the upper memory area.

The explanation below shows how to run the MEMMAKER Express Setup. If you wish to do a Custom Setup, then you can do so; however, DOS will ask you more questions, and you will have to be more knowledgeable. The Express Setup is easier. *However, you can still get into trouble.* If you are at all squeamish about making modifications to the AUTOEXEC.BAT and the CONFIG.SYS files (this means most, if not all beginners), you should probably have a dealer or experienced individual run the MEMMAKER program for you. *If you are a beginner, it is best not to fool with MEMMAKER at all.*

CAUTION: Before you run MEMMAKER:

1. If you have a CD-ROM, a scanner, or some exotic hardware installed, it would be best to have someone knowledgeable run the MEMMAKER program for you. MEMMAKER is known to have trouble configuring some hardware.

2. Back up your AUTOEXEC.BAT and CONFIG.SYS files on diskette. See pages 149 - 150 for details on how to do it. MEMMAKER does have an UNDO command, but unexpected things can happen. It is best to have backups.

3. For an added measure of security, run the MSD program and have it output the results on disk. See page 200. If you are running WINDOWS, the output from the MSD program will also have a copy of your important Windows SYSTEM.INI file.

4. Use the MEM command to report on your computer's memory. Turn your printer on, and at the system prompt type:

mem /c > prn <ENTER>

If you don't have a printer, you can display the information on your screen. To display your computer's memory information on your screen, type:

mem /c /p <ENTER>

It is a good idea to write down the information, so you can compare it after you have run the MEMMAKER program.

MEMMAKER—The Express Setup

Before running MEMMAKER, start any memory-resident programs that you usually use. You can determine if a program is memory-resident by reading the manual. These memory-resident programs are called TSR's (Terminate Stay Resident). After you get all your usual memory-resident programs running, go to the C prompt and type:

memmaker <ENTER>

Continue the process by pressing:

<ENTER>

You will then be prompted to choose between the Express or the Custom Setup. Choose the Express Setup by pressing:

<ENTER>

If you want more information about the Custom Setup, examine the DOS 6 manual and see the section on suggested reading on page 275.

Next, you will be asked if any of your programs require expanded memory. The manuals for your programs would have this information. If none of your programs require expanded memory or you don't know, answer NO by pressing:

<ENTER>

Those using Windows may be asked additional questions. Just answer the questions and follow the prompts. Eventually, you will be notified that it is time to restart your computer.

At this point, you should remove all diskettes from your floppy drives.

To restart your computer, press:

<ENTER>

If your computer doesn't start properly, just press:

<CTRL> <ALT> <DEL>

That is, hold down all three keys at once and then release them. MEMMAKER considers many possible configurations and makes some changes to your AUTOEXEC.BAT and CONFIG.SYS files. If you are running Windows, it may also change your SYSTEM.INI file. Then it asks you to restart your computer.

To restart your computer, press:

< ENTER >

The computer restarts with its new CONFIG.SYS and AUTOEXEC.BAT files. You will then be asked if your computer is working properly. If your computer seems to be working properly, choose YES by pressing:

< ENTER >

If your computer is not working properly, press the SPACEBAR for NO and then press:

< ENTER >

You will be prompted with more instructions. To get out of MEMMAKER, you can then press:

< ENTER >

To see what effect MEMMAKER had on your system's memory usage, type:

mem /c /p < ENTER >

You can print out a report by turning your printer on and typing:

mem /c > prn < ENTER >

Compare this report with the one you generated before you ran MEMMAKER.

For more information on the MEM command, type:

help mem < ENTER >

Undoing MEMMAKER's Changes

You can undo MEMMAKER's changes after quitting MEMMAKER by typing at the DOS prompt:

memmaker /undo <ENTER>

To restore your original start-up files, press:

<ENTER>

If you are prompted that MEMMAKER has finished restoring your start-up files, press:

<ENTER>

Just follow the screen prompts.

DoubleSpace

DOS 6 comes with a data compression program called DoubleSpace. It may almost double the size of your hard drive by compressing files. Compression programs use a kind of shorthand so that repeated data is stored in less space. Actually, a DoubleSpaced compressed drive is a single file on an uncompressed drive. Such files are called **Compressed Volume Files** (CVF). DoubleSpace is invisible to your programs. You can use DoubleSpace on both hard disks and floppy disks. *However, don't use it without reading the cautions below.*

Before you consider the new DOS 6 DoubleSpace program, you should understand that deleting files and directories are a necessary part of hard drive management. If you need help in this area, see pages 108 - 110. To determine how much space you have on any particular drive, use the CHKDSK command. See pages 56 - 57.

DoubleSpace Cautions:

1. **A DoubleSpaced hard drive is more likely to give trouble** than an uncompressed drive. If you have plenty of room on your hard drive, don't install DoubleSpace. You will be much better served with a large hard drive that is not compressed. *To date, there have been many reports of problems with DoubleSpace.* **If you need more room, my advice is to buy another or a larger hard drive.**

2. If you plan to use DoubleSpace, you should read the README.TXT file in the C:\DOS directory. For help, see pages 191 - 192.

3. You should not use DoubleSpace if your drive is already compressed with another compression program. You could lose all your files!

4.   If you run DoubleSpace, you will not be able to uninstall DOS.

5.   You cannot uncompress a drive that has been DoubleSpaced. Microsoft did not provide an uncompress command.

6.   DoubleSpace can compress a drive to a maximum of 512 megabytes.

7.   When you run DoubleSpace, DOS creates an extra drive. If you compressed drive C, you would then have a small uncompressed drive (perhaps drive H, it depends on your hardware). **Be careful not to move or delete any of the files in this new uncompressed drive, or it could result in the data loss of your entire C drive. The files on this uncompressed drive are: IO.SYS, MSDOS.SYS, DBLSPACE.BIN, DBLSPACE.INI, and DBLSPACE.000.** These files are Hidden and have a Read-Only attribute. To determine where DOS placed this uncompressed drive, run the MSD program (shown on page 200) or type DBLSPACE/INFO < ENTER > (shown on page 223) after you install DoubleSpace. If you want to see these hidden files, you can use the DIR/A command. *Remember, don't fool with these files!*

8.   Before you use DoubleSpace to compress a drive, it is a good idea to back up your drive. Not doing so could result in a permanent loss of all your data.

9.   If you plan to install Windows, you should do it before you run DoubleSpace. Windows has a swap file that should be stored on an uncompressed drive. If you install Windows first, DOS will automatically take care of this for you.

10.   Disable any screen blankers before you run DoubleSpace.

11.   DoubleSpace cannot be run from Windows. DoubleSpace should be run only at the DOS prompt.

Running DoubleSpace Express Setup

Do not run the DoubleSpace program until you have reviewed the eleven DoubleSpace cautions. Take special note of the first caution on page 220. To use DoubleSpace to compress your C drive, follow the steps below.

1.   Go to the DOS C prompt. (Do not attempt to run DoubleSpace from Windows or any shell or menu.) At the C prompt type:

dblspace <ENTER>

2.   To display the Express/Custom screen, press:

<ENTER>

3.   The cursor will be on the Express Setup. To select the Express Setup, press:
<ENTER>

Note: The Custom Setup is beyond the scope of this book. If you want more information, examine the MS-DOS 6 manual. Also, see the section on Suggested Reading on page 275.

4.   To continue the process and use DoubleSpace to compress drive C, press:
c

It can take quite a long time to compress a drive. You can *expect it to take about one minute for each megabyte of files*. Do not interrupt the process.

5.   When DoubleSpace is finished, press:

<ENTER>

To see how well DoubleSpace compressed the drive, type:

dblspace /info < ENTER >

A shortcut for the DBLSPACE /INFO command is:

dblspace /i < ENTER >

To get information about all your drives, type:

dblspace /list < ENTER >

or:

dblspace /l < ENTER >

To check how well DoubleSpace compressed individual files, change to the directory that contains the files you are interested in and type:

dir /c /p < ENTER >

Note that, if you had any files that were already compressed (such as .ZIP files), DoubleSpace may not have been able to compress them.

You can change the size of a DoubleSpaced compressed drive with the DBLSPACE /SIZE command. For more information on this type:

help dblspace /size < ENTER >

For help on how to change the estimated size of a compressed drive, type:

help dblspace /ratio < ENTER >

For more information on DoubleSpace, type:

help dblspace < ENTER >

223

Tips

- If you are using DoubleSpace, don't expect to gain space by compressing files with other compression programs such as PKZIP or LHA.

- If your machine has upper memory available, you should check to make sure that DBLSPACE is loaded into high memory. To check, type:

mem /c /p < ENTER >

If you have sufficient upper memory, you can load DOUBLESPACE high and save 43K of conventional memory by inserting the following line in the DEVICEHIGH section of your CONFIG.SYS file:

DEVICEHIGH = C:\DOS\DBLSPACE.SYS /MOVE

See the sample CONFIG.SYS file on page 209. To have DoubleSpace load into high memory, you can add this DEVICEHIGH line using EDIT. Make it the first DEVICEHIGH line in the CONFIG.SYS file. Like so:

```
DEVICE=C:\DOS\SETVER.EXE
DEVICE=C:\DOS\HIMEM.SYS
DOS=HIGH,UMB
DEVICE=C:\DOS\EMM386.EXE NOEMS
DEVICEHIGH=C:\DOS\DBLSPACE.SYS /MOVE
DEVICEHIGH=C:\MOUSE\MOUSE.SYS
FILES=30
BUFFERS=20
STACKS=9,256
NUMLOCK=OFF
```

Then restart your computer, and use the above MEM command to check that it loaded into upper memory.

224

Defragmenting a DoubleSpaced Drive

The DoubleSpace DEFRAGment command is used on a compressed drive. The program doesn't really defragment the drive, however it does consolidate the free space. Do this at least once a month. It should be considered routine hard drive maintenance. First use the CHKDSK command.

1. Change to the compressed drive and then issue a CHKDSK command like so:

   c: < ENTER >

   chkdsk /f < ENTER >

   The /F tells DOS to fix errors. See pages 56 and 57 for more information.

   Another option is to do it like so:

   dblspace /chkdsk /f < ENTER >

   A shortcut for the DBLSPACE /CHKDSK /F command is:

   dblspace /chk /f < ENTER >

2. Defragmenting a large hard drive can take a very long time. To consolidate a DoubleSpace compressed drive, change to the compressed drive and then issue a command like so:

   dblspace /defragment < ENTER >

   A shortcut for the above command is:

   dblspace /def < ENTER >

Using DoubleSpace on Floppy Disks

There are a few things you should know before you use DoubleSpace on floppy disks.

1.   You can't use DoubleSpace unless you have installed it on your computer.

2.   The floppy disk needs to have at least .65 Megabytes (665K) of free space. This means you cannot use 360K, 5¼" diskettes. Change to the appropriate drive, and use the CHKDSK command to check the capacity of a diskette.

3.   If you plan to share data with someone else, they will not be able to read a DoubleSpaced diskette unless they are using DoubleSpace on their computer.

4.   Before you can use a DoubleSpaced diskette, you will need to MOUNT it. This is not as painful as it sounds. It is explained on page 228.

5.   DOS will create a new drive where it will store information about this compressed floppy disk. It does this in the same fashion as it did when compressing a hard drive. See item number 6 on page 221.

Compressing a Floppy Disk

Make sure you read items 1-4 above. Then, to compress a floppy disk, do the following:

1. Place a formatted floppy disk in the drive of your choice.

2. If you want to compress a diskette in your A drive, type the following:

    dblspace /compress a: <ENTER>

    A shortcut for the DBLSPACE /COMPRESS A: command is:

    dblspace /com a: <ENTER>

    Change to the newly DoubleSpaced floppy:

    a: <ENTER>

    Then type:

    dblspace /info <ENTER>

    A shortcut for the DBLSPACE /INFO command is:

    dblspace /i <ENTER>

If you restart your computer or change floppy diskettes, you will need to MOUNT the floppy disk before it can be used. You will learn how to mount a floppy disk on page 228.

Mounting a Floppy Disk

To use a floppy disk that has been DoubleSpaced, you will need to MOUNT that disk. Change to the compressed diskette. If the disk in question is in your A drive, you would type:

a: <ENTER>

Then type:

dblspace /mount <ENTER>

A shortcut for the DBLSPACE /MOUNT command is:

dblspace /mo <ENTER>

You can now use this floppy disk. The disk will remain mounted until you restart your computer or you change to another floppy drive. Then you will need to MOUNT it again.

Unmounting a Floppy Disk

You can also unmount a DoubleSpaced diskette. With the compressed diskette in the current drive type:

dblspace /unmount <ENTER>

A shortcut for the above command is:

dblspace /u <ENTER>

Deleting a Compressed Drive

If you compressed a removable disk, such as a diskette, you may want to delete it so you can reuse it. For example, suppose you want to delete a compressed diskette in drive B. At the system prompt type:

dblspace /delete b: < ENTER >

A shortcut for the above command is:

dblspace /del b: < ENTER >

When you delete a compressed drive, you also delete all the files that were on that drive. DOS will not allow you to use this command on drive C.

Tips

- You may be able to recover a deleted DoubleSpace drive (a diskette drive or a hard drive) with the DOS UNDELETE command since a DoubleSpaced drive is really not a drive at all; in fact, it is a Compressed Volume File (CVF). If you UNDELETE a deleted compressed drive, you will have to mount the drive before you can gain access. See page 228 for more information on how to mount a compressed drive.

- One of my computers was running DoubleSpace and developed **cross-linked** files. Norton Disk Doctor in Norton Utilities fixed the problem. Norton Utilities is available from Symantec Corporation, 10201 Torre Avenue, Cupertino, CA 95014-2132. Phone 1-800-441-7234.

- If you want to compress files on a diskette, the shareware program PKZIP does a much better job than DoubleSpace. Another advantage is that you don't need DOS 6 to use PKZIP or PKUNZIP. See page 260.

Formatting a Compressed Drive

You can delete all the files in a compressed drive by formatting it with a special command. However, you cannot use this command on drive C and you will not be able to use UNFORMAT. You do it like this:

dblspace /format d: < ENTER >

Removing DoubleSpace

Suppose you decide that you don't like DoubleSpace and you want to remove it from your C drive. **If you want to get rid of DoubleSpace, it is important that you read the README.TXT file in the C:\DOS directory. See pages 191 - 192.** *There is no easy way to remove DoubleSpace; however, here is one way:*

1.   Format a diskette with the system on it that can be used in your A drive (format a: /s < ENTER >). *The B drive will not do.* See page 67 for more details. This makes a useful bootable floppy diskette. Label the disk and keep it in a safe place. You will need this disk for step 9 below. **Also, you will need your DOS diskettes for step 10.**

2.   Use the DOS EDIT program to delete the line in the CONFIG.SYS file that loads DBLSPACE.SYS. See page 209 for how to load the CONFIG.SYS file into EDIT. After you delete the line that loads DBLSPACE.SYS, save the file as shown on page 209.

3.   Use a backup program to back up everything on your C drive because soon all the data on your C drive will be destroyed. See pages 173 - 176 for help on using the DOS BACKUP or pages 236 - 252 for information on the DOS 6 MSBACKUP program. If you use MSBACKUP, save the settings as a backup setup file (see page 247).

4.   Type the following command:

dblspace /info <ENTER>

This will reveal which drive is the uncompressed host drive. For example, drive H might be the uncompressed host drive for the DoubleSpaced drive C. It depends on your hardware.

5.   Change to the uncompressed drive and type:

dir /a <ENTER>

6.   The above command tells DOS to show all the files in the current directory including hidden files. This should show the following files on this uncompressed drive: IO.SYS, MSDOS.SYS, DBLSPACE.BIN, DBLSPACE.INI, and DBLSPACE.000.

7.   To turn them into regular files, type:

attrib -s -h -r *.* <ENTER>

8.   To delete them all, type:

del *.* <ENTER>

9.   Place the bootable floppy disk you made in step 1 in drive A and reboot your computer.

10. Get out your DOS disks and reinstall DOS.

11. Get out your backup diskettes that you made in step 3 and restore your backups to the C drive. You may not be able to restore all your backup files because the C drive is now not compressed. Take a break, you deserve it.

Virus Protection

Viruses are insidious programs that infect a computer. Some viruses attach to files and are activated when you run that file. Others attach to the computer's memory, etc. Viruses can be very destructive. So with DOS 6, Microsoft included virus protection programs—one for DOS and one for Windows. They have also included a memory-resident virus protection program called VSAFE.

When DOS 6 is originally installed, there are three programs that can be installed in DOS, Windows, or both. These programs are MS Anti-Virus, MS Backup, and MS Undelete. If you have Windows already on your computer, the default is to install only the Windows versions of these programs. So, if you type the below MSAV <ENTER> command and get a "FILE NOT FOUND" error message, you can correct the problem. See page 191.

Before You Use the Anti-Virus Programs

To be safe, you should create a start-up diskette and copy the Anti-Virus files to this disk. Then, if your computer should get infected, you will have a clean (virus free) way to deal with the infected system. To make a start-up disk, you must use your A drive. The B drive will not do. At the system prompt place a blank diskette in drive A. This diskette needs to be one that corresponds to the full capacity of your A drive. If you need help, see pages 67 - 68. Then type:

format a: /s <ENTER>

Here the /S told DOS to put a copy of the system on the disk. After it is finished formatting, you can then copy the Anti-Virus files from your C:\DOS directory to the diskette in drive A by typing:

copy c:\dos\msav*.* a: <ENTER>

Now you should write protect the diskette and store it in a safe place where you will be able to find it in an emergency. If you need help with write protection or are unsure about diskette capacity, see pages 33 - 34.

Using the Anti-Virus Programs

To scan for viruses under DOS, at the system prompt type:

msav <ENTER>

You can use your arrow keys to choose the SELECT NEW DRIVE button. The drives show in the upper-left on your screen. Using your arrow keys, select the drive that you want to scan for viruses. If you want to detect and remove any viruses, select the DETECT AND CLEAN button. Just follow the screen prompts. If you need help, select the item you need help on and press:

<F1>

If you would like more information on the MSAV command, at the DOS prompt type:

help msav <ENTER>

VSAFE—for Memory-Resident Virus Protection

If you want to constantly check for viruses while you run other programs, you can do so with the VSAFE program. When it loads, it resides in memory and continually checks for viruses. VSAFE is what is called a memory-resident program. It will display a warning message if it finds anything suspicious. To run this program, at the DOS prompt type:

vsafe <ENTER>

If you regularly want to run the VSAFE program, you should add a line in your AUTOEXEC.BAT file. The AUTOEXEC.BAT file resides on the root directory of the start up disk (usually drive C). A good place to add the line would be right below the one which contains the PATH statement. The line would consist of one word which would be the command VSAFE. If you would like more information on VSAFE, type:

help vsafe <ENTER>

When you are running VSAFE, you can change various options. To start the procedure, press:

<ALT> v

If you want to modify an option, press the number that is next to the option you want to change. If the <ALT> V command did not result in a screen full of options, then you may not have loaded VSAFE into memory; or another memory resident program may be using that key combination.
To change the <ALT> V combination to <ALT> P, type:

vsafe /ap <ENTER>

If you have trouble with the <ALT> V key combination being used by other memory-resident programs, you may want to add the above line to your AUTOEXEC.BAT file.

Then, when you need to modify a VSAFE option, you can press:

<ALT> p

The options will appear.

To unload VSAFE from memory, type:

vsafe /u <ENTER>

Tips

● McAfee Associates makes a collection of shareware virus detection and clean up programs that are considered by many to be the industry standard. Some of the McAfee progams are: VIRUSCAN, CLEAN-UP, VSHIELD, and SCAN FOR WINDOWS. These are updated many times a year. See page 261 in the section on shareware.

MOUNTING A FLOPPY

235

Backing Up with DOS 6 MSBACKUP

DOS 6 has a new backup program called MSBACKUP. You should understand that the RESTORE function is included in the DOS 6 MSBACKUP program. It is not a separate program as was the case with older versions of DOS. DOS 6 does not include the old BACKUP program. If you upgraded from an earlier version of DOS and had the BACKUP program in your C:\DOS directory, then DOS 6 will retain it and you will also have the new MSBACKUP. For $5.00 you can order BACKUP along with other utility programs that Microsoft cut from DOS 6. They call this package "supplemental disks." See their offer in the back of the DOS 6 manual. The old BACKUP was dated and inefficient but easy to use! See pages 172 - 176.

DOS 6 does include the old DOS 5 RESTORE program; so if someone gives you some disks that were backed up with DOS 3.3 - DOS 5, you will be able to RESTORE them to your DOS 6 based computer.

It should be noted that the DOS 6 MSBACKUP program does not support tape backup systems.

Some people will find the new MSBACKUP too complicated to set up. There are sixteen excruciating steps just to run the MSBACKUP Compatibility Test! YIKES!! In fact, before your first attempt to use MSBACKUP, I would suggest that you allocate a couple of hours just to learn the ropes. If you manage to get through the MSBACKUP COMPATIBILITY TEST, it will all be downhill from there.

The easiest way is to have your favorite computer wizard configure the MSBACKUP program for you. Once it is set up, it is almost easy to use.

Getting Help

Before you even start playing with MSBACKUP, you should know that you can **get help with any backup operation** by first selecting the backup operation that you are interested in and then pressing < F1 > for **HELP**. Use your < **PG DN**> or < **PG UP**> keys to move around in the help information.

NOTE: When DOS 6 was originally installed, there were three programs that could be installed in DOS, Windows, or both. These programs are the MS Anti-Virus, MS Backup, and MS Undelete. If you had Windows already on your computer, the default was to install only the Windows versions of these programs. So, if you type the below MSBACKUP command and get a "FILE NOT FOUND" error message, you can correct the problem. See page 191.

Running the MSBACKUP Compatibility Test

Before you start, you will need **two blank diskettes.** These diskettes do not have to be formatted as the MSBACKUP program will format them if they need it.

Follow the sixteen steps outlined below:

1.   At the system prompt type **MSBACKUP < ENTER >**.

2.   Press < **ENTER** > for **START CONFIGURATION**.

3.   Read the VIDEO AND MOUSE CONFIGURATION screen. Such menu screens, Microsoft calls "dialog boxes." If everything looks good, select **OK** by pressing < **ENTER** >. If you want to make changes, you can use a mouse to click on a setting or use your keyboard by pressing < **ALT** > and the **first highlighted letter** of the option you

want to change.

4. Remove all diskettes from your floppy drives, and press <ENTER> to select **START TEST**.

5. Press <ENTER> for **OK** if drive types are displayed correctly. Remember, you can make changes using a mouse or by pressing <ALT> and the **first highlighted letter** of the option you wish to change, then select OK. MSBACKUP will then perform some diagnostic tests.

6. The **FLOPPY DISK COMPATIBILITY TEST** dialog box is shown on the screen. Read the screen. Select **START TEST** by pressing <ENTER>.

7. The FLOPPY DISK COMPATIBILITY TEST will pause, so you can select a diskette drive for the test. Press <ENTER> to **CONTINUE**.

8. The **BACKUP TO** dialog box is shown. Select the drive type that will match your two diskettes that you want to use for this test. You can use your mouse to click or press <ALT> and the **first highlighted letter** of the option you wish. When the cursor is on the desired drive and desired capacity disk that you want to back up to, press <ENTER> for **OK**.

9. You will be prompted to insert a floppy disk into the chosen drive. Use the first test diskette and label it TEST BACKUP #1. Place it in the selected floppy drive. Don't forget to close the drive door. Then press <ENTER> for **CONTINUE**. If you want to reuse a floppy disk with data on it, you can press <ALT> O for **OVERWRITE**. The backup test begins.

10. When the first diskette is full, you will be prompted to insert the second diskette. Remove the first diskette and keep it handy. Label the next

one TEST BACKUP #2. Insert the second disk and press <ENTER>.

11. When the backup compatibility test is finished, you will be prompted with a BACKUP COMPLETE dialog box. However, don't get excited. You are not even close to being finished! Press <ENTER> for **OK**. Now it is going to want to compare the backup data.

12. You will be prompted to insert the first backup test diskette into the drive. Do it and press <ENTER> to **CONTINUE**.

13. When it finishes, it will ask you for the second backup diskette. Replace the first backup diskette with the second backup disk. MSBACKUP will automatically detect the presence of a diskette so you will not even need to press <ENTER>.

14. When it finishes comparing data, you will be greeted with a COMPARE COMPLETE dialog box. Read the information on the screen. Now for the results. You will be informed if the backup test was successful. Press <ENTER> to select **OK**. If your machine does not pass the compatibility test, don't use the MSBACKUP program. If it did not pass the combatibility test, it means that MSBACKUP would not be reliable on your computer.

15. Select **OK** by pressing <ENTER>. You will now see the CONFIGURE dialog box. If you want to make changes, do so using a mouse; or use the keyboard by pressing <ALT> and the first highlighted letter of the option you wish to change. *If you make changes*, press <ALT> S for SAVE. This will save any new configuration settings. Then use your <TAB> key to move to OK and press <ENTER>.

16. The BACKUP dialog box appears again, and you can now press <ALT> Q to **QUIT**. WHEW!

The Different Backup Types

With DOS 6 and MSBACKUP, you have a choice of three different backup types. They are:

FULL BACKUP — This can be used for a **complete backup** of all the files on a particular hard drive or drives, *or* it can be used to **back up selected subdirectories** *or* even **selected files**. Most people would use it to back up an entire hard drive or a particular subdirectory with any underlying sub-directories.

INCREMENTAL BACKUP — This backup can be used to back up files that have changed since your last full backup *or* last incremental backup. Remember, an incremental backup only backs up the files that have changed. This makes the backup fast. The disadvantage of the incremental backup is that you must keep each incremental backup (between full backups), because each one builds on the last one. If you loose a backup set, you will be in trouble. Personally, I would not use an incremental backup for this reason. However, you may be better organized than I am.

DIFFERENTIAL BACKUP — A differential backup backs up all files that have changed since your last full backup. Perhaps you work with the same spreadsheet, database, or word processor. If you usually work with the same kind of files day after day, this may be your best choice after you have done a full backup.

You might ask, "How does DOS know if a file has changed since the last backup?" DOS knows by setting an archive flag. When a file is changed, DOS sets the archive flag to **on**. When DOS finds the archive flag on, it indicates that the file has not been backed up since it was last modified.

Selecting a Backup Type

First, you will need to run through the MSBACKUP COMPATIBILITY TEST (the sixteen steps starting on page 237). Then, to make a change in the backup type, do the following. At the DOS prompt type:

1.   **MSBACKUP <ENTER>.**

2.   Press **<ALT>** B for **BACKUP.**

3.   Press **<ALT>** Y for **BACKUP TYPE.**

4.   The BACKUP TYPE dialog box is displayed on your screen. Select the type of backup by pressing the **SPACE BAR.**

5.   Then press **<ENTER>** for **OK.**

Help with Backup Options

If you want to view or change your backup options, you would do the following. At the system prompt type:

1.   **MSBACKUP <ENTER>.**

2.   Press **<ALT>** B for **BACKUP.**

3.   Press **<ALT>** O for **OPTIONS.**

Then the **DISK BACKUP OPTIONS** is displayed. Most of these options need no explanation. If you need **HELP** with any of these BACKUP OPTIONS, press **<F1>**. Then **<TAB>** to the desired option and press **<ENTER>**. *Remember, you can get help with any backup operation by* *first selecting the backup operation that you are interested in and then pressing <F1>. Use your <PG DN> or <PG UP> keys to move around the help information.*

However, *if you choose to* **PASSWORD PROTECT BACKUP SETS** (<ALT> W), then <TAB> to **OK** and press <ENTER>. **You must not forget your password.**

You may wish to select **ALWAYS FORMAT DISKETTES** (by pressing <ALT> L), then <TAB> to **OK** and press <ENTER>. Then DOS will format all the floppy disks that you use for backing up.

Performing a Full Backup

Before you start a backup, you will need plenty of diskettes on hand. MSBACKUP will estimate how many diskettes you will need for this backup when you get to step 11 below. If you don't have enough, you can always cancel by pressing <ESC>. If you have high-density drives, I would suggest you get into the habit of using high-density diskettes. High-density diskettes will reduce the number of diskettes required for the backup.

To perform a full backup, do the following steps; at the system prompt type:

1. **MSBACKUP <ENTER>**.

2. From the opening screen, press **<ALT> B** for **BACKUP**; or select it by clicking on it with your mouse.

3. Select **BACKUP FROM** by clicking with a mouse or by pressing **<ALT> K**. (The K is the first highlighted letter of BACKUP FROM.)

4. Use your mouse or the **arrow keys** and the **SPACE BAR** to select the drive or drives you want to back up. If you intend to backup an entire drive or drives, make sure the BACKUP FROM indicates ALL FILES. If you only want to back up some files, make sure that ALL FILES is not marked. Use the SPACE BAR to change the ALL FILES statement. When you have it the way you want it, press **<ENTER>**.

5. **If you want to back up the entire drive or drives, go to step 8**. If you only want to back up certain files or directories, go to step 6.

6. To select specific files or directories, press **<ALT> L**. Use your mouse or the **arrow keys** to move to the directories or files that you want to back up. Press the right mouse button or the **SPACE BAR** to mark the files for backup. *Pressing the SPACE BAR again will undo*

243

the selection. If you wanted to back up the entire C drive, you can highlight the C:\ (root directory) and then press the **SPACE BAR** or press the right mouse button. Then all the files on the C drive will be selected and you will notice a triangle by the C:\ symbol for the root directory. You can tell that all the files on the C drive have been selected because you will see a check mark by each file. If you select a specific directory, you will see a triangle by that directory and a check mark by each file in the selected directory. If you only select some files in a directory, you will see a check mark by the selected files and a chevron > > by the directory containing the selected files.

7. Press the <**TAB**> key until the cursor is on the **OK** selection. Then press <**ENTER**>. If you are using a mouse, just click on OK.

8. Select the **BACKUP TO** dialog box by clicking on it with a mouse or by pressing <**ALT**> A on the keyboard. Use your mouse or **SPACE BAR** to select the disk type and drive that you want to use to **BACKUP TO**. Then press <**ENTER**>.

9. Take a look to make sure that the **BACKUP TYPE** is set to **FULL**. If you need to make changes press <**ALT**> Y and use the SPACEBAR to change it to FULL. If you want to save all the options you have selected as a backup setup file, do steps 1-5 on page 247.

10. Press <**ALT**> S for **START BACKUP**.

11. Read the screen. DOS will give you an estimate of *how many disks you will need for this backup.* If you want to cancel the backup, you can press <**ESC**> or choose <**ALT**> B for **CANCEL BACKUP**.

The MSBACKUP program will prompt you to insert your first backup diskette. Make sure you carefully number and date each backup disk. DOS will continue to prompt you for more backup diskettes as it needs them. Just follow the prompts.

Including or Excluding Files to Back Up

Suppose you only want to back up a single directory and all its subdirectories. Perhaps you want to INCLUDE only the directory C:\WP51 and its subdirectories. You should select **FULL BACKUP** for this operation. Below, you will see how to select the needed options using your keyboard. If you prefer, you can use a mouse to click on the options.

1. At the system prompt type: **MSBACKUP <ENTER>**.

2. Press **<ALT> B for BACKUP**.

3. If the **BACKUP FROM** does not have **ALL FILES** by the selected drive, press **<ALT> K** and use your arrow keys and **SPACE BAR** to change it to **ALL FILES**.

4. Press **<ALT> L for SELECT FILES**.

5. Press **<ALT> N** for **INCLUDE**. (If you want to exclude a subdirectory, you would choose Exclude.)

6. Press **<ALT> P** to edit the **PATH** and type: **C:\WP51**

7. Check to see that **FILE** is marked ***.***. If it is not, press **<ALT> F** to edit the FILE entry. Using *.* will include all files.

8. Make sure that the **INCLUDE ALL SUBDIRECTORIES** is marked with a check. If it isn't, press **<ALT> S** to edit.

9. Press **<ALT> E** to **EDIT INCLUDE/EXCLUDE LIST**.

10. Use the **up or down arrow keys** to place the cursor on an entry that you want to delete. To delete an entry, press **D**. When you have it the

way you want it, **use your arrow keys** to select **OK**. Then press
<**ENTER**>. You may have to press <TAB> before you can go to
OK.

11.   Press <**TAB**> until you select **OK**. Then press <**ENTER**>.

12.   Make sure that **BACKUP TYPE** is set to **FULL**.

13.   Press <**ALT**> S to **START BACKUP** and follow the prompts.

When you select EDIT INCLUDE/EXCLUDE LIST in step 5 above, the list
starts out with ALL files on the selected disk. The INCLUDE/EXCLUDE
statements are carried out in the sequence that they are listed. If you have an
INCLUDE statement that includes a certain group of files and then an
EXCLUDE statement that excludes that same group of files, then the exclude
statement will reverse the INCLUDE statement and the files will be excluded.

Now look at page 175 where you performed the same operation with the old
DOS BACKUP command.

Saving Your Backup Setups

You can save your setup options as a setup file with a unique name. This will really speed up your backup procedure. For example, suppose you want to save the setup you performed on pages 245 - 246. Perhaps you mainly work in WordPerfect, and you want to perform this kind of backup on a regular basis. When you finish step 12 on page 246 and all the settings are the way you want them, do the following:

1.   Press <ALT> F for the **FILE** menu.

2.   Press <ALT> A for **SAVE SETUP AS**.

3.   Type a name that makes sense to you, such as: **WP51**
     DOS will automatically add an extension of .SET to this file.

4.   If you want, you can <TAB> to the **DESCRIPTION** and type a description for this setup file.

5.   Press <ALT> S for **SAVE**. DOS will then save your setup file as WP51.

Then, when you want to back up your WP51 directory with all its subdirectories, you can issue the MSBACKUP command along with the name of the setup file you want to use. By issuing the command from the DOS prompt, you will save a lot of steps. Using the above example setup file to back up WP51 with all its subdirectories, you could type:

msbackup wp51 <ENTER>

Then all you have to do is press <ALT> B for BACKUP and <ALT> S to START the backup. If you have problems, find someone who is knowledgeable and ask them to please make your setup files for you.

Selecting Saved Backup Setup Files

You can also select a saved backup setup file from within MSBACKUP. You might need to do this if you forgot a setup file name. Follow these steps:

1. At the system prompt type: **MSBACKUP** **<ENTER>**.

2. Press **<ALT> B** for **BACKUP**.

3. Press **<ALT> P** for **SETUP FILE**.

4. Use your **arrow keys** to go to the setup file that you want from the **SETUP FILES list**. When the cursor is on the one you want, press the **SPACE BAR** to mark that setup file.

5. Press **<ALT> O** for **OPEN**.

6. Press **<ALT> S** for **START BACKUP**. Then just follow the prompts. Don't forget to label each backup diskette with the backup setup name, a disk number, and the date.

Developing a Backup Strategy

Suppose you have made a new year's resolution to turn over a new leaf when it comes to backing up your hard drive. Perhaps you have already lost your letter to Aunt Virginia which you had been working on for two months. You really should back up your important files. Things can happen. Things *will* happen. All hard drives eventually fail. Many people feel that they don't need to back up their entire hard drive, because they have their original programs on diskettes. However, most people do need to back up parts of their hard drive, especially those directories which contain important data files.

Take a look at the different backup types shown on page 240. You might like to do a **FULL BACKUP** on drive C and save that as a setup file called **FULL.SET**. See pages 243 and 244 for the details on how such a setup was accomplished. Then you might like to load that same FULL.SET backup and make one change. See step 3 on page 241. You could change the **BACKUP TYPE** to **DIFFERENTIAL** by pressing **Y** and then **D <ENTER>**. Then save this as a setup file named **MYDIF.SET**. Then you could on occasion do the full backup using FULL.SET for the backup setup, but mostly the differential backup using the MYDIF.SET. The differential backup would take a lot less time. If you think you will primarily be backing up a particular directory and any underlying subdirectories, review the procedure starting on page 245. Whatever you do, make some sort of decision. Avoid being diffident!

Backup Catalog Files

You can use the **RESTORE** option by pressing **<ALT> R** on the opening **MSBACKUP** menu to copy your backed up data to a hard drive. You will then be shown a **RESTORE** dialog box. When you use MSBACKUP to back up your files, DOS creates a **BACKUP CATALOG**. The backup catalog files are stored in two places—in your C:\DOS directory and on the last backup diskette. These backup catalogs contain the directory structure and the names of the backed up files. Backup catalog files use the extensions .FUL, .INC, and .DIF. These file name extensions indicate the type of backup—**FULL**, **INCREMENTAL**, or **DIFFERENTIAL**. See page 240. These backup catalog files are easy to identify. Suppose you saw a file named:

CC30420A.FUL

C	The first C represents the first drive that was backed up in the file.
C	The second C stands for the last drive backed up in this file.
3	Indicates that the year of the backup was 1993.
04	This represents the month that the backup took place.
20	Was the day that the backup was performed.
A	A letter sequence that differentiates this backup catalog from other backup catalogs with the same name.
.FUL	This file name extension indicates that this was a FULL backup.

So, from the backup catalog file name we are able to determine that this was a full backup; and it took place on 04/20/93.

There is another type of catalog called the **MASTER CATALOG**. This is used by DOS to correlate data when you restore files. A master catalog keeps a list of your backup catalog files. The master catalog uses the same filename as your SETUP files but with a file extension of **.CAT**.

Restoring a Backup

1.   At the DOS prompt type: **MSBACKUP** <ENTER>.

2.   Press <ALT> R for **RESTORE**.

3.   Press <ALT> K for **BACKUP SET CATALOG**.

4.   Select the desired backup catalog set using your **arrow keys**. Then press the **SPACE BAR**. Press <ALT> L to LOAD the selected catalog set. If you don't see the desired catalog set, press <ESC> and then press <ALT> G (for CATALOG). Then press <ALT> R to RETRIEVE the catalog from the *last disk* in the set of backup disks.

5.   If it is not showing the correct destination for your files, press <ALT> R for **RESTORE TO** and select the desired settings.

6.   If you want to restore your entire backup, press <ALT> I for **RESTORE FILES** and press the **SPACEBAR** to select **ALL FILES**. Then move to step 7 below. If you don't want to restore all the files, press <ALT> L for SELECT FILES. Use your arrow keys to move to the desired directories. Press the SPACE BAR to select each directory that you want to restore. Press the SPACE BAR again if you want to unselect a directory. If you want to select individual files, move to the desired directory and then <TAB> to the file area. Use your arrow keys to move to the desired file and press the SPACE BAR to select it. Then <TAB> to OK and press <ENTER>

7.   Press <ALT> S for **START RESTORE**. Then just follow the prompts.

If you need to restore a backup done with the BACKUP command (from an older version of DOS), see pages 174 and 175.

Tips

- If you need **HELP** with any MSBACKUP operation, you can select the operation; then press the function key labeled < F1 > . This kind of help is called "context sensitive help."

- If you have a large hard drive, you will want to **get a tape backup system**. If you shop around, you can find one for under $200.00. These come in different sizes and are a better media than diskettes for doing backup work. Instead of having to shuffle a hundred or more floppy disks, you just put in one tape! Think of the money and space you will save by not having to keep hundreds of diskettes on hand. *Think of your sanity.* Tape backup systems usually come with backup software. It is a good thing they do, because the MSBACKUP program does not support tape drives.

- If you have both size floppy drives, use 3½" diskettes instead of 5¼" disks to back up your data. Be sure to **use high-density diskettes** if your drive can handle them. The 3½" disks are more durable than 5¼" disks, and the high-density diskettes hold more data.

- If you want a particular backup setup file to be used whenever you are in MSBACKUP, save the setup file with the name **DEFAULT.SET**. See pages 247 - 248.

- When you are using MSBACKUP, you can often just press the first highlighted letter to make a selection rather than having to press the < ALT > key first. This may save you a bunch of key strokes. (If you have trouble, press the < ALT > key first).

Conserving Power on Laptops

If you have a laptop computer that conforms to APM (Advanced Power Management) specifications, you can use the DOS 6 POWER program to save up to 25 percent on battery power. It may save a little (about 5 percent) even if your laptop does not conform to APM specifications. To use the POWER.EXE program, you will need to add a device driver line to your CONFIG.SYS file like so:

DEVICE=C:\DOS\POWER.EXE

You can do this with the DOS EDIT program. See pages 162 - 163 for more on EDIT. Don't forget to save the file before exiting. Using the sample CONFIG.SYS file for an 80386 or a higher machine (see page 209), the modified CONFIG.SYS file for the laptop would look like:

DEVICE=C:\DOS\SETVER.EXE
DEVICE=C:\DOS\HIMEM.SYS
DOS=HIGH,UMB
DEVICE=C:\DOS\EMM386.EXE NOEMS
DEVICE=C:\DOS\POWER.EXE
DEVICEHIGH=C:\MOUSE\MOUSE.SYS
FILES=30
BUFFERS=20
STACKS=9,256
NUMLOCK=OFF

Remember that you need to restart your computer before the new CONFIG.SYS file will take effect. The default is for the POWER.EXE device driver to load into upper memory (providing that upper memory is available).

Then, to see your power savings, at the system prompt type:

power <ENTER>

Then you will see a screen showing your power setting and the percentage of time that the CPU (Central Processing Unit) on your computer is idle.

For more on the DOS 6 POWER command, at the system prompt type:

help power <ENTER>

Part 6

REFERENCE

CONVENTIONAL MEMORY | EXTENDED MEMORY | EXPANDED MEMORY

K. Rockwood

THE PHRENOLOGIST'S FIELD GUIDE TO MEMORY MANAGEMENT

Shareware Software

Shareware, or user-supported software, is a way of marketing software for the program's author. The manual for shareware is usually found on the disk, often in the form of a text file. Shareware software is copyrighted. The authors encourage you to copy their software and share it with friends. You can obtain shareware programs from shareware vendors, usually for just a few dollars per disk. This distribution charge does not cover the cost of the program. If you continue to use the software, you must send in the "registration fee." You can find out how to register the program by reading the manual. If you try it and don't wish to continue using the software, you owe the author nothing. This lets the user try the program first. When you register shareware software, you often get additional benefits. Depending on the author, you may get: free updates of the latest version, telephone support, a bound manual, customization and other goodies. Where else can you "TRY BEFORE YOU BUY!" Shareware software is becoming more popular all the time due to the geometric increase of excellent programs. In almost any computer magazine you will find advertisements for shareware software.

Public domain software is another type of software. Public domain software is not copyrighted and can be freely distributed without restrictions. With public domain software the author wants nothing in return for his efforts.

Freeware is a type of software that is similar to public domain software. A freeware program is copyrighted and has copyright restrictions; however, the author is not requesting a registration fee.

The programs listed below are all shareware products except for FDFORM which is public domain and ACD which is freeware. These programs are available from many shareware vendors. Below are what I consider to be some of the best programs available. Many of these programs take the place of specific DOS programs and are superior.

256

Shareware Software

4DOS is a DOS interface with replacement commands for traditional DOS commands. These replacement commands are better and more powerful than the DOS commands. 4DOS works with DOS 2.0 through DOS 6 and DR-DOS, and replaces COMMAND.COM. It is completely compatible with DOS commands. You can give file descriptions up to 40 characters long. With 4DOS, you have a CDD command which changes drives and directories in one command. It also has command line editing, history and recall which, along with 4DOS ALIAS, replaces the DOS 5 and DOS 6 DOSKEY features with more powerful ones. ALIAS allows you to create your own commands and make macros. The ALIAS feature is incredibly powerful. Automatic file name completion is marvelous. Suppose you wanted to run a program called RUMPLES.EXE. With 4DOS, you just type RU and press the <TAB> key, and the rest of the file name will be filled in for you. 4DOS will work with multiple commands on the same line. Example: COPY *.DOC *.TXT A:<ENTER> will copy both .DOC files and .TXT files to a destination drive. It also has a new kind of batch file that is 5 to 10 times faster than DOS's batch files and dozens of new batch file commands. When you need help with commands, you can press <F1>; and 4DOS gives you excellent help with examples. Symantec is under a license agreement with JP Software, the developer of 4DOS. Norton Utilities, by Symantec, includes many of these 4DOS features in their NDOS. 4DOS is still shareware and is from JP Software, P.O. Box 1470, East Arlington, MA 02174.

ACD is a freeware program that provides an easier way to change drives and directories. It will work across drives by using a database of all directories. If you were on the D drive and wanted to change to the C:\BRAXTON directory, you could type at the D prompt: ACD BR <ENTER>. If more than one directory started with BR, you would be presented with a menu of directories to choose from. ACD is by Arjen Merchkens, Gandhilaan 35, 1069 NC Amsterdam, The Netherlands.

Shareware Software

ASQ is a program that will analyze your computer system and tell you what you have. It gives information on memory, disk drives, type of monitor, and much more. It will take a "snapshot" of your system and save it as a text file. This shareware program is from Qualitas, Inc., 7101 Wisconsin Avenue, Bethesda, MD 20814.

BLANK-IT is a program to black out the computer's display after a certain "time out" period. This will prevent damage to the screen called "burn-in." This program works with all monitors. BLANK-IT is by Rhode Island Soft Systems, Inc., P.O. Box 748, Woonsocket, RI 02895.

CON > FORMAT is a program that allows you to format a disk while you do other work. The user is presented with a menu for formatting any size or type of diskette. This makes it easy. It is faster than DOS and just as reliable. This program is from SYDEX, 153 North Murphy Avenue, Sunnyvale, CA 94086.

COPYQM can replace the DOS DISKCOPY command. It will format, copy, and verify as it copies. It is faster than DOS and can make multiple copies from reading the source disk once. COPYQM is by SYDEX, the maker of CON > FORMAT. See address above.

FDFORMAT can format all sizes of diskettes to a greater capacity. FDFORMAT can format 360K disks to have 410K of space, 1.2MB disks to 1.48MB, 720K disks to 820K, and 1.44MB disks to 1.72MB. FDFORMAT is a Public Domain program. You will want to obtain FDFORMAT version 1.8 or later. FDFORMAT is by Christoph H. Hochsttter, Carl-Strehl-Strasse 20, D-3550 Marburg, West Germany.

Shareware Software

LIST is the very best replacement for the DOS TYPE command. Virtually all power users rely on LIST. It has so many features, yet it remains easier to use than TYPE. LIST is menu driven with "pop-up" help. With LIST, you can view text files and page up and page down to browse through files. LIST is very fast and can handle huge text files. Press F (for find) and LIST will search for a key word or phrase. LIST has scores of other unique features. Copy LIST to a subdirectory in your computer's path, and then it will be available from any drive or directory. Once you try LIST, you will not want to use the TYPE command again. LIST is by Vernon D. Buerg, 139 White Oak Circle, Petaluma, CA 94952.

PC-LEARN is a tutorial system on computers for beginners. It gives a history of computers, information on word processors, spreadsheets, and databases. It has excellent chapters on computer clubs, modems, online services, online databases, DOS, batch files, and a glossary of computer terms. PC-LEARN is by Jim Hood, Seattle Scientific Photography, P.O. Box 1506, Mercer Island, WA 98040.

PCOPY is a replacement for the DOS COPY commands. Unlike DOS, PCOPY will warn you if you are about to overwrite a file. PCOPY is more powerful than the DOS COPY commands, being able to split large files to multiple target disks; and it will even format your blank disks on the fly if needed. It will also move files. Try to obtain PCOPY version 9.0 or greater, so you won't miss any of the above features. PCOPY is by Patri-Soft, 5225 Canyon Crest Drive, Suite 71-358, Riverside, CA 92507.

PKLITE is a file compression program. It gives you more disk space by compressing .EXE and .COM files. *The compressed program runs as it normally would.* PKLITE is from Pkware, Inc., 9025 North Deerwood Drive, Brown Deer, WI 53223.

Shareware Software

PKZ204G is a self-extracting program that contains PKZIP, PKUNZIP, and other supporting files. PKZIP is a program for compressing files. PKUNZIP uncompresses ZIPped files. *Zipped files can be recognized by their .ZIP extension.* This new version can ZIP a directory and include the subdirectories. It also allows your ZIPped file to span multiple diskettes! If you intend to use a modem, you will find that most BBS's store their files in ZIPped format. See page 177 for how to unzip ZIPped files. PKZ204G is by PKWARE, Inc., the same people who offer PKLITE. The software version changes periodically. See the address for PKLITE.

POINT & SHOOT BACKUP/RESTORE is very easy to use. It makes backing up your hard drive easy. It is faster than the DOS BACKUP command and gives you the option of file compression. It will calculate the number of backup disks required and will format blank disks as needed. This program is by Applied Micro Systems Tech., P.O. Box 1784, Stillwater, OK 74076.

PSEARCH will search multiple files for *key words* or *phrases*. It will search an entire hard drive, or you can tell it to just search certain directories. Of course, wildcards can be used in the searches. PSEARCH then provides you with a list of documents that fit the search parameters, and they can be viewed one at a time. PSEARCH will view both text files and WordPerfect documents. It can also be used to find lost files. This program is by the same company who gave you PCOPY. PSEARCH is by Patri-Soft, 5225 Canyon Crest Drive, Suite 71-358, Riverside, CA 92507.

QEDIT is an extremely small editor which takes the place of the dreadful DOS editor EDLIN. QEDIT is perfect for writing batch files or CONFIG.SYS files. With QEDIT all you have to remember is Q <ENTER> starts it and <ESC> gives you pull down menus. QEDIT is

Shareware Software

by SemWare, 4343 Shallowford Road, Suite C-3, Marietta, GA 30062-5003.

QUIKMENU is a graphically beautiful menu system to make running your programs easy. You can use your keyboard or a mouse to click on the program you want to run. It has a particularly nice calendar and calculator, and a built in screen-blanker. It is easy to add new items to the menu and has file management features. QUIKMENU is from OSCS, 354 NE Greenwood, Suite 205, Bend, OR 97701.

STEREO SHELL is a wonderful shell for running your hard drive. You can view two directories at once, which is where it got the name. Copying software to and from your hard drive and between directories is made simple. It can also use your favorite viewing utility (mine is LIST) and editor (mine is QEDIT). It is very fast and provides an easy-to-use interface to compress and uncompress files using all the popular archive formats. STEREO SHELL is from M.R.E. Software, 150 Jones Street, West Point, MS 39773.

SST or Supersonic Search Tool, which used to be called "WHEREIS," provides a very fast way to find a file that you know is somewhere on your hard drive. It can search multiple hard drives and will even search archived files. This program is by Keith Ledbetter, 4240 Ketcham Drive, Chesterfield, VA 23832.

VIRUSCAN, by McAfee Associates, is considered by many around the world to be the industry standard in virus protection. They make a collection of virus protection programs. In addition to VIRUSCAN they also have: **CLEAN-UP** (which removes viruses), **VSHIELD** (for memory-resident virus protection), and **SCAN FOR WINDOWS**. These programs are updated often to keep up with the loathsome viruses that are generated by

Shareware Software

warped individuals. McAffee Associates, 3350 Scott Boulevard, Building 14, Santa Clara, CA 95054-3107.

ZDIR replaces the DOS DIR command. ZDIR will show you a sorted directory with *color coding* of the extensions. It gives you more information than DOS and will even show *hidden files*. ZDIR is from ZanySoft, 9303 Arabian Avenue, Vienna, VA 22182.

Tips

- You can obtain shareware software from a number of sources including: disk vendors, user groups, on-line services, bulletin boards, and other people with computers. A **"user group"** is a computer club consisting of a group of people who use computers. A Bulletin Board System (BBS) is a computer system that is set up with software and a modem(s) to allow other computer users with modems to access information on the computer. To access bulletin boards and other on-line services, you will need a modem. A **modem** is a device that allows your computer to communicate and transfer files with other computers over the telephone line. The easiest way to learn how to use a modem is to have someone who knows, teach you. If you would like a list of shareware vendors, bulletin boards, and a description of hundreds of shareware programs, you can contact:

  > Association of Shareware Professionals
  > 545 Grover Road
  > Muskegon, MI 49442
  > (616) 788-5131

  Most computer magazines contain ads for shareware software. You can usually find out about user groups in your area by contacting your local computer stores. Just ask, "Do you know about any user groups in the area?"

- The easiest way to learn how to use a modem is to have someone who knows teach you. However, if you can't find such a person, get the excellent book in its second edition by John V. Hedtke called **USING COMPUTER BULLETIN BOARDS,** by MIS: Press.

Summary of Important
DOS Commands

DOS Command	See Pages	
DOS Command	*See Pages*	
ASSIGN	124 - 125	The ASSIGN command is used to reroute disk drive requests from one drive to another. This command was dropped from DOS 6.
BACKUP	172 - 176	The BACKUP command does just what its name suggests. It is for backing up your files and was included through DOS 5. BACKUP can be used on hard or floppy disks. You need to use the DOS command RESTORE to reinstate the data.
CD	102 - 103	This is the **C**hange **D**irectory command. Instead of typing CD, you can type **CHDIR**. Most people prefer the shortened version of just CD. If CD is issued alone, it will display the current or active directory. If issued with a path specified, it will cause you to change to the specified directory. Example: At the C> type: CD \GAMES <ENTER>. This would result in changing over to the games directory on the C drive.

Important DOS Commands

Important DOS Commands

DOS Command	See Pages	
DBLSPACE	220 - 231	**DouBLeSPACE** is new with DOS 6. It provides data compression to increase the available space on hard and floppy drives.
DEFRAG	195 - 196	A disk optimizer which is new with DOS 6.
DEL	87 - 90	This is the **DEL**ete command. It is used to delete a file, or group of files. If you use wildcards in the command, it will delete a group of files. You can use **ERASE** instead of DEL to delete files. It is really the same command. Most people prefer DEL.
DELTREE	197 - 198	DELTREE is new with DOS 6. It deletes a specified directory along with its files and subdirectories.
DIR	35 - 37 116, 129	Shows what files and subdirectories are on a disk or directory.
DISKCOPY	70 - 73	For making an exact duplicate of a diskette.
EDIT	48	An editor that comes with DOS 5 and later. You can use EDIT or most other editors to make, change, view, and print text files.
FORMAT	59 - 69	Prepares a disk for use.

266

Important DOS Commands

Important DOS Commands

268

Important DOS Commands

DOS Command	See Pages	
RD	108	This command is used to **R**emove a **D**irectory. Before you can remove a directory, all files in the directory must be deleted and all subdirectories must be removed. You cannot remove a directory if the directory you want to remove is the current directory. Instead of issuing the command with RD, you can use **RMDIR**. Most people prefer RD for brevity.
REN	94	The **REN**ame command is used to rename a file or subdirectory name. Instead of issuing the command with REN, you can use **RENAME**. Most people prefer REN to keep the keystrokes down to a minimum.
RESTORE	174 - 175	The RESTORE command is used to restore files that were backed up using the DOS BACKUP command.
TIME	28 - 29	This command is used to change the time that is maintained by DOS.
TREE	100	The TREE command is used to display the directory structure of a disk or a directory.
TYPE	46 - 47	This primitive DOS command is used to display a text file.

Important DOS Commands

DOS Command	See Pages	
UNDELETE	91 - 92 202 - 204	UNDELETE comes with DOS 5 and DOS 6. You can sometimes restore a deleted file with UNDELETE.
UNFORMAT	64 - 65	The UNFORMAT command comes with DOS 5 and DOS 6. If you accidently format a disk, UNFORMAT can sometimes help to restore your files.
VER	29	This command tells you which **VER**sion of DOS you have.
VSAFE	234 - 235	This new DOS 6 program is a ram-resident virus scanner.
XCOPY	80 - 85 120 - 122 130 - 133 138 - 139	The XCOPY command provides a way of copying both files and subdirectories. The XCOPY command is more powerful than COPY.

Tips

- With *DOS 5* you can type **HELP <ENTER>** at the system prompt to get a brief one line description of each DOS command. If you type **HELP <ENTER>** with DOS 6, you will get a table of contents of commands that have help information. You can use your arrow keys to move to the command you want help on and press <ENTER>.

  To get help *with DOS 5 or DOS 6*, type the name of a DOS command at the system prompt and add a /? switch. This will show you what the command does and provide a summary of the available switches. Example:

  xcopy /? <ENTER>

  With *DOS 6* you can type **FASTHELP <ENTER>** at the system prompt to get a brief one line description of each DOS command. They greatly improved the help with DOS 6. To get more information, type HELP and a space followed by the command. For example, suppose you would like help with the UNFORMAT command. You could type:

  help unformat <ENTER>

  For more information on DOS 6 HELP see the section starting on page 192.

The Most Common
DOS Error Messages

BAD COMMAND OR FILE NAME

This is the most common error message of all. Usually it means you have misspelled a file name or DOS command. DOS is completely unforgiving about spelling. Check the spelling by doing a directory—DIR <ENTER>. It can also mean you are not in the right directory to execute a file. If that is the case, change to the proper directory and try again.

DIVIDE OVERFLOW

The program tried to divide something by zero; and, of course, you can't do that. There is probably something wrong with the software program.

FORMAT FAILURE

The disk you attempted to format may be bad. Try formatting it two more times. If you get the same message, try using another diskette.

GENERAL FAILURE READING DRIVE A

You probably have not formatted the diskette. Before a disk can be used, it must be formatted.

INSUFFICIENT DISK SPACE

You do not have enough free space left on the disk to copy all the files.

DOS Error Messages

INSERT DISK WITH BATCH FILE
PRESS ANY KEY TO CONTINUE

You probably removed a diskette that contained files with the extension .BAT. To continue, put that disk back into the drive and press a key. If you would rather terminate the processing of the batch file, press <CTRL> C. That is, hold down the <CTRL> key; and while the <CTRL> key is being held down, press C. Then follow the prompts.

INSERT DISK WITH \COMMAND.COM IN DRIVE A
AND STRIKE ANY KEY WHEN READY

The diskette which has the file COMMAND.COM has been removed from the drive. Put it back in and press a key.

NOT READY ERROR READING DRIVE A
ABORT, RETRY, FAIL?

You forgot to close the drive door or have no disk in the drive. Put the disk in the drive and close the drive door. Then press R for RETRY. Pressing A for ABORT will take you back to the DOS prompt. If you press F for FAIL, sometimes the computer will not respond right away. You may have to press F a number of times before it responds with:

CURRENT DRIVE IS NO LONGER VALID>

Then change to the drive of your choice by typing the drive letter followed by a colon and press <ENTER>. For example: **C: <ENTER>**.

DOS Error Messages

SECTOR NOT FOUND

Try the command again. If you still get this error message, try using another diskette.

SYNTAX ERROR

You gave an incorrect command. Consult your DOS book. Remember, DOS is so very fussy about syntax. Syntax is the governing rules for the DOS "language." If you get a syntax error, you said it wrong. Sometimes it helps if you whisper "Please" near the drive lights before you issue a command.

WRITE PROTECT ERROR WRITING DRIVE A
ABORT, RETRY, FAIL?

The disk that you are trying to copy the file to is write protected. Remove the write protection and proceed. See pages 31 - 32 if you need help. Anytime DOS presents you with "ABORT, RETRY, FAIL?" you can press the first letter of your choice, and it will take effect. So, if you want to RETRY, all you would have to do is press R. If you press A for ABORT, you will go back to the system prompt.

NON-SYSTEM DISK OR DISK ERROR

The disk in the A drive does not contain a copy of DOS. Remove all diskettes from the drives and let DOS start from the C drive. If you don't have a hard drive, then you need to place a diskette with the system on it in drive A. See page 67 for information on how to make a bootable diskette.

274

Suggested Reading

As was explained in the Introduction, this book was not intended as a comprehensive DOS manual but only as an introduction to DOS. Once you know the commands in this manual, the other books on DOS will not be so intimidating. There are a lot of books on DOS out there, but a seven hundred page book can quickly overwhelm a novice. Remember, when you are reading a big reference book, you need to make continuous use of the **INDEX**. The index is located in the back. I think some people attempt to read an entire reference book straight through! If that is the case, it is no wonder so many novices are overwhelmed by DOS. Before you buy any reference book, it is wise to check the quality of the index. A reference book with a poor index can be a nightmare to use.

One of the best books on DOS 5 is **PC MAGAZINE DOS 5 TECHNIQUES AND UTILITIES, by Jeff Prosise,** published by Ziff-Davis Press. The ISBN number is 1-56276-007-6. It weighs almost four pounds and is 1012 pages thick but is full of good stuff. Jeff Prosise will undoubtedly update his DOS 5 book to cover DOS 6. It should be out by time you read this.

After you have mastered my book, you will be ready for **Alfred Glossbrenner's** excellent book, **DOS 6.** It is published by Random House and has an ISBN number of 0-679-74470-3. It has 633 pages and plenty of information for intermediate and advanced users that is hard to find elsewhere. Alfred Glossbrenner has written over a dozen computer books. Another new book of his is called **POWER DOS!** which is also published by Random House.

If you are using DOS 5 or DOS 6 and want to fine tune your machine, get **PC MAGAZINE DOS 6 MEMORY MANAGEMENT WITH UTILITIES, by Jeff Prosise**, published by Ziff-Davis Press. The ISBN number is 1-56276-097-1. Mr. Prosise is a veritable DOS guru and has tips to squeeze all the memory that is available from your machine. He covers DOS 5 and

Suggested Reading

DOS 6. The book comes with a diskette full of fourteen memory management utilities that Mr. Prosise wrote. One of the utility programs will save your CMOS RAM setup information to diskette. Another one will restore your CMOS RAM setup from diskette.

A modem is one of the more difficult computer peripherals for the beginner to conquer. If you want to get the most out of your modem, buy **John Hedtke's** book, **USING COMPUTER BULLETIN BOARDS**, by MIS: Press. The ISBN # is 1-55828-196-7. The book is now in its second edition. He not only covers BBSs but also has information on all the popular online information services.

Once you triumph over your modem, you may want to attempt to keep up with the changes in online information services. If that is the case, I would suggest acquiring **ONLINE ACCESS** magazine. This fine quarterly publication is published by Chicago Fine Print, Inc., 920 N. Franklin Street, Suite 203, Chicago, IL 60610.

After you get hooked on shareware from downloading it from all those online sources, you may find it is hard to go into those high priced software stores. Shareware software is constantly changing. To keep up with all the best shareware programs, subscribe to **SHAREWARE MAGAZINE**. This bimonthly magazine is published at 1030-D East Duane Avenue, Sunnyvale, CA 94086.

As software changes, you will find that you need a more powerful computer. To keep informed about the latest technological changes in the PC marketplace, you can subscribe to **COMPUTER SHOPPER** magazine. This huge magazine has many fine articles as well as some of the best prices for computer hardware and software. Furthermore, it weights more than all the others combined. COMPUTER SHOPPER, One Park Avenue, 11th Floor, New York, NY 10016.

101 Computer Acronyms

ANSI	American National Standards Institute.
AOL	America OnLine.
APM	Advanced Power Management.
ASCII	American Standard Code for Information Interchange.
ASP	Association of Shareware Professionals.
BASIC	Beginner's All purpose Symbolic Instruction Code.
BBS	Bulletin Board System.
BIOS	Basic Input/Output System.
BIT	BInary digiT.
BOF	Bottom Of File.
BPS	Bits Per Second.
CAD	Computer Aided Design.
CD-ROM	Compact Disk Read Only Memory.
CGA	Color Graphics Adapter.
CIS	CompuServe Information Service.
CMOS	Complementary Metal Oxide Semiconductor.
COBOL	COmmon Business Oriented Language.
COM1	COMmunications port 1 (the first serial port).
CPM	Control Program/Microcomputer.
CPU	Central Processing Unit.
CRC	Cyclic Redundancy Check.
CRT	Cathode Ray Tube.
CVF	Compressed Volume File.
DAT	Digital Audio Tape.
DIN	Deutsch Industrie Norm.
DIP	Dual In-line Package.
DIX	Dec-Intel-Xerox.
DMA	Direct Memory Access.
DOS	Disk Operating System.
DRAM	Dynamic Random Access Memory.
DTP	DeskTop Publishing.

101 Computer Acronyms

DS/DD	Double-Sided Double-Density.
DS/ED	Double-Sided Extended-Density.
DS/HD	Double-Sided High-Density.
EEMS	Enhanced Expanded Memory Specifications.
EEPROM	Electrically Erasable Programmable Read Only Memory.
EGA	Enhanced Graphics Adapter.
EISA	Enhanced Industry Standard Architecture.
EMB	Extended Memory Blocks.
EMS	Expanded Memory Specifications.
EOF	End Of File.
EPROM	Erasable Programmable Read Only Memory.
ESDI	Enhanced Small Device Interface.
FAT	File Allocation Table.
FORTRAN	FORmula TRANslator.
GB	GigaByte.
GUI	Graphical User Interface pronounced "Gooey."
HGC	Hercules Graphics Card.
HMA	High Memory Area.
IBM	International Business Machines Corporation.
IDE	Integrated Drive Electronics.
IEEE	Institute of Electrical and Electronics Engineers.
I/O	Input/Output.
IRQ	Interrupt ReQuest.
ISA	Industry Standard Architecture.
ISAM	Indexed Sequential Access Method.
KB	KiloByte.
LAN	Local Area Network.
LCD	Liquid Crystal Display.
LED	Light Emitting Diode.
LIM	Lotus-Intel-Microsoft.
LPT1	Line PrinTer 1.
MB	MegaByte.

101 Computer Acronyms

MCA	Micro Channel Architecture.
MDA	Monochrome Display Adapter.
MFLOPS	Millions of FLoating Point Operations Per Second.
MFM	Modified Frequency Modulation.
MHz	MegaHertz.
MIPS	Million Instructions Per Second.
MODEM	MOdulator-DEModulator.
NEAT	New Enhanced Advanced Technology.
OCR	Optical Character Recognition.
OEM	Original Equipment Manufacturer.
OLE	Object Linking and Embedding.
PC	Personal Computer.
PGA	Professional Graphics Adapter.
POST	Power-On Self-Test.
PROM	Programmable Read Only Memory.
RAM	Random Access Memory.
RGB	Red Green Blue. Also known as CGA.
RISC	Reduced Instruction Set Computer.
RLL	Run Length Limited.
RNG	Real Nice Guy.
ROM	Read Only Memory.
SCSI	Small Computer System Interface pronounced "Scuzzy."
SIMM	Single In-line Memory Module.
SIP	Single In-line Package.
SVGA	Super Video Graphics Array.
SYSOP	SYStem OPerator.
TOF	Top Of File.
TSR	Terminate-and-Stay-Resident.
UMB	Upper Memory Blocks.
VAR	Value Added Reseller.
VESA	Video Electronics Standards Association.
VGA	Video Graphics Array.

101 Computer Acronyms

VRAM   Video Random Access Memory.
WORM   Write Once Read Many.
WYSIWYG What You See Is What You Get pronounced "Wizzy Wig."
XGA   EXtended Graphics Adapter.
XMA   EXpanded Memory Adapter.
XMS   EXtended Memory Specification.

Also, see the Glossary of File Name Extensions on page 281. Some extensions are acronyms.

If you want to have some fun, go to the largest super computer store that you can find. One with plenty of salespeople. Find a salesperson who looks eager. Tell him you are new to computers; however, a friend told you to get an internal **modulator demodulator** for your computer. One salesperson will ask another and so on up the chain. If it gets to the top, you might be nice and give them a hint. "I believe he said it was also called a modem."

It is easy to misuse acronyms. The following is an example of how annoying acronyms can be:

ISAM, who was a NEAT RNG, RISCed everything to take IDE to the PROM. On the way, he took an IRQ for the Kernel, a VAR. ISAM used VESA to order. When IDE BIT, she found a FAT GUI SCSI WORM and shouted, "IEEE!" When the couple complained, the cashier exclaimed, "You DRAM people are all the same! WYSIWYG."

Glossary of File Name Extensions

.$$$ A temporary work file. *Any file name extension that starts with a .$-- is probably a temporary work file.* These are often erased (or should be) by the program which created them.

.1ST   Usually a text file with the name README.1ST. These often contain instructions for running software.

.AFM   An Adobe PostScript font support file.

.ALL   A WordPerfect file containing printer and font definitions.

.ANS   An ANSI graphics file.

.ARC   A compressed archived file. You can usually uncompress these by using PKUNPAK.EXE by PKWARE, Inc.

.ARJ   A compressed archived file. You can extract these files using ARJ.EXE by Robert K. Jung. This is a shareware program.

.ART   A graphics file for First Publisher.

.ASC   An ASCII text file.

.ASM   A file that is in assembly language source code.

.ASP   A script file used by Procomm.

.BAK   A backup file. A backup file may save the day.

.BAS   Indicates the program is written in BASIC language. You need to load a BASIC language program to run these.

.BAT   A batch file. These can be run by just typing the file name.

.BIN   A binary file.

.BIT   A LOTUS Manuscript graphics file.

.BLD   A BSAVEd BASIC binary file. These are loaded with BLOAD.

.BMP   "Wallpaper" graphics file for Microsoft Windows.

.C   Indicates the source code for a program written in C language.

.CAL   A calendar file.

.CAT   A master catalog file used with MSBACKUP (DOS 6).

.CDR   A graphics file for Corel Draw.

.CFG   A configuration file. Sometimes it is necessary to modify these with your text editor.

.CFN   A configuration file.

Glossary of File Name Extensions

.CGM	Computer Graphics Metafile.
.CHK	A file produced by the DOS CHKDSK command. These files are written to the root directory when you convert lost chains to files.
.CLP	A Windows file that has been saved to the clipboard.
.COB	A source code for COBOL language.
.COD	An object code file used by compilers.
.COM	A command file. These can be run by just typing the file name and pressing <ENTER>.
.CPI	Code page information files for foreign character sets.
.CPL	A Windows control panel file.
.CRD	A card file for Windows.
.CRF	A cross reference file.
.CUT	Halo I, II, III graphics file. Used by Dr. Halo program.
.DAT	A file containing data.
.DB	A Paradox data file.
.DB2	A dBASE II file.
.DB3	A dBASE III file.
.DB4	A dBASE IV file.
.DBF	A database file. Used with dBASE or compatible programs.
.DCT	A dictionary file.
.DEV	A device driver file.
.DHP	A Dr. Halo PIC graphics format file.
.DIB	A device-independent bitmap graphic file.
.DIC	A dictionary file.
.DIF	Data Interchange Format. ASCII files used by spreadsheets. Or a differential backup catalog file used with MSBACKUP (DOS 6).
.DIZ	A text file found in shareware that describes the software.
.DJP	An HP softfont file for a Deskjet printer.
.DLL	Windows Dynamic Link Library file.

Glossary of File Name Extensions

.DOC	Documentation text file. DOC files are often the manual for programs. It is IMPORTANT TO READ THESE FIRST. Use the DOS TYPE command, or you can use a text editor or most word processors. Just to keep you on your toes, Microsoft Word uses a .DOC extension for files it creates.
.DRV	Hardware driver. These interface your hardware.
.DRW	A graphics file used by Corel Draw.
.DVP	A DESQview configuration file.
.DVR	A device driver file.
.DWG	Autocad drawing file.
.DXF	An Autocad graphics file.
.EPS	Encapsulated PostScript file used by desktop publishing programs.
.EXE	Executable file. To run these, just type the file name and press <ENTER>. Look for these when you do a directory.
.FMT	A formatting file used by dBASE III.
.FNT	A font file.
.FON	A font file.
.FOR	A FORTRAN language source code file.
.FOT	A Windows file for a TrueType scalable outline font.
.FOX	A FoxBASE database file.
.FRM	A form file.
.FUL	A full backup catalog file used with DOS 6 MSBACKUP.
.GDI	A GEM Metafile.
.GIF	A CompuServe graphics file. Graphics Interchange Format.
.GRP	A Windows Group data file.
.GX1	Show Partner graphics file.
.H	A C language header file.
.HLP	A help file. Sometimes these are text files.
.HNT	A file containing hints. Usually a game.
.HPF	HP/PCL printer Bitstream soft Fonts.
.HPG	A Hewlett Packard Graphics language file.
.HST	Often a text file showing the history of a particular program.

Glossary of File Name Extensions

.HYC	A hyphenation list file for WordPerfect.
.ICE	A file compressed by LHice.
.ICO	Icon graphics file used by PROGMAN in Microsoft Windows.
.IDX	A FoxBASE database index file.
.IFF	A Deluxe Paint II graphics file.
.IMG	A GEM Paint graphics file which can often be used by desktop publishing programs.
.INC	An incremental backup file used with the DOS 6 MSBACKUP.
.INF	An INFormation file, usually a text file. Read it first.
.INI	A Windows initialization file.
.ISF	An IBM image support facility file.
.JPG	JPEG–Joint Picture Experts Group compressed graphic image file.
.KEY	KEYboard macro definition files.
.LBM	An IFF graphics file used by Deluxe Paint and others.
.LIB	A Library file used by a computer language compiler.
.LST	A text file consisting of a list of files.
.LTR	A letter file.
.LZH	A compressed archived file. To uncompress this type of file, you need LHA.EXE by Haruyasu Yoshizaki. This is freeware.
.MAC	A MacPaint graphics file or a MACRO file.
.MAN	A file that contains the manual for a program. This is usually in the form of a text file.
.ME	Usually a text file with the name READ.ME. These can be read with the DOS TYPE command. You can also use an editor or word processor to view and print these files.
.MID	A MIDI audio file.
.MNU	A menu file or a mouse control file.
.MOD	A file to support data exchange between DOS and Windows.
.MSP	Microsoft Windows graphics file.
.NAM	A Print Shop "name file."
.NDX	A dBASE database index file.
.NG	A database file for Norton Guides.

Glossary of File Name Extensions

.NTX	A dBASE index file.
.OBJ	An object code file.
.OLD	A file that has been backed-up by renaming the file.
.OVL	An overlay file.
.OVR	An overlay file.
.P	A text file that indicates Pascal language source code.
.PAK	A compressed archived file. To uncompress, you need a shareware program called PAK.EXE by NoGate Consulting.
.PAS	A PASCAL programming file. The source code file.
.PCC	A graphics file used by Z-Soft. HINT—Rename these with a .PCX extension, and you can often use them in other programs.
.PCD	Kodak Photo-CD graphic files used for their CD-ROM format.
.PCX	A PC Paintbrush (Z-Soft) graphics file. These can often be used by desktop publishing programs.
.PDF	A Printer Definition File.
.PDV	A Microsoft Paintbrush device driver file.
.PDX	A Paradox file.
.PGM	A program binary file.
.PIC	A LOTUS graphics file, or a graphics file used by PC Paint +, Grasp, and others.
.PIF	A Windows Program Information File
.PIM	A permanent image file used by some graphics programs.
.PNM	A New Print Shop "name file."
.POG	A New Print Shop graphic file.
.PRD	A printer definition file used by Microsoft Word, etc.
.PRG	A programming source file.
.PRN	Usually a text file that should be printed.
.PRS	A WordPerfect printer definition file.
.PRT	A file to be printed. Sometimes these are text files and contain the documentation or manual.
.PSO	PostScript PDL printer Bitstream softfonts file.
.REC	A Windows macro recorder file.

Glossary of File Name Extensions

.RLE	A Run-Length-Encoded graphics file.
.SAV	A file that has been backed-up or a saved position in a game.
.SCR	A script file used by a telecommunications program or a screen file.
.SCT	A Lotus Manuscript screen capture text file.
.SCX	Graphics file for RIX/EGA and ColoRix programs.
.SDR	A Printmaster "name file."
.SET	A backup set used with MSBACKUP.
.SFL	An HP PCL 4 bitmapped SoftFont file (Landscape orientation).
.SFP	An HP PCL 4 bitmapped SoftFont file (Portrait orientation).
.SFS	A SoftFont file indicating a Screen font.
.SHP	A Printmaster graphics file.
.SK	A SideKick Plus utility file.
.STY	Style files for WordPerfect.
.SYS	A device driver file. Usually you need to add a line to the CONFIG.SYS file to install these. The CONFIG.SYS file resides in the root directory of the boot disk.
.TGA	A file used by Targa 16.
.THS	A thesaurus file for WordPerfect.
.TIF	A graphics file called Tagged Image Format. Used by Aldus Pagemaker and other desktop publishing programs.
.TMP	A temporary file.
.TST	A test file.
.TTF	A Windows header file for a TrueType scalable outline font.
.TUT	A tutorial file.
.TXT	A text file. These often contain the directions for how to run a program. ASCII text files can be viewed using the DOS TYPE command or loaded into most editors and word processors.
.UPD	An updated text file usually containing history.
.VBX	A Visual Basic control file.
.VOC	A Soundblaster sound file.
.WAV	A Windows sound file.

Glossary of File Name Extensions

.WK1	A LOTUS spreadsheet file for version 2.0.
.WKE	A LOTUS educational worksheet file.
.WKQ	A QUATTRO spreadsheet file.
.WKS	A LOTUS spreadsheet file for version 1A.
.WMF	A Windows Metafile graphics format file.
.WPG	A WordPerfect Graphics file for version 5.0 and later.
.WPK	A WordPerfect keyboard macro file.
.WPM	A WordPerfect Macro file.
.WQ1	A spreadsheet file for Quattro 1.0.
.WRI	A text file for Windows Write.
.WRK	A Symphony spreadsheet file.
.XLS	An Excel spreadsheet file.
.XLT	A file containing translation tables.
.XTP	An Xtree overlay file.
.ZIP	A compressed archived file. You need PKUNZIP.EXE to uncompress and use these files. This is a shareware program. PKUNZIP is by PKWARE, Inc. You will want the latest version. It changes periodically.
.ZOO	A compressed archived file. Requires ZOO.EXE to uncompress.

Glossary of Computer Terms

ACTIVE DIRECTORY: The current directory. The directory that you are working in is the active directory.

APPLICATIONS PROGRAM: These are simply software programs that you use for specific applications. A word processor, a spreadsheet, or a data base are all examples of application programs.

ASCII: Pronounced ASK-EE. An ASCII file is a file saved in a format called ASCII, also called a text file. ASCII stands for American Standard Code for Information Interchange.

AUTOEXEC.BAT FILE: This is a batch file that has user defined commands. DOS executes the AUTOEXEC.BAT file upon start-up. An AUTOEXEC.BAT file resides in the root directory of the start-up disk.

\ BACKSLASH: The backslash (\) is used in DOS commands to indicate a directory. Don't confuse the backslash character with the forward slash which looks like this (/).

BASIC: A programming language. BASIC stands for Beginner's All-purpose Symbolic Instruction Code.

BATCH FILE: A text file with .BAT extension. Batch files contain DOS commands that execute when the batch file is run.

BAUD: The speed at which data can be transmitted. This term comes from J. M. E. Baudot (1845-1903) who was a French pioneer in printing telegraphy. **Bits Per Second (BPS)** is the usual way BAUD is expressed. Ask about the BAUD rate when you consider a modem.

Glossary of Computer Terms

BIOS: A chip that contains programs in ROM, **R**ead **O**nly **M**emory, that manage the computer's hardware. BIOS stands for **B**asic **I**nput **O**utput **S**ystem.

BIT: BIT stands for **BI**nary digi**T** which is the most basic unit of information in the binary numbering system.

BOOT: To start the computer. Please don't kick your computer!

BULLETIN BOARD: A **B**ulletin **B**oard **S**ystem (BBS) is a computer system that is set up with software and a modem(s) to allow other computer users with modems to access information on the computer.

BYTE: A byte contains eight bits. A byte can store one letter or other character. A byte is a unit of measure for a computer's memory and also for disk data storage. The disks we buy are expressed in how many bytes of storage that they will hold. One kilobyte (k) is 1,024 bytes.

C PROMPT: The system prompt which tells you that you are on C drive and that DOS is ready to accept commands. It may look something like: C> or C:\DOS>.

CGA: Color Graphics Adapter. Provides low resolution (640 x 200) with up to 16 colors. Avoid, if possible. Also see EGA, VGA, and XGA below.

CLONE: An IBM clone is a computer that works the same as, and runs the same programs as an IBM PC.

COLD BOOT: This means to turn on the computer by using the power switch or reset button. Also see WARM BOOT below.

Glossary of Computer Terms

COM1: The first serial port which is also called a communications port. See RS-232 below.

COMMAND LINE: The DOS system prompt. You know you are at the DOS command line when you see something like: A>, B>, C>, etc.

CONFIG.SYS FILE: This is a text file residing in the root directory of the start-up disk that is read by DOS when DOS starts up. This file is defined by the user and contains DOS commands that configure the system.

CONVENTIONAL MEMORY: The memory between 0 and 640K is known as conventional memory. Unless instructed otherwise, DOS only uses the first 640K of memory for applications and data. The memory between 640K and 1024K is reserved memory or Upper Memory Area. Memory management software can make use of this Upper Memory Area to load device drivers and memory-resident programs. The Upper Memory Area is used in units or blocks called Upper Memory Blocks (UMB's). When programs are loaded into the Upper Memory Area, it provides more room for your application programs and data in the first 640K of memory. See UMB.

CPU: Stands for Central Processing Unit. DOS CPU's are known as 8088, 8086, 80286, 80386 or 80486. A computer with an 80286 CPU is known as a 286 machine, an 80386 is called a 386 machine, and an 80486 is a 486 machine. The Pentium is the new Intel CPU chip one step above an 80486.

CURRENT DIRECTORY: The directory in which you are currently working. This is also called the active directory. The current directory is the directory that DOS searches for files (unless told otherwise). DOS keeps track of the last current directory that you were in for each drive. If you change drives, DOS will take you to the last directory you were working in for that drive. If you have not used that drive since turning on the computer,

290

Glossary of Computer Terms

DOS will take you to the root directory.

CURSOR: The cursor is the blinking character that shows you where you are on your screen.

CVF: Compressed Volume File. With DOS 6 you can use DoubleSpace to increase the capacity of your drive. It creates a Compressed Volume File that appears as a disk drive. DoubleSpace employs data compression techniques to almost double the capacity of your drive.

DATA FILE: A file that is used by another program to store information. For example, your word processor may store the letters you write in a special kind of data file.

DEFAULT DRIVE: The current drive that is being used.

DEFAULTS: Programs often come with designated values which are called the default values. If you don't enter your own values, you can often just press <ENTER>; and the program will accept the *default values*.

DEFRAGMENTATION: A procedure where a special program re-writes files on a disk, so each file (and the parts of each file) are stored in adjoining sectors.

DESTINATION DISK: When you copy a file, the disk that you are copying the file to is called the destination disk. A destination disk is also called the target disk.

DEVICE DRIVER: A program (usually with the extension .SYS) that is called up by a statement in the CONFIG.SYS file. There are lots of possible device drivers. A mouse might come with a device driver on disk by the name MOUSE.SYS.

DIRECTORY: A directory can mean several things in computer jargon. Directory can mean a *list of files* displayed when you issue the DOS DIR command. Also, the files on a disk are organized in directories and subdirectories. So, a directory can also mean *an area on the disk where a certain group of files are stored.*

DISK: A disk can mean a hard disk or a floppy disk. See floppy drive.

DISKETTE: A floppy disk. Please note that a diskette can also be called a disk or a floppy.

DOCUMENTATION: The instructions for running software are called the "documentation."

DOS: Stands for **D**isk **O**perating **S**ystem. PC-DOS is what DOS is known as when it comes with an IBM PC computer. MS-DOS is what DOS is called if it comes with an IBM clone. Both of these are made by Microsoft Corporation. DOS coordinates the computer's operation and all its parts.

EDITOR: A software program used to make or change a text file. An editor is sometimes called a text editor.

EDLIN: The name of a dreadful DOS text editor. Edlin should be avoided in this writer's opinion. There are plenty of inexpensive alternative text editors that are easy to use.

Glossary of Computer Terms

EGA: Enhanced Graphics Adapter. Introduced in 1984. Provides medium resolution (640 x 350). Much better than CGA but not as good as VGA.

EXPANDED MEMORY: Memory that is not normally in an IBM PC or compatible computer. Usually expanded memory is purchased in the form of an expansion card with device driver software, and this memory must conform to LIM (Lotus-Intel-Microsoft) EMS (Expanded Memory Specifications). Expanded memory can be used with all types of IBM PC's and compatibles.

EXTENDED MEMORY: On an 80286, an 80386, or an 80486 machine the memory above 1MB is called extended memory. Often, a software program called an extended-memory manager is used to make efficient use of extended memory.

EXTENSION: The up to three letter suffix that helps identify a file. Extensions give valuable clues to help identify file types. The extension comes after the file name. When you do a directory—DIR <ENTER>, you will see the list of file names with their extensions. Learning about extensions is one of the most important things a beginner can do. Suppose you did a directory on a disk and saw a file called JUMP.EXE. The example file's name is JUMP and the extension is .EXE. See pages 39 - 45.

FILE: A collection of information that is stored on a disk as a single unit and has a file name.

FLOPPY DRIVE: A diskette drive. DOS users are likely to have either a 5¼" drive and/or a 3½" drive. Even though the 3½" disks are hard, they are not called hard disks because they are not fixed. They are removable. A 3½" disk is called a floppy disk.

Glossary of Computer Terms

FORMAT: Before a disk can be used, it must be formatted. When you format a disk, you prepare it for use.

/ FORWARD SLASH: This character is a key on the keyboard which is on the same key as the question mark. It is often used with DOS commands as a switch. See switch below. Don't confuse the forward slash (/) with the backward slash (\).

FREEWARE: This is a program that is similar to public domain software, except that it is copyrighted. A freeware program has copyright restrictions; however, the author is not requesting a registration fee. Also, see SHAREWARE and PUBLIC DOMAIN SOFTWARE.

FUNCTION KEY: Those keys that are marked F1 through F12. Older keyboards only had function keys F1 through F10.

GIGABYTE: One thousand megabytes.

HARD DRIVE: A large capacity disk (storage system) that is not removed from the computer. These usually range in size from twenty megabytes to one gigabyte. A hard disk is also called a fixed disk. See FLOPPY DRIVE above.

HARDWARE: Computer hardware is computer equipment and its physical components like: power supply, mother board, disk drive, monitor, keyboard, printer, etc. Computer programs are called software.

KILOBYTE (K): A unit of measure for computer memory. One kilobyte is 1,024 bytes. *K* or *KB* is often used as an abbreviation for kilobyte.

Glossary of Computer Terms

LPT1: The first parallel port where you attach a printer. LPT stands for Line PrinTer.

MEGABYTE (MB): A unit of measure equal to 1,048,576 bytes. Note that a megabyte is equal to a little over one million bytes. An abbreviation for megabyte is *MB*.

MENU: A display on screen that lets the user make a choice--often by choosing a number or letter. A software menu is kind of like a restaurant menu; except instead of listing food items, it lists specific functions or programs.

MODEM: A modem is a device that allows a computer to communicate and transfer files with other computers over a telephone line.

MOUSE: A device that is rolled on a flat surface and is used as a pointer. By moving the mouse you move the mouse pointer on the screen. When you have the mouse pointer on the desired menu option, you can select the item by pressing a mouse button.

OPTIMIZATION: The process of defragmentation. This is done with a software program. With active use, a hard drive becomes fragmented. A fragmented drive is one where the files are not stored in an efficient manner.

PATH: The term PATH can have several meanings. PATH can mean the *directories that DOS searches for programs to run when the programs are not in the active directory.*   Path can also mean *the full directory name where a particular file is stored.* For example, C:\GAMES\PINBALL might be the directory where you keep your favorite pinball game. If that were the case, C:\GAMES\PINBALL would be the PATH to your pinball game.

Glossary of Computer Terms

PENTIUM: The Intel CPU microprocessor chip that is one step above the 80486. Unofficially, it will be known as the 586.

PUBLIC DOMAIN SOFTWARE: Software that is not copyrighted and can be freely distributed without restrictions.

QBASIC: A BASIC language that comes with *DOS 5* and later. QBASIC will not run earlier BASIC programs.

RAM: This stands for **Random Access Memory**. RAM is the computer's primary working memory.

RAM DRIVE: A simulated disk drive made using special software and random access memory (RAM). This is also called a virtual disk or electronic disk.

REBOOT: To restart the computer.

ROM: This stands for **Read Only Memory**. You can only read information from ROM; you can't write data to ROM.

ROOT DIRECTORY: The first or top level directory on a disk. This is the directory that was made when the disk was formatted.

RS-232: A serial port. You plug mice and modems and other goodies into serial ports.

SELF-EXTRACTING FILE: A self-extracting file is a compressed file. The file contains a file or group of files that has been compressed to save space. When a self-extracting file is run, other files pop out (emerge) from it. These are often found on BBSs (**B**ulletin **B**oard **S**ystems) and in shareware. It is best to copy self-extracting files to the hard drive where they will have plenty of room to expand.

SHAREWARE: Shareware is a method of marketing software for the program's author. Shareware programs are copyrighted. The manuals for these programs are usually found on the disk in the form of a text file. You can print the manuals using your printer. You can obtain these programs for *trial use* from shareware distributors for a copying fee of just a few dollars per disk. *Shareware programs require a separate payment to the author if found useful.* Shareware is a wonderful deal for the consumer, because you get to "*Try before you buy.*" There are some great programs that are distributed as shareware.

SHELL: A program that tries to make DOS easier to use. There are hundreds of shells on the market. DOS 4.0 and later come with a built in shell. Some people don't like DOS shells. A shell is easier to use once you know DOS. Some programs will not install properly from a shell or menu.

SOFTWARE: The programs that are used in a computer. Software is to a computer what a record is to a record player. The computer would be a big paperweight without software. Just think how useless a record player would be without records. Also, see hardware above.

SOURCE DISK: When you want to copy a disk, the one you want to copy is called the SOURCE disk. The disk you want to copy the file or files to is called the TARGET disk or DESTINATION disk.

SUBDIRECTORY: A directory that is subordinate to another directory. For example: C:\GAMES\PINBALL. PINBALL is a subdirectory of the GAMES subdirectory which is subordinate to the C:\ root directory.

Glossary of Computer Terms

SWITCH: A code in a command to indicate a particular way that the command is to be used. For example: DIR /W. The */W* in this command tells DOS to show the directory in wide fashion.

SYSTEM PROMPT: This is also called the *command line*. See command line and C PROMPT above. These are the characters that DOS displays on the screen to indicate that it is ready to accept commands. An example would be: C>.

TARGET DISK: When you are copying files to a disk, the disk that you are copying the files to is called the target disk. The target disk is also called the destination disk. Also, see source disk above.

TEXT FILE: A file saved in a format called text or ASCII. See ASCII above.

TSR: A memory-resident program. TSR stands for **T**erminate and **S**tay **R**esident. When a TSR program is run, it stays in memory and can be called up by pressing a key or combination of keys. Such a key is called a "hot key."

UMB: Upper Memory Blocks. This is an area in upper memory that is not used by video memory or ROM's. DOS 5 and DOS 6 come with EMM386.EXE which is used with 80386 and 80486 machines to simulate expanded memory. The EMM386.EXE works to allow loading memory-resident programs and device drivers into UMBs with the LOADHI and DEVICEHIGH command. With DOS 5 and DOS 6, you can't use UMBs with 80286 and 8088 machines. There are third-party vendors that have extended memory managers that will work with 80286 and 8088 machines.

Glossary of Computer Terms

UTILITY: A program that performs a specific job to help with the routine tasks of operating the computer. People who use utilities find them incredibly valuable. For example, the shareware program LIST is a utility program to help you view and print text files. It replaces the barbaric DOS TYPE command which is hard to use and has few features. See page 259 for more on LIST.

VGA: Video Graphics Array. Introduced in 1987. Provides medium to high resolution (640 x 480). Better than CGA or EGA but not as good as Super VGA or Super VGA PLUS. Super VGA was introduced in 1988 and has a resolution of up to 800 x 600. Super VGA Plus has a resolution of up to 1024 x 768. See XGA below.

VIRTUAL DISK: A ram drive. See ram drive above.

VIRUS: A software program designed to destroy data or cause problems with your computer.

VOLUME LABEL: A name which can be up to eleven characters long to identify a disk. It is not necessary that a volume label be given to each disk. The volume label is optional.

WARM BOOT: To restart your computer by pressing <CTRL> <ALT> <DEL>. These three keys are all held down at the same time. If your computer locks up, this can provide your best way to get back to work.

WILDCARD: A DOS wildcard character is a special symbol that is used to represent any character. This is like the wildcards used in the game of poker. The asterisk looks like (*) and is used to represent any character or number of characters. The question mark (?) is used to represent any single character.

WORD PROCESSOR: Software that is a fancy text editor used to write letters, books, etc.

WRITE PROTECTION: If you use a write protect tab to cover up the small rectangular notch in the edge of a 5¼" disk, then information can't be written to that disk. It is then write protected. The 3½" disks have a little switch on the top left corner on the back side for write protection. The switch on the 3½" disks is placed in the up position (so you can see through the hole) for write protection. On those disks to which you are constantly writing information, write protection is not practical.

XGA: EXtended Graphics Adapter. Introduced in 1990. Provides high resolution of up to 1024 x 768. It can have up to 256 colors in 640 x 480 resolution. To the human eye it looks like 32,000 colors.

ZIPPED FILE: A compressed file that contains a file or a collection of files. A zipped file has an extension of .ZIP. You need the shareware program called PKUNZIP.EXE to unzip a zipped file.

INDEX

Bulletin Board System, 177, **263**, 289
"burn-in," screen, 31
byte, 11, 289

BYTES
defined, 11, 289
determining BYTES with **CHKDSK**
available, 56
of conventional memory, 57
of free memory, 57
of memory used by files, 56

With DOS 5 & DOS 6 (see MEM), 58

C

C>, 26
C drive, changing to, 30
C prompt, 289
caches (disk),
  SMARTDRV.EXE (DOS 6), 205-207
  SMARTDRV.SYS (DOS 5), 162-165,
canceling a DOS command, 9
capacity of (determining the)
  floppy disks, 33-34, 56, 200
  hard drive, 56, 200
<CAPS LOCK>, 7, 182
CD command (Change Directory), 97, 102,
  103, 105, 263
    determining current directory with, 103
    shortcuts, 112-114
CD \, (command to move to the root
  directory), 97, 101, 105
CD.., for moving to parent directory, 113
CD-ROM, 215
CGA (Color Graphics Adapter), 214
changing directories (CD command), 97, 102,
  103, 105, 112-114, 264
changing drives, 30
CHDIR command (another name for CD), 264
CHKDSK command, 33, **56-57**, 220, 265
  /F switch (for fix), 57, 225

clean boot (DOS 6), 213
CLEAN-UP, 235
CLEAN-UP (shareware), 261
CLEAR SCREEN (see CLS)
clone, 289
CLS, clear screen command, 29, 265
clusters, lost, 57
CMOS (Complementary Mental Oxide
  Semiconductor), 201
    WARNING, 201
"code to get in," 16
cold boot, 289
.COM (files), 39
COM1, 11, 290
COMMAND.COM, 67, 98, 117
command line, 11, 26, 27, 290

COMMANDS (also see DOS commands)
canceling, 9
history with DOSKEY, 171
repeating last command with <F3>, 8
Summary of Important DOS
  Commands, 264-271

common computer acronyms, 277-280

COMPRESS, (a program in PC TOOLS), 185

Compressed Volume File (CVF), 220
compressing floppy disks (DOS 6), 227
compressing hard drives (DOS 6), 222

COMPUTER
Acronyms, 277-280
Glossary of Terms, 288-300
  Introductory, 11-14

turning off, 31
turning on, 26

Computer Shopper Magazine, 276
CON>FORMAT (shareware), 66, 258

<CTRL> C, 9, 173, 183
<CTRL> key, 8
<CTRL> S, 10, 47
<CTRL> Z, 64
CURRENT DIRECTORY, 11, 77, 290
  displaying, 103
  symbol (.), 104
current drive, 26
cursor, 7
CVF (Compressed Volume File), 220

D

.DAT (files), 40
data file, 40, 291
DATE command, 28, 265
date and time of files, 29
date and time, setting, 28

DBLSPACE (DOS 6), 220-231, 266
  Cautions, 220-221
  compressing floppy disks, 227
    a better alternative, 229
  deleting a compressed drive, 229
  maximum compressed drive size, 221
  problems, 221
  removing DoubleSpace, 230-231
  switches
    /CHKDSK/F, 225
    /CHK/F (shortcut), 225
    /COMPRESS, 227
    /COM (shortcut), 227
    /DEFRAGMENT, 225
    /DEF (shortcut), 225
    /DELETE, 229
    /DEL (shortcut), 229
    /FORMAT, 230
    /INFO, 227
    /I (shortcut), 227
    /LIST, 223
    /L (shortcut), 223
    /MOUNT, 228
    /MO (shortcut), 228

/RATIO, 223
/SIZE, 223
/UNMOUNT, 228
/U (shortcut), 228

DBLSPACE.000 (file), 117, 221
DBLSPACE.BIN (file), 117, 221
DBLSPACE.INI (file), 117, 221
default drive, 11, 291
defaults, 11, 291
DEFAULT.SET (file), 252
DEFRAG command (DOS 6), 195-196, 266
defragmentation, 11, 185, 195-196, 291
defragmenting a DoubleSpaced drive, 225
DEL command, 7, 87-90, 109, 113, 266
  shortcuts, 90, 113-114
Delete Sentry, 202-204
  installing, 203-204

DELETING
  characters, 7
  directories, 108
    using DELTREE (DOS 6), 197
  FILES, 87-90, 109, 113, 266
    a single file, 87, 109
    all files in a directory, 88, 90, 113, 197
    CAUTION, 88
    groups of files, 88-90, 109-110
    on a diskette
      all files using an unconditional
        format, 63-64
    on a hard drive, 109
      WARNING, 110
      with wildcards, 109
    Tips, 90, 113
    undeleting files, 91-92, 270
    with wildcards, 88-90, 109
      del *.*, 88, 109-110
        shortcut (del .), 90, 113
        shortcut
          (del directoryname), 113
  SUBDIRECTORIES, 108, 197, 266
    difficult ones, 116-117

deletion tracking,
  with DOS 5, 91
  with DOS 6, 202-204
DELTREE (DOS 6), 197, 266
  caution, 197
destination disk, 12, 70, 291
device drivers, 291
  adding to CONFIG.SYS, 160-165, 224
DEVICEHIGH, 164-165, 209-210, 224
different backup types, 240
differential backup (defined), 240
DIR command, 35, 115-116, 129, 171, 266
DIR... (displaying subdirectories), 116
DIR /A, (displaying all), 116, 221
DIR /A:D (showing just subdirectories), 116
DIR /C /P (showing Compression Ratio), 223
DIR /P, (showing a page at a time then
  pausing), 36, 126, 171
DIR > PRN, (redirecting the output to the
  printer), 36
<DIR> "thing," 77, 98
DIR /W, (showing in wide style), 36, 171

DIRECTORIES 96-116
  creating, 101, 105
  deleting, 108, 197
  first (1st) generation, 98
  making for installing software, 119
  number of, determining with CHKDSK, 56
  removing, 108, 197
  removing difficult ones, 116-117, 197
  root, 13, 96-97
  structure, 97-100
  Summary, 111
  Tips and Shortcuts, 112-117
  TREE command, 100

DIRECTORY
  ambiguity of the term, 12, 292
  displaying a directory, 35
    one page at a time, 36
    wide, 36
  listing the parts of, 38

  making sense of, 38
  printing a directory listing, 36
    to issue a form feed, 50

DISK (also see diskettes)
  auto-booting, making a program
    start automatically, 151-155, 184
  cache, 162-165, 206-207
  drives, changing, 30
  operating system (DOS), 2, 292
disk space, determining with CHKDSK, 56
DISKCOPY, command, 70-73, 266
  Tips, 73

DISKETTES, 292
  3½" and write protection, 32, 34
  5¼" and write protection, 32-33
  auto-booting, 67-69, 154-155, 184
  capacity, checking for, 33, 34, 56, 200
    by visual inspection, 33, 34
  COPYING, (see COPYING above)
  formatting, 59-69
  precautions, 34
  subdirectories on, 96
  types of, 32-34, 62
  write protection of, 32-34

displaying a directory, 35-37
displaying all files in a directory, 116
divide overflow, (error message), 272
.DOC (files), 41, 46
documentation, 12, 292
DOS 6 (book), 275

DOS
  COMMANDS
    ASSIGN, 124-125, 264
    ATTRIB, 84, 116, 131-133
    BACKUP, 172-176, 264
    CD (CHDIR), 102-103, 264
    CHKDSK, 56-57, 265
    CLS, 29, 265
    COPY, 74-79, 127-129, 134-137

E

/E switch with XCOPY, 81, 82, 120-121
ECHO <CTRL> L > PRN, form feed, 50
ECHO OFF command, 147, 151-153, 205-206
EDIT, command, **48**, 162-163, 205, 209, 212, 266
editing include/exclude MSBACKUP list, 245-246
editor, 292
EDLIN, 48, 292
EGA (Enhanced Graphics Adapter), 293
ejecting a page from a printer, 50
EMM386.EXE, 164-166, 209
end of file <F6>, (see F6 and COPY CON)
environmental variable, 205-206
ERASE (another name for DEL), 266
erasing files, 87-90, 109
error messages, the most common, 272-274
<ESC>, 7
.EXE (files), 39
executable files, identifying, 39
expanded memory, 293
exploding..., 23-24, 179
Extended-Density (ED) diskettes, 34
extended memory, 215, **293**

EXTENSIONS, 12, **39-45**, 281-287, 293
GLOSSARY OF, 281-287
identifying
data files, 40
executable files, 39
files that run, 39
manuals (files), 41, 46
text files, 41
Key to Computing Success ☺, 39
Summary, 45

F

/F SWITCH
used with BACKUP command, 173-175

used with CHKDSK, 57, 195, 225
used with formatting, 62, 68
<F1> often a "HELP" key, 8
<F1> - <F12>, 8
<F3>, 8
to exit the DOS SHELL, 26
to repeat last command, 8, 84, 132
<F5> (DOS 6) for a clean boot, 213
<F6>, used with COPY CON, 64, 91, 103, 141, 155, 157, 184
<F8> (DOS 6) for an interactive boot, 214
FASTHELP (DOS 6), 192
FAT GUI SCSI WORM, 280
FDFORMAT (public domain), 86, 258

FILE, 6, 12, 293
file compression, 220, 300
file extensions, 39-45, 281-287
importance of, 39

FILE NAME
and rename, 93-94
CAUTION, 93
character restrictions, 93
conventions, 93
extensions, **38-45**
glossary of, 281-287
names which are likely text files, 42, 47

file types, 39-45, 281-287

FILES
accessing, 39-45
backing up, 70-73, 83-86, 172-176
copying, (see copying)
creating text, (see COPY CON, editor, and word processors)
defined, 6, 12, 293
deleting, (see deleting)
file paths, 13, 17, 144-145, 268, 295
FILES= statement in CONFIG.SYS file, 157-158, 209
identifying files that run, 39, 45

308

kilobyte, 13, 294

L

laptops, conserving power, 253
laser printer form feed, 50
lightning storms, 31
LIST (shareware), 49, 51, 123, 259
listing files, see DIR command
LOADHI command in
  AUTOEXEC.BAT file, 165-166, 208
loading DoubleSpace high, 224
loading software, **39**, 40-45
  on the hard drive, 118-123
    Do I have to?, 23
logging on, 102
lost clusters, 57
  fixing with CHKDSK /F, 57
lost files, finding, 115, 170, 260-261
low capacity diskettes, 33-34, 60-62, 169
LPT1, 13, 295

M

/M switch with XCOPY, 84, 132
macro, 169
Making a Directory (MD), 101, 105, 267
.MAN (files), 41, 46
MANUAL (files), 41, 42, 46-47
manuals
  tips on how to read and navigate, 6, 49,
    275
  where to get third-party manuals
    for commercial software, 20
MB (megabyte), 33, 295
McAfee Associates, 235
MD command, 101, 105, 112, 267
  automatically make directories using
    XCOPY, 84-85, 120-124, 132, 139
.ME (files), 41, 46
megabyte, 13, 295
MEM command, memory information, **58**, 267

MEM /C command, 58
MEM /C |MORE command, 58
MEM /C /P (DOS 6), 58, 212, 216, 218

MEMMAKER (DOS 6), **215-219**, 267
  CAUTIONS, 215-216
  Express Setup, 216
  /UNDO switch, 219

MEMORY
  conventional, 215
  expanded, 217
  extended, 217
  finding out what you have
    with ASQ, 19, 258
    with CHKDSK, 56-57
    with MEM, 58
    with MSD, 200-201

  HMA (High Memory Area), 163
  RAM, (Random Access Memory), 296
  ROM, (Read Only Memory), 296
  UMB (Upper Memory Blocks), 164-165
    298
memory management, 162-168, 190, 215-219
  third-party, 167
memory management (book), 167, 275
memory-resident programs, 215
menu removal from
  AUTOEXEC.BAT file, 154, 207-208
menus, 187-188, 295
Microsoft Corporation, 2
MicroSoft Diagnostic Utility (MSD), 200-201
Microsoft Tools group, 191
Microsoft supplemental disks, 124, 236
MIRROR command, 65, 91-92, 267
MIRROR, unloading, 91
MKDIR (another name for MD), 267
modem, 31, 263, 295
  the easiest way to learn to use, 263

311

SHELL, 26, **187-188**, 297
getting out of a, 26
removal from AUTOEXEC.BAT file, 154,
207-208
Tips on shells and menus, 188

<SHIFT>, 8
<SHIFT> <PRT SC>, 10, 51-52
SMARTDRIVE.SYS disk cache, 162-166

SMARTDRV /C switch to flush the disk
cache, 206
SMARTDRV.EXE (DOS 6), 205-207

SOFTWARE, 14, 297
finding lost files, 116, 170, 261
installing, 43
on a hard drive, 118-123
Summary, 122
requirements, 18-19
running software, **39**, 40-45, 181-182
where to purchase third party manuals
for commercial software, 20

source disk, 14, 70, 80, 297
space problems, help solve, 86
split files to multiple disks, 86, 259, 260
SST (Supersonic Search Tool shareware),
115, 261
STACKS= (in CONFIG.SYS file), 162-164,
209-211
START (files), 43
starting computer, 26
starting DOS, 26
start-up diskette, making, 67-69, 149
STEREO SHELL (shareware), 117
stopping programs, 7, 9, 31, 183
stopping the computer, 31

SUBDIRECTORIES
copying, 81-86, 136-140
defined, 96, 297
finding lost ones, 115
how to tell if they exist, 98
RD, command for removing, 108-110
removing with RD command, 108-110
removing difficult ones, 116-117
removing with DELTREE (DOS 6), 197
using on floppy disks, 96

SUGGESTED READING, 275-276
supplemental disks, 124, 236
surge protection, 31
swap file for Windows, 221

SWITCHES
defined, 14, 298
power, 26
software switches, (defined), 14, 298

syntax, 274
syntax error, 274

SYSTEM, command, 183
system files, 117
system files, turning into regular files, 116
SYSTEM.INI file, 216
system prompt, 14, 26, 298

T

/T switch used with UNDELETE 91, 203
<TAB>, 7
tape backup systems, 176, 252
target disk, 14, 70, 80, 298

TERMS
101 Computer Acronyms, 277-280
Glossary of, 288-300
Introductory Computer, 11-14

TEXT FILES
  defined, 298
  identifying, 41-42
  making with COPY CON, 64
  printing, 50-51
  viewing, 46-49
    Tips, 49
    with
      a word processor, 49
      EDIT command, 48
      LIST, 49, 259
      TYPE command, 46-47

three fingered salute, 10
TIME, command, 28, 269

TIPS, 37, 49, 66, 69, 73, 79, 86, 90, 112-117
  129, 140, 143, 176, 180, 184, 188, 198,
  201, 208, 211-212, 224, 229, 235, 252, 263,
  271

TREE, command, 100, 269
tricking software
  using the ASSIGN command, 124-125
"TRY BEFORE YOU BUY!",
    software, 256-263
TSR (Terminate Stay Resident), 216, 298
turning the computer off, 31
turning the computer on, 26
.TXT (files), 41, 46

TYPE command, 46-47, 269
  replace with LIST (shareware), 49, 259
  to stop the scrolling
    with <CTRL> S, 47
    with |MORE filter, 47
    with <PAUSE>, 47

typeover mode, 8

U

/U switch in formatting, 63, 64
UMB, **Upper Memory Blocks**, 164-166, 209,
  298
unconditional format, 63, 64
UNDELETE command, 91-92, 202-204, 270
  importance of recovering files quickly, 92,
    203
underscore character instead of space, 93
undoing MEMMAKER's changes, 219
UNFORMAT command, 64-65, 270
unmounting a floppy, 228
unzipping zipped files, 177-180
Upper Memory Blocks, 164-166, 298
user group, defined, 263
USING COMPUTER BULLETIN BOARDS
  (book), 263, 276
utility program, 299

V

VENDOR (files), 42
VER command, 29, 270
version, your DOS, 29
version, your software, 20, 22
VGA (**Video Graphics Array**), 299
virtual disk, 296, 299

VIRUS (defined), 232, 299
  cleaning, 233
  protection, 232-235
  removal, 233

VIRUSCAN (shareware), 235, 261
volume label, 60, 299
VSAFE (DOS 6) command, 232, 234-235, 270
  help, 234
VSHIELD (shareware), 235, 261

W

/W switch with DIR command, 36
warm boot, 10, 158, 299
wildcards, 14, 127-129, 299
  Tips, 79, 90, 113, 129

WINDOWS
  and DoubleSpace, 221
  modifying an AUTOEXEC.BAT file to
    prevent Windows from starting
    automatically, 154, 208
  MSD, 201
  SYSTEM.INI file, 216-217
  Undelete (program), 202
  WIN, 205

word processors, 300
  and ASCII files, 49, 143, 151, 159

write cache disabling, 206
write cache flushing, 206

WRITE PROTECTION
  3½" disks, 34
  5¼" disks, 33
  error writing drive A (error message), 274
  notch, 32
  tabs, 33

X

XCOPY, 81-85, 120-122, 130-133,
    138-139, 270
  CAUTION about hidden files, 81
  using XCOPY to automatically make
    directories, 84-85, 120-122, 133, 139
XGA (EXtended Graphics Adapter), 300
XTREE GOLD, 187

Y

Y/N abbreviation, 72

Z

ZDIR (shareware), 37, 261
.ZIP (files), 177-180, 299
zipped files (.ZIP), 177-180, 299

NOTES

NOTES

NOTES

NOTES

Book Order Form

**MAIL the order
form below**

OR

CALL Toll-Free
1-800-330-3311
Visa/MasterCard

OR

FAX your order to us
813-845-8522
Visa/MasterCard

Learning DOS For The Complete Novice, 2nd Edition

(ISBN# 0-9623898-9-7)
$15.95 plus shipping
(US funds only)

_____ at $15.95 Each _____

Shipping and Handling _____

SUBTOTAL _____

Florida orders add 6% sales tax _____

TOTAL AMOUNT _____

Shipping and Handling :

VIA	USA	Canada	International
SURFACE BOOK RATE (Allow 2 weeks US & Canada Up to 6 weeks International)	Add $2.00	Add $3.00	Add $3.00/book
AIR MAIL	$3.50	$4.50	$10.00/book
Shipping for each additional book ordered	$1.00	$2.00	(above)

Payment:

☐ Check to Celestial Press ☐ MasterCard ☐ VISA

Card number: _____

Name on card: _____

Signature: _____

Credit card: Exp. date _____ / _____

Ship to:

Date: _____

Your name: _____

Address: _____

City: _____ State: _____ Zip: _____

Telephone: (_____) _____

Send this order form to:
CELESTIAL PRESS, 4424 Dohrcrest Drive, #6, New Port Richey, FL 34652-5542